Stuart's Finest Hour

General James Ewell Brown Stuart
Library of Congress

STUART'S FINEST HOUR

The Ride Around McClellan, June 1862

John J. Fox III

Angle Valley Press
Winchester, Virginia

For information contact:
Angle Valley Press, P. O. Box 4098, Winchester, VA 22604
www.AngleValleyPress.com

Designed and printed in the United States of America.

First Edition, First Printing

Jacket Design: Radford Wine—www.RWAdvertising.com
Modern Images: Randall Flynn—www.rflynnphotography.com
Author Image & Copy Editor: Nancy Jones Fox
Interior Design: 1106 Design—www.1106design.com
Cover images: J.E.B. Stuart Portrait, National Archives
Stuart Monument Photo, Library of Congress
Maps: George Skoch

Publisher's Cataloging-in-Publication Data

Fox, John J., 1959–
    Stuart's finest hour : the ride around McClellan, June 1862 /
John J. Fox III.
        p. cm.
    ISBN: 978-0-9711950-5-9 (hardcover)
    Includes bibliographical references and index.
    1. Stuart, Jeb, 1833–1864—Military leadership. 2. United States—
History—Civil War, 1861–1865—Cavalry operations. 3. Virginia—
History—Civil War, 1861–1865—Campaigns. 4. Virginia—History—
Civil War, 1861–1865—Personal narratives.   I. Title.
E467.1 F69 2013
973.7—dc23
                                    2013911131

For Anna and Jay
May your quest for knowledge always strive
to find the truth

ALSO BY JOHN J. FOX III

Red Clay to Richmond:
Trail of the 35th Georgia Infantry Regiment

A History of Opequon Presbyterian Church:
"Mother Church of the Valley"
co-written with C. Langdon Gordon and Arthur L. Stanley

The Confederate Alamo:
Bloodbath at Petersburg's Fort Gregg on April 2, 1865

Contents

Maps

Numerous illustrations have been placed throughout the text.

Preface

"HE IS A RARE MAN, wonderfully endowed by nature with the qualities necessary for an officer of light cavalry. Calm, firm, acute, active, and enterprising, I know no one more competent than he to estimate the occurrences before him at their true value."

August 1861 letter from General Joseph Johnston to President Jefferson Davis recommending Colonel Jeb Stuart to command a cavalry brigade.[1]

Many people, even those remotely interested in U. S. military history, have heard the name Jeb Stuart and are aware that he was a famous cavalry general who rode for the Confederacy. Yet, in the spring of 1862, James Ewell Brown Stuart was an unfamiliar name to many soldiers and to the civilian population throughout the country. How did this twenty-nine-year-old former U. S. Army lieutenant become the 1860's version of a media sensation? What did he do to make his name a household word that struck pride in the hearts of Southerners and fear in the minds of Northerners, especially Union soldiers?

At the beginning of June 1862, General George McClellan's huge Union army stood poised to decimate the Confederate capital of Richmond. The city faced chaos as thousands of civilians fled. The newly appointed Confederate army commander, Robert E. Lee, knew that Richmond could not long withstand a siege of Union naval and land-based artillery. Lee wanted to launch his own attack, but he needed to know what stood on McClellan's right flank.

Lee called for a little-known meeting with Stuart on June 10, 1862 to discuss a cavalry reconnaissance along the Federal right flank located in central Hanover County. Using numerous eyewitness accounts, this book places the reader in the dusty saddle of both the hunter and the hunted as Stuart led 1,200 hand-picked cavalrymen deep behind Union lines. Close on his tail rode numerous Federal horsemen led by Brigadier General Philip St. George Cooke, Stuart's father-in-law.

Three days and 110 miles later, Stuart and his men returned to a heroes' welcome in Richmond. Newspaper headlines in both the North and the South hailed Jeb Stuart's success and introduced the public to names like Mosby, Latane and von Borcke. Stuart's ride around the Union army boosted morale for the Confederacy and its people, who in the spring of 1862 craved any piece of positive news. This expedition gave them something to celebrate, and its success raised Stuart's image and reputation for the ages.

More importantly though, Stuart brought General Lee information that changed the tactical and strategic situation in Virginia. This intelligence gave Lee the impetus and the confidence to split his army and to launch the Seven Days' Battles that eventually pushed the Army of the Potomac away from the Confederate capital. Almost three more years would pass before Federal soldiers faced another such opportunity to seize Richmond.

While George McClellan and his supporters brushed off Stuart's Chickahominy Raid as merely a nuisance, Union colonel William W. Averell later recognized the uniqueness of Stuart's leadership during the ride. He wrote, "This expedition was appointed with excellent judgment, and was conducted with superb address." Averell also noted that Stuart's mission forever changed American cavalry tactics by launching the lightning raid, deep behind enemy lines, accompanied by horse artillery.[2]

Stuart's raid confirmed the importance of the cavalry mission on the battlefield and it revealed that an unexpected swift strike behind enemy lines could not only gather intelligence, but it could also sever enemy supply and communication lines; create chaos in the enemy command structure; and disrupt small unit cohesion.

John Mosby insisted that the raid placed the first tarnish on McClellan's heretofore stellar career. The expedition also created dissension amongst some Union officers and gave an opportunity for some Northern newspapers to question the Federal generalship in Virginia.[3]

This book is not intended to be a biography of Jeb Stuart nor a synopsis of the Peninsula Campaign. Instead, this story covers General Stuart's dramatic raid from June 12–15 of 1862 that helped stymie George McClellan's grand plans. This cavalry chase highlights how the fog of war and the fear of the unknown created confusion and danger for officers and enlisted men in both armies. During three years of fighting, Jeb Stuart led his men into many tight situations; however, just before his combat death in 1864, he acknowledged to Captain John Esten Cooke that he considered the June 1862 Chickahominy Raid to be the most dangerous mission of his war experience.[4]

Acknowledgments

I WANT TO THANK the many people who have helped me to assemble the various parts of this remarkable story. I am especially grateful to Robert E. L. Krick, Chris Ferguson and Jeb Stuart IV for reading an early version of the manuscript and making helpful and accurate corrections and suggestions. Bobby Krick also pointed me toward numerous pertinent documents and he coordinated access to key Chickahominy River places.

In August of 2011, I bumped into Latane (Harry) Campbell at my regular job. When I saw his name on his I.D. card I knew there was a good chance he was related to Captain William Latane from the 9th Virginia Cavalry. After some conversation I discovered that Harry is a Latane descendant. Harry gave me all kinds of information related to Hanover County and he took me along the back roads to Westwood and Summer Hill before we stopped at Captain Latane's grave. Without his help I would still be lost somewhere along the Pamunkey River.

Richmond-based photographer Randall Flynn supplied most of the modern images that appear on these pages. Randy chased down numerous leads on local information and I am indebted for his time and expertise as we travelled many dirt and hard-surface roads in Henrico, Hanover, New Kent and Charles City counties. Elwood (Woody) Harrison provided background info and gave an excellent tour of his property near the Forge Bridge on the Chickahominy River. Historians Charles Knight and Eric Wittenberg sent me excellent images related to the project.

Horace Mewborn's great article titled "A Wonderful Exploit: Jeb Stuart's Ride Around the Army of the Potomac," in the August 1998 *Blue & Gray Magazine,* served as a blue-print that helped me initially sort through the chaos and confusion of June 12–15, 1862. He also provided me with additional information that clarified my many questions.

David Deal, director of the Hanover Tavern Foundation, gave me a tour of the beautifully restored Hanover Tavern and provided documentation about some of the area residents and the events swirling around Hanover Court House in June 1862. Gayle Stewart from Old Church's Immanuel Episcopal Church gave me a pamphlet that outlined the church's long history and the difficulties encountered by the pastor and the members during the war. David Auerbach answered questions and allowed us to photograph the Old Church Hotel which is now a private dwelling. B. T. (Bernard) Smith who lives next to the White House Landing area spent time with us discussing the war's affect on the citizens and their property and he allowed us to take photographs.

I am also thankful that I spoke to the Roanoke Civil War Roundtable in May 2013 because one of their members, J.B. Mead, gave me copies of a letter that his relative, the 1st Virginia Cavalry's William Z. Meade, wrote about the expedition. This letter stood out as one of the best Confederate accounts of those three days and William had indicated that he hoped to write an article some day about his experience on the ride. Sadly, he was killed in action at Resaca, Georgia in 1864 before he could pen his article.

I visited numerous research facilities in my quest for primary documents related to what some Civil War era newspapers referred to as the Great Chickahominy Raid. Several of these places and their staff members deserve special mention. Teresa Roane and her staff at the Museum of the Confederacy's Brockenbrough Library; Becky Ebert and Jerry Holsworth at the Handley Library Stewart Bell Archives room; the Virginia Historical Society Library staff; Tom Buffenbarger, Rodney Foytik and Rich Baker from the U.S. Army Heritage and Education Center's Military History Institute research library; and the National Park Service's Richmond National Battlefield Park research library.

My book production team has done a great job getting this project ready for print. Radford Wine did phenomenal work taking my ideas and turning them into a beautiful book cover. He also came up with the idea for the book's title. Nancy Jones Fox, my wonderful and patient wife, provided editorial expertise as she read numerous iterations of the manuscript. George Skoch has again been fantastic to work with as he perused numerous old sketches and old maps to turn out seven new maps that will aid the reader in following Jeb Stuart's trail. I previously noted the great efforts of team member Randall Flynn and his camera. Michelle DeFilippo and Ronda Rawlins and their staff at 1106 Design have again put together another eye-catching book interior that I know the reader will enjoy.

I especially want to thank my wife and children for their love and patience as I have worked to put together another time consuming book project.

CHAPTER 1

On to Richmond

D URING THE LAST WEEK of March 1862, numerous heavily laden ships rode low in the water as they floated down the Potomac River from Alexandria, Virginia. The decks of these boats held precious cargo, soldiers from Major General George McClellan's Army of the Potomac. These soldiers, dressed in Union blue, shared space with horses, wagons, cannons and the myriad of supplies that this army of 100,000 men needed to sustain themselves for the coming spring offensive.

McClellan wanted to attack Richmond, but an overland march that sliced through Major General Joseph Johnston's Confederate defense lines in northern Virginia seemed risky. Instead, McClellan visualized using the Potomac River as an end-run around the Rebel army. The transports docked at wind-whipped Fortress Monroe, the largest coastal fort in the country. This hexagonal rock-and-brick bastion guarded Point Comfort, which jutted into Hampton Roads, the name of the body of water where the James River churned into the Chesapeake Bay. McClellan planned to march his army northwest, up the Virginia Peninsula to Richmond about 100 miles away.

The 6th United States Cavalry regiment boarded the boats at Alexandria on March 27, 1862. The vessels creaked and groaned as they plowed through the waves of a freak snowstorm. Touching dry land three days later at Fortress Monroe reminded these horse soldiers of the benefits of the army over the navy. The regiment had formed a year earlier as the 3rd Cavalry; hence, it was re-designated as the 6th U. S. Cavalry in August 1861. Most of these men came from Ohio, Pennsylvania and western New York and numbered about 34 officers and 950 enlisted men. This unit would be the only regular United States cavalry regiment raised during the war.[1]

Meanwhile, the members of the 5th U. S. Cavalry had also boarded boats at Alexandria on the same day. This regiment had originally formed as the 2nd U. S. Cavalry in 1855, and numerous important men had served in the unit before the Civil War. Both Albert Sydney Johnston and Robert E. Lee had commanded the 2nd Regulars. Other familiar names included George Stoneman, Earl van Dorn, John B. Hood, and Fitzhugh Lee. In the summer of 1861, the regiment was re-designated as the 5th U. S. Cavalry. By late May 1862, the 5th U. S., the 6th U. S. and the 6th Pennsylvania Cavalry regiments formed Brigadier General William H. Emory's brigade, which was part of Brigadier General Philip St. George Cooke's Cavalry Reserve.

As McClellan's invasion force assembled, concern grew in the port towns of Norfolk and Portsmouth. Both of these places stood across the water from Fort Monroe. By May 9, the Confederate military evacuated both towns. A parade of demoralized citizens followed the soldiers. Fear of the Yankee invaders soon spread west, and many Richmond area women and children left that city. Even Confederate President Jefferson Davis' family fled to safety in Raleigh.[2]

General Joseph Johnston's 75,000-man army had arrived in mid-April from their northern Virginia defense lines to join Major General John B. Magruder's small force near Yorktown. Magruder had deceived McClellan into thinking he had more than his 8,000 men. Thus, the Union army dug defensive positions at Yorktown and built numerous small forts and batteries all in the face of a weak but theatrical foe.

Johnston not only feared McClellan's numerically superior army but also the big shells from nearby Union gunboats. The Confederate commander soon ordered a withdrawal up the Peninsula toward

Richmond. He also worried that a Union infantry move via boat up the York River might cut off his left flank. A rapid movement by his army toward the capital would alleviate this potential problem. The Army of the Potomac followed and over the next several weeks, the two armies clashed at Yorktown, Williamsburg and Eltham's Landing.

On May 11, with the C.S.S. *Virginia* [*Merrimac*] trapped near Norfolk, her crew scuttled the ironclad to prevent her capture. This unsettling event opened the river approach to Richmond for the Union navy.

By May 14, Johnston's men had run out of space. The gray army stood five miles east of Richmond. Many politicians and citizens voiced displeasure over Johnston's apparent lack of aggressiveness, for they knew that neither the Confederate army, the Confederate government nor the citizens could long endure a siege against the city. Joseph Johnston had to go on the offensive.

"Much anxiety is felt for the fate of the city," noted John B. Jones, one of the city's numerous war clerks. "Is there no turning point in this long lane of downward progress?" Then, the next day the alarm bells sounded on Capitol Hill as word spread that a string of Federal warships chugged up the James River to shell Richmond. The sound of gunfire reached the city as the enemy boats rounded a sharp bend in the river eight miles away and faced the Confederate guns at Drewry's Bluff.[3]

The Union army's proximity to Richmond plus the approach of the gunboats buoyed McClellan's confidence and his ego in a May 15 telegram to his wife. "My troops are in motion, all in splendid spirits. We may have a severe battle to fight but I know that I will win it and we'll be together again."[4]

The May 15 edition of the Richmond *Dispatch* stressed that the "greatest anxiety was manifested by our citizens" despite several bold notices seeking brave men to impede the approach of the Federal flotilla. One notice requested "[a]ll young men out of the army who are familiar with the use of the Rifle" to come to the Washington statue next to the capital building to form teams of sharpshooters to roam the banks of the James River to pick off enemy sailors.

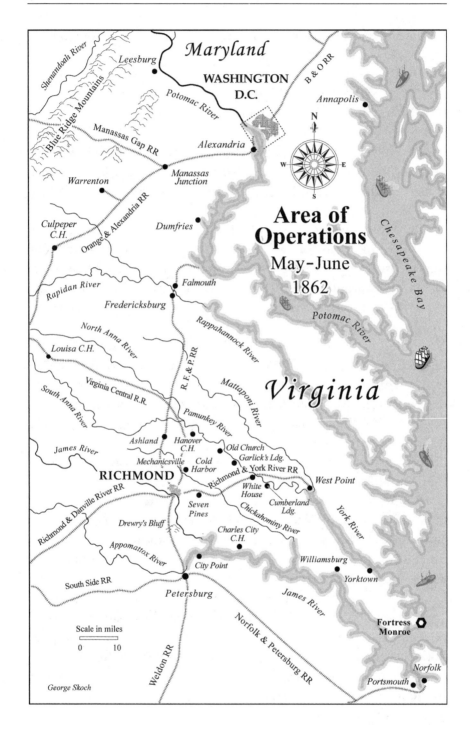

Area of
Operations
May–June
1862

George Skoch

Another person with the pen name "Corinth", presumed to be a soldier or sailor from Mississippi, stated he would join about 100 other "determined and resolute" men who would seize the enemy fleet of gunboats "at all hazards."[5]

A rival paper, the Richmond *Examiner,* assumed a more cavalier attitude toward the possible naval bombardment of the city. Comparing the fortitude of Richmonders to war-weary Venetians in 1848, the writer welcomed the attack if that was to be the fate of the Confederate capital [fait accompli]. With "bombs crashing through every roof" the Venetians had survived "famine and pestilence" by eating rats and making soup from old shoe leather. The writer urged his fellow citizens to be no less defiant or brave.[6]

Vermin and shoe leather soup aside, General Robert E. Lee decided that he did not want his wife, Mary, to endure the potential siege of Richmond either. He sent her and several daughters to a safer place on some family land in Hanover County on the bank of the Pamunkey River. The Lee family had called the property White House Landing for many years.[7]

The war had also displaced Judith McGuire. She and her family had fled their home in Alexandria in 1861 to escape the invading Union army, which she called the "locusts of Egypt … carrying the bitterest enmity and desolation wherever they go." Judith's pedigree placed her in the category of FFV — First Family of Virginia. She was born in Richmond and her father, Judge William Brockenbrough, had served on the Virginia Supreme Court. She married a prominent Episcopal minister, John P. McGuire, who was headmaster of the well-heeled Episcopal School in Alexandria when the war began. Both their sons had enlisted in the Confederate army while they had sent their daughters farther south to safety. Now Judith found herself in Richmond. She soon departed the city for safety with family at Summer Hill, an estate in Hanover County.[8]

Late on May 15, the capital's citizens cheered news that the rapid plunging fire from the Drewry's Bluff garrison had caused enough damage both to the Federal boats and their sailors to turn the flotilla back downstream. Residents breathed a collective sigh of relief. Then, word spread that the Union army had halted their slow march toward the city as McClellan had ordered his men to dig defensive positions. However, President Davis knew that the Federal army and navy would threaten the city again soon. He called for May 16 to be a day of "fasting and prayer," and many residents streamed in to fill church pews.[9]

However, where Richmond citizens gathered, the talk inevitably turned to their apprehension that Confederate authorities would abandon the city once the Union army began to move again. John Jones, privy to much military and political correspondence, sent a letter to President Davis reminding him of the "demoralization and even insubordination in the army" should Richmond be evacuated. The Confederate Congress had even given political cover to the Davis administration and senior military leaders by passing resolutions urging the army to stay and fight. Jones reflected the view of many when he told his diary, "Better die here!" On May 20, Jones' noted that Davis had stated that the city would be defended. His pen flowed to the melodramatic when he wrote, "A thrill of joy electrifies every heart, a smile of triumph is on every lip. The ladies are in ecstasies."[10]

As the residents waited, the continual bang and pop of artillery and musketry from the east and northeast kept their worries alive. Hospital Hill, on the northern outskirts of Richmond, became a popular place as residents flocked there to listen to the sounds of the guns and to swap rumors. The appearance of one, two and even three balloons floating high above the trees along the Union lines created a stir. Thaddeus Lowe's invitation by Union authorities to use his gondola balloons for observation represented the first use of an airship in combat and a huge technological leap forward. John Jones was not alone in his concern when he wrote "they can not only see our camps around the city, but they can view every part of the city itself."[11]

However, despite his advantage in men and supplies, George McClellan had a problem that increased the closer his army came to Richmond. He seemed convinced that he was outnumbered two-to-one thanks to some dubious arithmetic from members of his staff and a civilian named Allen Pinkerton, who was hired to make intelligence assessments. A telegram McClellan sent on May 14 to Lincoln reflected this obsession: "Casualties , sickness, garrisons, and guards have much weakened my force and will continue to do so. I cannot bring into actual battle more than eighty thousand men at the utmost, and with them I must attack in position, probably entrenched, a much larger force, perhaps double my numbers."[12]

A British military observer later commented on McClellan's perceived numerical disadvantage. Lieutenant Colonel Garnet Joseph Wolseley, who later became field marshal and commander in chief of the British army, arrived in Richmond in the fall of 1862. Wolseley knew that the Comte de Paris had observed the inner workings of McClellan and his staff during the Peninsula Campaign. Both foreign officers agreed that McClellan "had a tendency to greatly exaggerate the numbers," but this affliction caused him to hesitate, "which was of great advantage to his opponents."[13]

While Richmonders feared for their future, George McClellan had other problems to think about as well. While his troops marched up the Peninsula they increased their line of communication from Fort Monroe. The massive job of moving the Union army's supplies across a broad front fell to a forty-two-year-old West Pointer named Rufus Ingalls.

CHAPTER 2

White House Landing on the Pamunkey River

MID-MAY 1862

UNION LIEUTENANT COLONEL Rufus Ingalls paced along the half-moon dusty road that fronted a plain house on the south bank of the Pamunkey River. Several mature locust trees, their strands of small white flowers highlighted by new green leaves, provided shade from the midday Virginia sun, already stifling for May. The shade also invited unwanted guests as the quartermaster officer instinctively swatted at the buzzing insects that followed him. The infernal mosquitoes that inhabited the Peninsula southeast of Richmond had plenty on which to feast as more than 100,000 Union soldiers moved toward a cataclysmic collision with some 75,000 Confederate defenders.

Once George McClellan's army had landed at Fortress Monroe, on the southeastern tip of the Peninsula, Ingalls had leap-frogged his supply depots up the York and Pamunkey rivers as the blue juggernaut creeped past Yorktown and Williamsburg toward Richmond. As the assistant quartermaster for the army, Ingalls now needed to find a harbor where wharves could be quickly built for supply boats brimming with material for the Army of the Potomac. Ingalls had previously served as the chief quartermaster in northern Virginia until March 1862 and then had supervised the "embarkation of the army to the Peninsula."[1]

Ingalls realized that the scalloped shoreline near the house seemed a natural harbor, especially at high tide. Charred abutments and beams from the Richmond & York River Railroad Bridge poked out of the water. Confederate troops had recently torched the bridge to West Point to prevent its use by the Federal army. The damaged single-track line, commonly referred to as the York River Railroad, pointed to the west toward Richmond. Ingalls knew that once the line was repaired, the rails would help move supplies quickly toward the frontline troops as they attacked and captured the Rebel capital.

The small white-washed house, flanked by a chimney at each end, faced the water. Ingalls climbed up three steps, and his boots echoed on the floor of the covered porch. Inside he surveyed the four small rooms in the main part of the house. A small wing bookended each side of the structure. On one end was a tiny first floor room. On the other end was a pantry with steps that led down to a noxious cellar. He decided the place would provide an adequate headquarters for the army's supply depot. Once Ingalls discovered who owned the property, his decision was perhaps easier.[2]

The house and land had been owned by Martha D. Custis, who married George Washington. The property later passed to their grandson, George Washington Parke Custis whose daughter, Mary Anne Custis, later married a career army officer named Robert Edward Lee. In the 1850s, the 4,000 acre estate had passed to their son William Henry Fitzhugh "Rooney" Lee, who had farmed the property until the war began. Rooney Lee now commanded the 9th Virginia Cavalry Regiment. The Lee's had named the place White House Landing years before simply because of the brightness of the whitewash, yet one Union newspaperman thought the color of the wood frame house was more pink than white. A correspondent for *The New York Times* ignominiously referred to Rooney Lee as "the skedaddled owner of the White House property."[3]

Mrs. Robert E. Lee and her daughters had made several moves as they tried to stay ahead of the U. S. Army. They first headed to Richmond after their property at Arlington was seized by Federal troops in 1861. Then Mrs. Lee, Annie and Mildred went to the anticipated safety of White House Landing. On May 10, they had to flee again at the approach of Union soldiers into Hanover County. One report indicated that Lee's wife tacked a note to the front door imploring McClellan's men to leave her property alone.[4]

After the Lee women left White House, they dawdled too long at Marlbourne, the home of staunch secessionist Edmund Ruffin. Union cavalry rode up and discovered the unexpected prize. Mrs. Lee later admitted to the 6th Pennsylvania Cavalry commander, Colonel Richard H. Rush, that nobody had expected the Union advance into Hanover along the Pamunkey River. The Lee ladies would spend the next several weeks under house arrest pending negotiations to deliver them back to the Confederate line near Mechanicsville.[5]

When Lieutenant Colonel Ingalls finished his interior inspection of White House, he walked back out onto the porch. The short pudgy officer made some mental notes about where he wanted the livestock pens to be built and where the various wharves would be anchored onto the bank. However, he knew that his first priority would be fixing the railroad and ordering locomotives and rolling stock. Ingalls' boss, Brigadier General Stewart Van Vliet, visited the site several days later. The chief quartermaster must have liked what he saw as he reported on May 20 that the White House depot was established, but much still needed to be done before the hundreds of large transport ships and barges would be able to offload the cargo that McClellan's men needed.[6]

Lieutenant Colonel Rufus Ingalls, Army of the Potomac assistant quartermaster. Ingalls was born in Maine in 1819 and graduated in West Point's 1843 class. While in school he roomed with U. S. Grant. Ingalls ran the massive supply depot at White House Landing and he organized the defense of the depot and awaited an attack on the night of June 13. He became Quartermaster for the Army of the Potomac in July 1862 when van Vliet requested to be relieved. This image was taken in 1864 when Ingalls was a brigadier general. MOLLUS Collection, USAHEC.

White House. The Pamunkey River ancestral home of 9th Virginia Cavalry commander Colonel William H. F. "Rooney" Lee. Used by Federal army as main supply depot until abandoned and burned in latter part of June 1862. Library of Congress.

The balding Ingalls sometimes swirled his long side hair to try to cover the vacancy on top. Born in Denmark, Maine in 1819, he entered West Point in 1839, where he graduated with Ulysses S. Grant in the class of 1843. He gained combat experience in the Mexican War and then served in various quartermaster roles on the west coast until being recalled east when the war erupted in 1861. An affable and competent officer, his many years of active service gained him good contacts amongst senior officers who knew of his superb leadership and organizational skills. He joined McClellan's staff as an aide in the summer of 1861, and he soon received more responsibility. His logistical experience would be noticed and he later became McClellan's chief quartermaster when Van Vliet retired in July 1862. The reputation that Ingalls gained from his 1862 duties benefited his career as he pinned on a brigadier's star the following summer. His ability to resupply the army despite the weather, the terrain, and the inevitable combat confusion would be why Grant retained him as the quartermaster during the 1864 Overland Campaign. Grant later recalled in his memoir, "[t]here never was a corps better organized than was the quartermaster's corps with the Army of the Potomac in 1864."[7]

Some of the initial troops who arrived to help Ingalls came from the 6th U. S. Cavalry Regiment. These horsemen rode into the clearing at White House Landing on May 12. The remainder of the regiment trickled in over the next few days. One trooper described what he discovered there: a "magnificent plantation" manned by numerous servants "who informed us that they were the property of General Robert E. Lee." George McClellan soon ordered that the home be protected, and guards from the 6th Cavalry began to turn away curiosity seekers who ventured too close to the house.[8]

The 6th U.S. Cavalry's senior captain rejoined his men about the time of their arrival at White House. The cold wet voyage down the Potomac River at the end of March had sapped the energy from August V. Kautz, a sturdy officer who stood nearly six feet tall. The German-born Kautz headed straight for the Fort Monroe hospital when he disembarked, and they kept him there for twenty-eight days. A bout with rheumatism the previous fall had landed Kautz on the sick list then, so it is possible that the affliction had returned.[9]

Just after his 1828 birth, Kautz's family had moved from Germany to Baltimore and eventually settled in Georgetown, Ohio. August enrolled at a local school run by schoolmaster John White. The youngster probably knew a fellow student named Hiram Ulysses Grant although Grant was six years older. When he was eighteen, Kautz had enlisted in an Ohio regiment and fought in several battles in Mexico in 1846. Upon his return to Ohio he received an appointment to West Point, where he graduated in 1852 with an undistinguished academic record and a ranking of thirty-fifth in a class of forty-three. He served at various army posts and by early 1861 when the war began, he was an infantry lieutenant in the Washington Territory. A determined officer, outspoken against mediocrity and injustice, he would rise to division command before the war's end. He later served on the military commission that tried the Lincoln assassin conspirators.[10]

The Fort Monroe hospital discharged Kautz when he was well enough to ride a horse. His arrival at White House Landing renewed simmering leadership problems for the regiment. Kautz harbored intense dislike for the regimental commander, Major Lawrence Williams. Their stormy relationship dated back to their classmate days at West Point.

Brigade commander Brigadier General William H. Emory had been rebuffed in his bid to have Kautz command the 6th Regulars. Kautz believed that McClellan had made overtures to assign the command to Williams since the latter had served McClellan as an aide in 1861. The simmering feud between Kautz and Williams would only get worse.[11]

Members of the 11th Pennsylvania Cavalry soon arrived at the supply depot too. The vastness of the property, "many hundred acres," surprised some of the Pennsylvanians although one trooper described the White House as "an unassuming structure" that stood "on a high bluff" that provided the occupants an excellent view both up and downstream. Some Pennsylvanians grumbled because they could not understand the reason for guarding a home owned by a Confederate officer.[12]

One 6th U. S. Cavalry trooper, Sidney Morris Davis, complained about their mission for a different reason. George McClellan had handed the cavalry a difficult job because there were too few horsemen to guard the numerous roads in New Kent and Hanover counties. Davis frequently found himself alone atop his horse for stints of "twelve hours at a time without relief or food." Sometimes the next nearest picket sat from "one to four miles" away.[13]

Davis detailed his first picket guarding the road network near White House:

> I must confess that, sitting there on my horse, alone in those
> dark woods, fully a mile from any of my companions, in the
> midst of a hostile community, armed only with a revolver
> and sabre — though weapons are of little account when one

is so exposed to assassination by an unseen enemy — I felt considerable uneasiness.[14]

In the darkness one night, Davis no doubt recalled an ugly sight he had seen on a previous day — the body of a Union prisoner, propped against a tree, with the head "riddled with bullets." When some nearby leaves rustled, Davis' finger looped over the trigger. He stared toward the noise as his heart pounded. Seconds later, a big dog walked into view and then moved away to Davis' relief.[15]

The Army of the Potomac's chief surgeon Charles S. Tripler arrived at White House to establish a general hospital on May 16. The conditions that he found there disappointed him. "There were no buildings at all fit for the purpose, so to meet present necessities I resorted to the use of tents." He regretted "not having appropriated the dwelling at White House to the general hospital." However, after a closer inspection he decided the house was unfit as a hospital because "[t]he cellar is dark, damp, and foul," and the small rooms could only accommodate twenty-four patients "leaving no room for the nurses." Over the next four days, Tripler's men wrestled 100 large white tents into the air and threaded guide and support poles under the canvas. The solid "thunk" of sledgehammers echoed in the hospital area as men pounded wooden anchoring stakes into the ground. Others dug fire pits for cooking caldrons, erected beds and gathered bedding material before the inevitable onslaught began of the sick, the wounded and the malingerers. Before May 21, some 260 patients had been loaded onto a hospital ship en route to Boston.[16]

Even after several days of work, the hospital situation still displeased Tripler. He wrote to the Surgeon General in Washington and he pleaded for more steam boats outfitted as hospital ships and staffed with medical personnel. He worried where he would put the wounded if a battle erupted. Seven civilian doctors from Boston and New York soon arrived to help the overwhelmed Tripler, but it was not enough. He immediately sent one of these doctors to the 1st U.S. Cavalry because their assistant surgeon was ill. "I have but one assistant surgeon for each regiment of regular cavalry," Tripler noted, "and less than that for each regiment of regular infantry. When one of them falls sick I have no one to replace him." This paucity of doctors both in the field hospital and at the small unit level resulted in the misdiagnosis of many soldiers' maladies, but it also enabled more soldiers to feign illness. Soon after medical workers drove the last tent stakes into the ground the flood of patients that Tripler had worried about began to come. The beds in the hospital tents quickly filled with 1,020 men. The dirty work begun by the squadrons of mosquitoes and the swampy tepid Peninsula water exacted its toll. The gnats, flies and numerous snakes added to the problems. Cases of typhoid, malaria, and dysentery soon overwhelmed the Union medical staff, and even some cases of scurvy appeared from a lack of fresh vegetables.[17]

These maladies soon gained the generic name of Chickahominy fever or camp fever. The sad result brought death to many soldiers from both North and South. New York reporter George Alfred Townsend walked off a boat at White House Landing and remembered the busyness of the embalmers. A nearby steam coffin factory added to the macabre atmosphere. The operation employed twenty men who hammered and sawed pine coffins all day.[18]

Several days later, Townsend visited an ill friend at the White House hospital, as the man fought the spiking temperatures of fever. Each white wall tent housed about twenty sick soldiers. This "town of sick men" tried to stay cool, as the sun heated the canvas like a furnace or else they tried to stay dry as the frequent rain leaked through. As the reporter became more familiar with the military operations at the supply depot, he expressed concern that some officers "lived like princes, and behaved like knaves" as they "robbed the Government" of equipment and food.[19]

Meanwhile, Rufus Ingalls and his men continued their mighty task of changing the flat peaceful fields of White House Landing into a bustling modern-day port facility. During high tide, engineers, boat captains, soldiers, and free blacks worked to maneuver barges and canal-boats into the proper position to stake or to tie them down. Teams of men then carried stacks of thick planking onto these vessels while carpenters sawed, hammered and nailed this decking across the gunwales of these boats in order to transform them into instant wharves. Others erected fencing to corral a herd of cattle driven from Fort Monroe.[20]

Ingalls soon discovered that the railroad damage was minimal except for two inland creek bridges that the Southerners also had burned. As rows of wharves grew into the river, he dispatched teams of carpenters and engineers to repair these railroad bridges too. Soon several boats loaded with rail equipment arrived from Baltimore. Horse teams and men wrestled "five locomotives, eighty cars, 3 miles in length railroad iron, 30,000 feet" of timber and other items off the ships.[21]

The large number of soldiers and workers at the supply depot attracted sutlers, who hoped to ply their products. The high prices on some items angered many soldiers, who frequently sought ways to even a score with these merchants. One night, under cover of darkness, several men in the 11th Pennsylvania Cavalry, sneaked off with a barrel full of eggs. When the men reached a safe spot, they cracked open the shells only to shrink back from the noxious smell of rotten eggs.[22]

White House Landing with Union supply boats. MOLLUS Collection, USAHEC

White House Landing with Union supply boats which shows view of scallop-shaped shore which made a good harbor. MOLLUS Collection, USAHEC.

White House Landing view circa 1954. Note Richmond & York River RR bridge in upper right background. Brick building in left foreground dates to Civil War era. Charles R. Knight Collection.

Stewart Van Vliet indicated in a May 23 letter to Quartermaster General Montgomery Meigs that he hoped to have the railroad bridges repaired and the line operational in two days. He lamented that supplies for McClellan's men had to be offloaded from the supply ships and then reloaded onto wagons for movement to the line troops. Muddy roads inundated by spring rains and churned by thousand of wheels and horses slowed the resupply effort. Van Vliet assured Meigs that with the railroad running in two days "all anxiety with regard to supplies may be dismissed." The railway trains soon began to chug westward almost twelve miles to Dispatch Station, where supplies still had to be offloaded onto wagons and then sent to Union troops north of the Chickahominy River. The train would then cross this swampy, snake-infested river and continue west almost three more miles to Savage Station to replenish the troops there.[23]

To complicate matters, Van Vliet and his staff had to keep track of 3,600 wagons and 700 ambulances, not to mention the 405 vessels strung out from the Chesapeake Bay to the new depot at White House. He later lamented that the immense rain that fell during the last week of May washed out some of the rail bed, "injuring the railroad and impairing the wagon roads."[24]

A glance at the map revealed another problem. The Union line of communication extended for twelve miles from White House to the Chickahominy River along the York River rail line. The track ran only nine miles to the rear and parallel to the main Union line. A lightning enemy raid might be able to punch through and quickly cut the railroad. To prevent this possibility, McClellan decided to keep his largest corps, Major General Fitz John Porters' 5th Corps, to guard the right flank between the banks of the Pamunkey and the Chickahominy rivers. McClellan expected his cavalry to fill in any gaps in this area.

McClellan organized the 5th Corps Provisional in mid-May by taking Porter's division and combining it with Major General George Sykes' division of U. S. Regular infantry. Two months later, "Provisional" would be dropped as army authorities decided to permanently retain the corps.

Throughout May, Lieutenant Colonel Rufus Ingalls' job of providing for the needs of the 100,000 men in the Army of the Potomac became more difficult, as he tried to ensure the safe, free-flow of supplies toward the front. The troops devoured about "150 wagonloads of subsistence daily" not to mention the other wagons that carried ammunition, clothing, medical supplies and other needed items to the front. The scale for food and forage alone tipped toward 700 tons each day.[25]

Almost all of the items needed for the upcoming attack against Richmond would come ashore at White House Landing. The vulnerability of this spot, on the Union army's right flank, would soon present an irresistible opportunity for a young Confederate cavalry commander and his hand-picked band of horsemen.

CHAPTER 3

Jeb Stuart and Philip St. George Cooke: The In-Law Problem

MAJOR GENERAL GEORGE McCLELLAN's lack of understanding and misuse of his mounted arm would ensure the poor performance of the Union cavalry during the first two years of war. During this same period, what would allow the Confederate cavalry to tally so many successes against their foes?

To gain an answer to this question, one has to look at several factors. General Joseph Johnston and his replacement, General Robert E. Lee, both understood the benefits of keeping their Confederate horsemen consolidated into cavalry regiments under the direct control of their own cavalry officers. The agrarian South also had more experienced horsemen who were attracted to the cavalry arm. The first Rebel cavalrymen also brought their own horses and received a per diem stipend from the Confederate government. Since these men owned their mounts, they tended to take better care of their animals. During the Peninsula Campaign, many of the Virginia cavalrymen fought in and around their own homesteads, which bred familiarity plus steadfastness and enthusiasm to oust the invading Federal army from state soil. Another factor that cannot be discounted is the difference between the commanders of the opposing armies and their subordinate cavalry commanders.

The main reason for Confederate cavalry success in Virginia during the first two years of the war landed squarely on the broad shoulders of James Ewell Brown Stuart. Stuart was born to a prominent Patrick County, Virginia family on February 6, 1833. As the youngest son in a family of six girls and four boys, he had an ever-present need to prove himself.

A story of a young James Stuart revealed his perseverance and bravery amidst pain. He and his brother, William, discovered a hornet's nest in a tree at the family farm named Laurel Hill. The two boys climbed the tree to beat the nest into submission with sticks. When things went awry, William dropped out of the tree and retreated as fast as his legs would carry him. James however, remained in the tree, despite multiple stings, and continued to batter the nest until the broken pieces fell to the ground.[1]

The rural lifestyle in southwest Virginia provided Stuart the skills needed to become an excellent horseman and weapons expert. Farm life also gave him an independent and sometimes impulsive streak.

Jeb Stuart as West Point cadet taken in 1854. The Museum of the Confederacy, Richmond, Va.

Young James entered West Point as a plebe in July 1850. He graduated in 1854 and was ranked thirteenth in a class of forty-six. His fun-loving spirit combined with his refusal to back down from confrontation garnered the young Virginian 129 demerits during his four year stay.[2]

An important part of Stuart's West Point experience came during his third or junior year, when Colonel Robert E. Lee arrived to become the school's superintendent. Stuart and Custis Lee, the eldest Lee son, had already become best friends. Familiarity with the Lee family would hold Stuart in good stead for the remainder of his life. Historian Jeffry Wert noted that once war came, "[n]o subordinate commander enjoyed Lee's personal affection more than the twenty-nine-year-old cavalryman Brigadier General Jeb Stuart."[3]

Stuart's post-West Point assignments brought him vital opportunities as a military leader. His first assignment in a mounted rifle company carried him to south Texas to fight Indians. In 1855, then Secretary of War Jefferson Davis ordered the formation of the 1st and 2nd Cavalry regiments and Lieutenant Stuart soon received an assignment to Fort Leavenworth, Kansas and the 1st U.S. Cavalry.

His arrival at Fort Leavenworth gave him new introductions and experiences with officers who would also play a prominent role in his military career. Colonel Edwin "Bull" Sumner commanded the 1st Cavalry, and Joseph Johnston served as lieutenant colonel. Captain George McClellan also joined the regiment at the same time.[4]

At this new post, fate came into play as Stuart met his future wife, Flora Cooke, the daughter of Colonel Philip St. George Cooke. He noted several positive attributes when he first met Flora. She was a Virginian, and her father commanded the 2nd Dragoons. At twenty-years-old, she was also an accomplished horsewoman who could shoot a gun straight. The pair married in late 1855.[5]

In 1857, Stuart galloped from one end of Kansas to the other as he attempted to keep the peace between Free-Soil and Pro-Slave groups. He encountered abolitionist John Brown, who had moved to the state with his sons to stir up trouble. Later, while fighting Cheyenne Indians, a cornered brave fired point blank at a charging saber-wielding Stuart, and the bullet flew true and hit the young officer square in the chest. When the doctor finally arrived, he discovered that the round had luckily deflected off some cartilage and bone into a shallow lodgment in the left side of the breast. The doctor saw no vital organs damaged, so he bandaged Stuart up.[6]

The Virginian soon recovered from the wound, and the latter half of 1857 saw the birth of the first Stuart child, a daughter named Flora. The 1st Cavalry next transferred to Fort Riley, Kansas. Perhaps with another mouth to feed and the potential fatal consequences of his wounding, Stuart sought other ways to supplement his meager lieutenant's salary. He looked into purchasing land, and he fiddled in a workshop with several ideas that he believed would make life easier for a cavalryman. One of these inventions was a saber hook, which allowed a horseman to detach his sword and scabbard from a waist belt and quickly reattach it to the saddle. The idea showed enough promise that the War Department requested that he return east to patent, demonstrate and negotiate the sale of his device.[7]

Historical fate next found the twenty-six-year-old Stuart in Washington D.C. on the morning of October 17, 1859. He waited at the War Department for his appointment with Secretary of War John B. Floyd to discuss his invention. Before Stuart met with Floyd, he detected a flurry of alarmed activity amidst the War Department employees. The telegraph wires hummed while rumors swirled that a slave insurrection was underway at a remote place called Harper's Ferry. A Federal armory stood in this town that guarded the confluence of the Potomac and Shenandoah rivers.

Stuart, at Floyd's request, soon crossed the Potomac River to the Virginia side and rode up hill to Arlington, the family home of Colonel Robert E. Lee. Stuart carried a note ordering Lee to make all haste to the War Department. Stuart and Lee then raced back to Washington and met with Floyd and President James Buchanan. Floyd placed Lee in command of the militia force that was already en route to Harper's Ferry. Stuart, never one to shy away from adventure, requested to accompany Lee as his aide. Lee accepted the offer.

Several hours later, Stuart and Lee arrived at Harper's Ferry and met with the ninety marines and militia reserves who had already staked out positions around the small stone-and-brick engine house where the invaders had retreated. They learned that the gang had already murdered several men, including a free black man employed by the Baltimore and Ohio Railroad. Colonel Lee was in no mood to negotiate. At first light the next morning, Lieutenant Stuart walked toward the building with a white flag in one hand and a surrender ultimatum for the group's leader. Hundreds of eyes peered from window sills and around building corners as the unarmed officer neared the wooden double-doors. He called out, and one of the doors inched open. The dark circle of a carbine barrel poked through the crack and pointed directly at Stuart's chest. Stuart recognized the face of John "Osawatomie" Brown, murderer of five pro-slave Kansas residents in 1856.

When Stuart realized that Brown would not surrender, he stepped to the side and gave a signal. Twelve marines rushed forward and battered the door open. They overwhelmed and arrested John Brown and his lawless minions.[8]

The attack at Harper's Ferry proved to be a flashpoint for the upcoming tragic Civil War, and Jeb Stuart had been right there with Robert E. Lee to play a key part. On this day, Stuart's bravery and frontline leadership stood on full display. The future would hold many more such days for the young cavalry officer.

Eight months later, on June 26, 1860, the Stuarts welcomed the birth of a son. They named him Philip St. George Cooke Stuart after her father. The following year, the clouds of war swept over the country. For Jeb Stuart there was never any doubt that if Virginia seceded from the Union, he would resign his U. S. Army commission and join the Confederate effort. While still a U. S. Army lieutenant, he wrote his older brother, William Alexander Stuart, in March 1861 from Kansas Territory that "I would rather be a private in Va's army than a General in any army to coerce her." He then stressed the reality of the situation: "I am looking forward with considerable certainty to resignation."[9]

His father-in-law, Philip St. George Cooke, like many southern-born U.S. Army officers, had to make a delicate decision intertwined between family, state, country and conscience. Cooke selected his country, and he would be rewarded with a U. S. Army brigadier general's commission in November 1861. Cooke's son, John Rogers Cooke, selected his state and became a Confederate brigadier. Two of Cooke's daughters and their husbands sided with the South while his other daughter and her husband remained loyal unionists.

Brigadier General Philip St. George Cooke. MOLLUS, USAHEC.

Once Colonel Philip St. George Cooke made the decision to remain in the Union army, Stuart wanted nothing more to do with his father-in-law. Beset by anger, Stuart decided to change his son's name and settled on James Ewell Brown Stuart, Jr. In a letter written to Flora in November 1861, Stuart urged his wife "to act well *our* parts & bear with the mistakes & errors of others however grievous with the charity of silence but by no means attempt justification of what must be condemned. Read well & con well those words my darling, and be consoled in what you rightly regard as very distressing, by the reflection that your husband & brothers will atone for the father's conduct." In January 1862, Stuart wrote a letter to his brother-in-law who commanded Virginia's Stafford Light Artillery Battery. He stressed to Captain John Rogers Cooke his "great mortification at Colonel Cooke's course. He will regret it but once and that will be continually." Stuart insisted that the blame for "the separation in the family rests entirely with the Colonel. Let us bear our misfortune in silence."[10]

Stuart initially commanded the 1st Virginia Cavalry Regiment, and then he received a promotion to brigadier general in late 1861 and the command of a cavalry brigade. Stuart made known his

desire to meet and beat his father-in-law on the field of battle. He intended to "wipe out every stain on the name." The middle of June 1862 would present that opportunity.[11]

Captain Johann August Heinrich Heros von Borcke, who later became a close member of Stuart's staff, noted that Stuart envied the idea of capturing his father-in-law. Von Borcke recalled that "it would have given him [Stuart] greater satisfaction to send General Cooke under escort to Richmond than to capture the mighty McClellan himself." Stuart affirmed this desire in a letter he wrote to Flora in early May 1862. He indicated

Brigadier General James Ewell Brown Stuart. USAHEC.

that the 6th U. S. Cavalry's commander, Major Lawrence Williams, had related to the "bearer of a flag of truce" that during the Battle of Williamsburg "I [Stuart] came within an ace of capturing my father-in-law" during a close fight between Union troopers and the 4th Virginia Cavalry.[12]

Stuart's talent for reconnaissance meant that he and his men would soon be busy gathering intelligence for the undermanned Confederate army. His penchant for fancy dress was also well known. Yet, most of his men loved him because he led from the front. They knew that he would never send them anywhere that he would not go himself. He also had a strong sense of duty as exhibited by a request from Flora in late 1861 to come visit her and the children in Richmond. He responded: "As for my going to Richmond — I don't care what other Genl's do, all I have to say is that while this war lasts I will not leave the van of our Army unless compelled to. Let that answer put to rest any hope of seeing me in Richmond."[13]

In the spring of 1862, with George McClellan's army parked just east of Richmond, there was a good chance that a physical collision between the father-in-law and his young, upstart son-in-law might become a reality.

CHAPTER 4

More Indecision Near Richmond

LATE-MAY 1862

THE SUN AND RAIN of May 1862 ushered in welcome changes to the fields of Hanover County as stalks of corn poked above the fallow soil near the Pamunkey River. Snaking green-leafed vines of beans swallowed up some fields. However, the arrival of huge numbers of Union soldiers tramping along the roads, across the fields, into the barns and sometimes barging into homes brought some unpleasant encounters with the locals. Many of the residents tried to stay inside and off the roads to prevent interaction with Union soldiers. With all the local military-age men serving in Confederate units, only the eyes of the females or the eyes of the very young and the very old peered out the windows of the farm and plantation houses when the Federal soldiers appeared outside.

Many Hanover civilians who lived near the Pamunkey River became familiar with troopers from Colonel Richard H. Rush's 6th Pennsylvania Cavalry. This regiment received orders from army headquarters on May 22 detaching them from Brigadier General Philip St. George Cooke's Cavalry Reserve. Over the next several days, these Pennsylvanians then scouted and picketed the Pamunkey River crossings that stretched from Piping Tree Ferry northwest to Hanovertown Ferry.[1]

On May 25, several squadrons from Rush's regiment trotted into the crossroads village of Old Church, which stood south of the Pamunkey River and about twelve miles northwest of White House Landing. Many members of this unit came from prominent Philadelphia families, and some had served before the war in the First Troop Philadelphia City Cavalry, which had roots as an escort to George Washington in the American Revolution. Thomas Smith wrote that many of the men in his regiment came from Philadelphia's "Ginger Bread Aristocracy." The regimental chaplain, Samuel L. Gracey, admitted "most of the recruits were raw city boys, unaccustomed to riding and caring for horses." One company in the regiment did come from Reading.[2]

Thomas Smith revealed that he did not care for Colonel Rush, and he was not alone in his ill feelings. In one letter to his brother, Smith referred to Rush as a "Tyrent to Perfection." Major Alexander Biddle, 121st Pennsylvania Infantry Regiment, considered Rush "a very unnecessarily mean and severe officer." Biddle knew Rush well as he was married to one of the colonel's cousins.[3]

Over the next several weeks Rush's men performed more scout duty. They also burned bridges over the Pamunkey River near Hanover Court House and participated in the battle there on May 27 to clear Confederate units away for the arrival of Major General Irvin McDowell's 1st Corps from Fredericksburg.

McDowell's anticipated move would bring some 30,000 more soldiers to reinforce the Army of the Potomac. Fearing that he lacked men, McClellan continued to besiege the War Department and President Abraham Lincoln with appeals for more troops. He did not want to spare any front line men from the coming battle, so on May 24 he requested from Secretary of War Edwin Stanton an order for a regiment to be moved from Norfolk to White House Landing on the Pamunkey River to guard the supply depot. General John Wool, commanding Union troops at Norfolk, refused. This rebuff began McClellan's tug of war with other commanders for men. Stanton placated the squabble by sending troops from the New York area — a trip of several hundred miles versus the forty miles between Norfolk and White House Landing.[4]

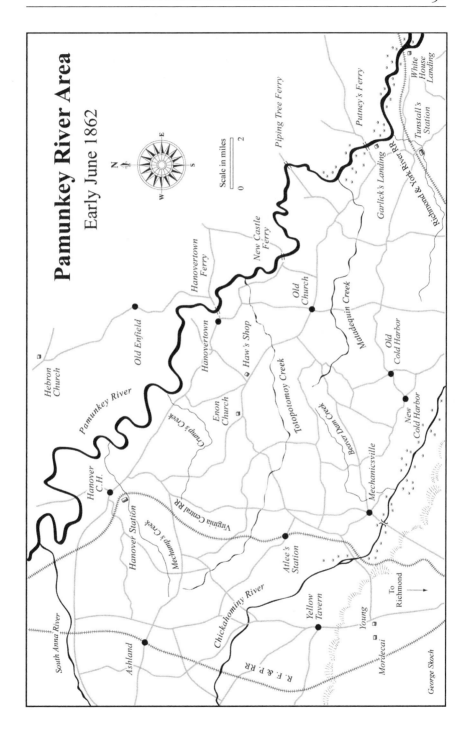

Pamunkey River Area
Early June 1862

Scale in miles
0   2

White House Landing
Puney's Ferry
Tunstall's Station
Garlick's Landing
Piping Tree Ferry
Richmond & York River RR
New Castle Ferry
Old Church
Matadequin Creek
Hanovertown Ferry
Old Cold Harbor
Hanovertown
Haw's Shop
New Cold Harbor
Old Enfield
Enon Church
Totopotomoy Creek
Hebron Church
Cramp's Creek
Beaver Dam Creek
Pamunkey River
Mechanicsville
Hanover C.H.
Virginia Central RR
Hanover Station
Mechump's Creek
Atlee's Station
To Richmond
Yellow Tavern
Chickahominy River
Young
Mordecai
South Anna River
Ashland
R. F. & P. RR
George Skoch

In late May, details of the exploits of General Thomas J. "Stonewall" Jackson in the Shenandoah Valley reached Richmond. John Jones referred to Jackson as "lightning in the Northwest" for "sweeping everything before him" in defeating three Union armies. This distraction was not lost on the Lincoln administration, as they cancelled the southward move of McDowell's troops from Fredericksburg.[5]

McClellan fumed over this change, and he continued to pester the Lincoln administration with his manpower problems. On May 26 he complained that he had lost the service of 3,000 men over the previous ten days due to sickness and casualties.[6]

McClellan's dithering was evident to many enlisted men, as they grumbled through their daily duties of digging trenches and pulling picket duty. The 4th U. S. Cavalry's private Charles E. Bates wondered about the timing for the inevitable attack against Richmond. His squadron worked as the headquarters' guard for McClellan's staff. Bates wrote to his father back in Connecticut: "I think I have the solution of the reason why McClellan wont attack the rebels. It is my belief that he is going to extend his right far enough to get possession of the railroad running through Fredericksburg and thus kill two birds with one stone. Join McDowells forces to his, and alas get the famous Stonewall Jackson on the hip." Yet, as George McClellan delayed his attack against Richmond, he unwittingly allowed time for reinforcements to strengthen Joseph Johnston's army.[7]

Unfortunately for the Union cavalrymen, George McClellan harbored misconceptions about the use of cavalry despite having served in pre-war cavalry assignments. He seemed unable to contemplate a role for cavalry beyond headquarters' guard, escort duty and limited scout missions. The 1861 Federal general-in-chief Winfield Scott believed that the wooded hilly terrain of Virginia coupled with newly designed rifled weapons rendered the traditional role of cavalry — scouting and flank screening — obsolete. Scott believed "the role of the cavalry in the approaching contest would be unimportant and secondary in its character." McClellan also shared this theoretical use of the mounted arm. Thus, he decided that his cavalry should be split up amongst the five corps in his army, which he enacted with Special Orders 90 on March 24, 1862. The Union corps commanders then further divided the blue horsemen, splitting regiments up and sending mounted companies to support the various infantry divisions and brigades. The anti-cavalry bias dated back to 1861 when the Federal army had only five mounted organizations, and some senior officers looked askance at horse units.[8]

By the spring of 1862, a stark contrast existed between the organization and the mission of the cavalry forces in each army. Generals Joseph Johnston and later Robert E. Lee supported a centralized cavalry command led by Brigadier General James Ewell Brown (Jeb) Stuart. Civil War historian Jeffry Wert noted that the organization of the Union cavalry "suffered from bureaucratic myopia and McClellan's view of its role."[9]

Joseph Johnston had the utmost confidence in Stuart and viewed him as the consummate leader of men. In August 1861, Johnston had noted in a letter to President Davis that he needed more cavalrymen:

> Our men, and we can find thousands like them, are good horsemen, well mounted. Can you not give them to us, and with Stuart to command them? He is a rare man, wonderfully endowed by nature with the qualities necessary for an officer of light cavalry. Calm, firm, acute, active, and enterprising, I know of no one more competent than he to estimate the occurrences before him at their true value. If you add to this army a real brigade of cavalry, you can find no better brigadier-general to command it.[10]

During the same period, George McClellan harbored suspicion toward volunteer cavalry regiments, as he believed these soldiers would need more than two years of training to become competent horse soldiers. His belief that the war would be over before the volunteers could become effective cavalrymen made it easier to break down the regimental structure and attach individual volun-teer cavalry companies to serve with infantry brigades. He placed more faith in his regular cavalrymen, many of whom had seen prewar service out west guarding forts, wagon trains and hunting Indians. His preference to use his horsemen to carry messages or serve as headquarters and escort guards was a flashy but poor use of the mounted arm. This misuse of the cavalry trickled down-ward as subordinate commanders elected to use the horsemen in a similar fashion.[11]

McClellan's failure to understand the varied uses for horse soldiers would eventually lead to immediate problems during the Peninsula Campaign. He refused to view the cavalry arm as an independent force "nor did he seem to understand the tactical role of a unified cavalry command." Meanwhile, Jeb Stuart used his visionary talent and realized that brigade-sized cavalry units were perfect for con-ducting deep raids and for screening army movements.[12]

Union captain Wesley Merritt who would later rise to brigadier general issued an unflattering description of McClellan's command capabilities. He found McClellan "was especially deficient in the instincts which characterized the great army commanders of history, with reference to the proper uses of cavalry." The rushing hither and yonder by Union cavalrymen frequently in bad weather on the Peninsula only served to wear the horses and the riders down. In Merritt's view, Little Mac's abuse and scattering of his mounted assets ensured that when they would be needed they would not be ready or able.[13]

Two experienced officers commanded the bulk of the Army of the Potomac's cavalry arm during the Peninsula Campaign. Brigadier General George Stoneman led the Advance Cavalry Guard which included the 2nd Rhode Island Cavalry, the 98th Pennsylvania Infantry and the 8th Illinois Cavalry plus several artillery batteries. Several other volunteer cavalry regiments had been parceled out to the army's various corps.

Stoneman had graduated in the famous West Point class of 1846. He ranked number thirty-three to his friend and classmate George McClellan who stood number two in the class. Stoneman had also roomed with Stonewall Jackson while there. He had served on McClellan's staff during the 1861 campaign in western Virginia.[14]

Brigadier General Philip St. George Cooke commanded the army's Cavalry Reserve, a quasi-division. By May 1862, the Cavalry Reserve included two undersized brigades that consisted of the 5th U. S. Cavalry, the 6th U. S. Cavalry and the 6th Pennsylvania Cavalry brigaded with Brigadier General William H. Emory. Colonel George A. H. Blake commanded the other brigade with the 1st U. S. Cavalry and the 8th Pennsylvania Cavalry.

Philip St. George Cooke was born in Leesburg, Virginia in 1809. He had graduated from West Point in 1827, and he spent the next thirty years involved in mounted operations on the western plains, an area that nineteenth century geography books referred to as "The Great American Desert." He combined his extensive outpost experiences into two books: *Scenes and Adventures in the Army* (1845) and *The Conquest of New Mexico and California* (1858). A short time after he received a promotion to colonel of the 2nd U.S. Dragoons, Cooke sailed to Europe to serve as an observer in the Crimean War in 1859–1860. The War Department acknowledged that he was the expert on cavalry operations and asked him to work on a cavalry tactics manual. Shortly after the Civil War began his name graced the cover of a book titled *The 1862 U.S. Cavalry Tactics.*[15]

Wesley Merritt had worked for Cooke in the prewar 2nd Dragoons, and then he became his aide as McClellan's army approached Richmond. Merritt would remain one of Cooke's staunchest allies, and he noted that Cooke had studied the cavalry tactics of Frederick the Great and Napoleon. Cooke had stressed to his troopers the importance of "the mounted charge." He "was opposed to fighting on foot save in cases of necessity." Merritt recalled that his old commander had insisted on "[s]harp sabers, and sharp spurs" to overwhelm the enemy during a horseback charge. Although Cooke commanded the Cavalry Reserve composed of two brigades, prior to the war he had never commanded more than a regiment.[16]

When McClellan became commander for the Army of the Potomac, he appointed Stoneman as his chief of cavalry even though Cooke was thirteen years older and had more mounted experience than Stoneman. Stoneman became a brigadier general in August 1861, which was three months ahead of Cooke's promotion to the same rank. Many officers knew that McClellan took care of his friends, and perhaps this was one of those cases. Stoneman would survive the war and later be elected as governor of California in 1882.

As McClellan's army approached Richmond in late May, his lines stretched from the Pamunkey River south to the James. A ride between both rivers would take all day. However, McClellan thinly

6th Pennsylvania Cavalry known as Rush's Lancers. Note lances on right festooned with red pennants on end. MOLLUS, USAHEC.

stretched his cavalrymen north of the Chickahominy River which resulted in gaps in the line. The bulk of the cavalry operations on the army's right flank would fall to Cooke and his Cavalry Reserve.

The stagnated thinking at the Army of the Potomac command levels might explain why Colonel Rush's 6th Pennsylvania Cavalry troopers carried nine-foot-long wooden lances. An eleven-inch steel blade tipped the pike giving it some heft at eight pounds. A scarlet pennant festooned the sharp end of the lance. This primitive weapon earned the regiment the moniker of Rush's Lancers. One trooper considered the weapons "a decided nuisance in a wooded country" while an infantry officer observed

Colonel Richard H. Rush, commander of 6th Pennsylvania Cavalry. A Philadelphia native, Rush graduated in the same West Point class as George McClellan. His regiment became known as Rush's Lancers because of their primitive weapons. MOLLUS, USAHEC.

that some soldiers called the red pennants "'hospital flags.'" Other soldiers derisively referred to the Pennsylvanians as "Lancer's Rushes" because they flitted back and forth providing escort duty for senior officers and visiting dignitaries.[17]

The idea to arm a cavalry regiment with lances came from McClellan. In fact, McClellan had also traveled to Europe to serve as an observer in the Crimean War, and he believed that the European-style weapon would give the cavalry a unique flashy look. The unfortunate recipient of this idea was McClellan's West Point classmate Richard Rush.

Richard Rush had also graduated in the West Point class of 1846 with fellow plebes Stonewall Jackson, A.P. Hill, and George Pickett. Rush's Philadelphia family roots traced quite a historical pedigree. His paternal grandfather, Benjamin, was a signer of the Declaration of Independence. Rush's namesake father served in several presidential cabinet positions while he also represented the United States as a Minister to Great Britain and later to France. The thirty-eight-year-old Richard had fought in the Mexican War and had served in the artillery for several years afterward. Rush left the army in 1854 and returned to Philadelphia to join the business community until the war erupted.

During most of May, Rush and his Lancers spent their time learning the Hanover County roads and guarding the Pamunkey River crossings. Meanwhile, McClellan continued to delay his attack while more Confederate regiments arrived in Richmond. Rebel war clerk John Jones counted the increase in Confederate numbers each day, and he believed that McClellan "is doomed to defeat." In contrast, northern newspapers reveled in the coming great battle and the certain destruction of Richmond. Some of these Union forecasters saw June 15 as the latest that the city could survive.[18]

As the end of May arrived, civilians and soldiers alike waited for this inevitable clash. McClellan finally placed his overwhelming force on the move as he planned an attack with his right flank. However, Mother Nature would soon intervene, and would provide Joseph Johnston an opportunity to save Richmond.

CHAPTER 5

Big Decisions for General Lee

EARLY JUNE 1862

THE GREAT BATTLE in front of Richmond, long forecast by many, did come, but not before a violent thunderstorm hurled rain and lightning across the Richmond area on the evening of May 30. The banks of the Chickahominy overflowed, which left two U.S. Army corps commanded by brigadier generals Erasmus Keyes and Samuel Heintzelman stranded south of the river near a place called Seven Pines. Joseph E. Johnston saw the opportunity to overwhelm the pair of Federal corps, and he put his gray army into action on May 31. Through miscommunication and delays, the Confederate attack began five hours late, and the divisions moved forward on one muddy road instead of the planned three parallel roads. The result became a chaotic mess.

The 6th U. S. Cavalry's private Sidney Morris Davis remembered being at bivouac near Cold Harbor on the afternoon of May 31 when "muttering of cannon and small arms could be heard away off towards the south." Davis' fellow cavalrymen passed several newspapers around camp while they waited for orders to move toward the fighting. The headlines brought grumbles amongst the men thanks to Major General Nathaniel Banks' Union defeat at Winchester in the Shenandoah Valley. Darkness ended the sounds of battle only to return with sunrise the next morning. Davis remembered many of his colleagues expressed enthusiasm for the battle that they believed would open the way into Richmond. However, hours after the firing had ended, no orders came for the regiment to pack "up our military fixtures and entering the Capital of the Confederacy, as we had hoped."[1]

At the height of the fighting that day, George McClellan lay on a bed in his headquarters' tent north of the Chickahominy River. His body sweated and shook from his "Mexican disease," recurring malaria that had plagued him since the Mexican War.[2]

What Sidney Davis and his fellow 6th Regular cavalrymen did not know was that a valiant effort on May 31 by Union engineers saved the day. They reconstructed the flooded Grapevine Bridge which enabled Brigadier General Edwin "Bull" Sumner's corps to slog across the Chickahominy River to reinforce the Union line at Seven Pines. As darkness swept the field that day burial details scoured the area. The fighting continued on June 1 and ended in a stalemate. Davis later lamented about the Battle of Fair Oaks/Seven Pines because "instead of culminating in the capture of Richmond, it had almost ended in irretrievable disaster to our arms." Casualties for both sides were high, but the most significant loss was one man who wore gold wreathed stars on his gray collar.[3]

On the first day of the battle, while Joseph Johnston sat atop his horse a bullet struck him in the shoulder. Seconds later, shards from an overhead shell-burst broke some ribs. This wounding brought more darkness for the Confederate army as the one man who knew the battle plan joined the ranks of wounded.

Few people could have foreseen the strategic impact that Johnston's replacement would have. Fifty-five-year-old General Robert E. Lee's move from military advisor for Jefferson Davis to command of the Confederate army defending Richmond did not elicit unanimous cheers from Confederate soldiers or military officials. Some did not believe that Lee was up to the biggest task that the Confederacy had faced — defending the new country's capital. The editor of the Richmond *Examiner* newspaper showed his dislike of Lee in noting his uneven performance commanding troops in southwest Virginia in 1861.

A short time after Lee's appointment, Major Edward Porter Alexander, the army's ordnance chief, expressed his doubts about Lee too. He questioned allowing an overwhelming "enemy to take his own time, & to perfect all his plans, & accumulate all his forces, & to choose his own battle." Alexander discussed the situation with a member of President Davis' staff, Colonel Joseph C. Ives, and he sadly noted that waiting for McClellan's inevitable attack would end in defeat. "Our only hope," Alexander reasoned, "is to bounce him & whip him somewhere before he is ready for us, and that needs audacity in our commander. Has Gen. Lee that audacity?" Ives dispelled Alexander's fears by assuring the young Georgian that "Lee is audacity personified."[4]

Brigadier General Jeb Stuart seemed pleased with Lee's new position. However, six months before, Stuart had expressed reservations about Lee in a letter to his brother, William Alexander Stuart. Jeb Stuart had considered Joseph Johnston "head and shoulders above every General in the southern Confederacy." William must have shuddered when he heard of Lee's appointment as he recalled Jeb's unflattering assessment: "With the profoundest personal regard for Genl Lee — he has disappointed

General Robert E. Lee, commander of the Army of Northern Virginia. MOLLUS, USAHEC.

me as a General." The cavalry general had also noted to his wife in December 1861 that "Jo Johnston is as good a friend as I have in C. S."[5]

Richmond war clerk John Jones supported Lee's appointment as he scribbled in his diary, "[t]his may be hailed as the harbinger of bright fortune." However, Jones did not indicate his source of optimism over Lee's new position.[6]

Certainly George McClellan did not foresee the significance of Lee's new assignment. He had written a letter to President Lincoln on April 20 and included harsh words about Lee. The young Union commander indicated that he preferred to face Lee rather than Johnston because Lee "is too cautious & weak under grave responsibility — personally brave & energetic to a fault, he yet is wanting in moral firmness when pressed by heavy responsibility & is likely to be timid & irresolute in action." This misjudgment would later come back to haunt McClellan.[7]

Robert E. Lee's orders during the first week of June to strengthen and to lengthen the defense lines sent many dispirited Southern soldiers to work with their shovels hacking into the muddy soil, swatting mosquitoes and sawing logs. "Granny" Lee soon earned a new moniker amongst the troops — "king of spades." What the new commander witnessed as he rode the lines on the back of Traveller bothered him. "Our people are opposed to work. Our troops officers community & press. All ridicule & resist it."[8]

The typical Union soldier who manned defense lines a short distance to the east experienced similar frustrations. The 4th U. S. Cavalry's private Charles E. Bates informed his parents of one prominent Peninsula problem. "[T]he flies and musquitos being as thick and voracious. The musquitos are commonly called gallon-sippers here and I think the flies should be called two gallon sippers, for they have twice the powers of suction that musquitos have. Perhaps they think the order for rations applies to them and they are getting five days ahead. The torments."[9]

The acerbic editor of the Richmond *Examiner*, John M. Daniel, scolded both army commanders when he wrote on June 10, "As for this city, if its fate depends on a game in which 'spades are trumps,' played by two eminent hands of the old army, each knowing every thing that the other knows, there is no doubt but that the Confederate Government will, sooner or later, be spaded out of Richmond."[10]

Lee sent a letter to Jefferson Davis on June 5 outlining his strategy. If Jackson could be reinforced with troops brought in from the Carolinas and Georgia, he could carry his Shenandoah Valley success into Maryland and Pennsylvania. This move would certainly create hysteria in Washington and distract McClellan's mission against Richmond. Lee actually knew and understood McClellan — much better than McClellan understood Lee. He figured that McClellan would move from one fortified line to the next and always remain under cover of artillery and naval gunboats. Lee estimated that the defense of Richmond would require 100,000 troops, "which perhaps would only prolong not save" the Confederate capital. Unbeknownst to most of his staff, Lee wrote Davis: "I am preparing a line that I can hold with part of our forces in front, while with the rest I will endeavour to make a diversion to bring McClellan out."[11]

The new Confederate army commander massaged his plans during this first week of June. He believed that McClellan's left was too strong. However, as he looked over his maps he could see that a move across the Chickahominy River into the enemy's right flank would threaten the Richmond & York River Railroad and McClellan's main supply depot at White House Landing. If successful, the move would force the enemy out of his defense lines and possibly into a retreat.[12]

The rainy weather continued to be bothersome for both sides. A Mississippi cavalryman in the Jeff Davis Legion reported that he had grown accustomed to being wet. Private Joseph Dunbar Shields wrote to his father on June 8, "If it does not rain every twelve hours we think there is going to be a drouth." He admitted that "the only thing I want is to get the Yankees started towards Washington City." However, he realized "we are going to have a pretty hard time getting them started as they are throwing up fortifications."[13]

Shields also indicated that increased time spent caring for his horse meant that he minimized other essential tasks. "I generally sleep every morning so as to forget my breakfast and then wake up and carry my horse to water and graze him and then come back and eat my breakfast, dinner and supper all in one which answers very well."[14]

A Georgia officer in the Jeff Davis Legion mulled over army life in their camp along the Charles City Road east of Richmond. He noted that he had already plucked a bunch of ticks off of himself, but the real problem seemed to be the "redbugs" also known as chiggers.[15]

During June's first week, McClellan moved more troops south, across the Chickahominy, to reinforce his left flank. By the end of that week, only Major General Fitz John Porter's 5th Corps held McClellan's right flank on the river's north bank. McClellan had invited an attack against his left at the end of May by splitting his army, and now he invited an attack against his right. Fitz John Porter commanded the largest corps in the army, and this assignment angered other Union officers who were not members of McClellan's inner circle. McClellan did express some concern about his right flank's vulnerability, which might explain why the largest corps remained near Mechanicsville. Perhaps a glance at his own maps revealed the ease of supplying his army from a depot on the James River rather than trying to run trains from White House Landing eleven miles to Dispatch Station and almost four more miles to Savage Station.

On May 31, in response to concerns about the Union right flank, Philip St. George Cooke had received orders from Army of the Potomac headquarters which directed him to send two cavalry squadrons to Old Church, a crossroads village located about fourteen miles southeast of Hanover Court House. The order stressed that "great vigilance" should be exercised as "[s]couts will be thrown well to the front and flanks to watch well the movements of the enemy." Cooke gave the assignment to thirty-seven-year-old Captain William B. Royall.[16]

Royall rode into Old Church on June 1 with men from companies B, C, F, and H of the 5th U. S. Cavalry. For the next two weeks, Royall sent out daily patrols to Hanover Court House, and he established pickets on the roads that led into Old Church.

These patrols watched and listened for any danger to the Army of the Potomac. Royall had served in an infantry unit during the Mexican War and then returned to civilian life only to rejoin the army as a cavalry officer in 1855. Though a native Virginian, he had remained in the U. S. Army with the outbreak of the Civil War.[17]

On June 2, Major Lawrence Williams received orders for his 6th U. S. Cavalry to report to Brigadier General Philip St. George Cooke at Cavalry Reserve headquarters near Johnson's farm, about a mile southwest of Bethesda Church. After these troopers arrived, most of the men then spent much of the day "standing to horse" in anticipation of an attack on the right flank while the distant guns still banged away at Seven Pines.[18]

On the same day, Cooke sent Captain August Kautz's squadron (two companies) of the 6th U. S. Cavalry plus two squadrons from the 6th Pennsylvania Cavalry toward the Pamunkey River. Kautz's team set out to burn any viable bridges and ferries between Piping Tree Ferry and Dr. Carter Warren Wormley's place that might make the right flank vulnerable to an attack across the Pamunkey River. Cooke also warned Kautz to look and to listen for any enemy force assembling across the river in King William County. The troopers hoped to find and arrest Dr. Wormley too. The Lancers and the Regulars galloped north toward the river. Some of Kautz's men no doubt shook their heads at the Pennsylvanian's unwieldy lances. The column reached the south bank at dark. Captain Kautz and some of his officers ate supper at the home of an overseer named Patterson. Later that night, the rumble of thunder grew as lightning shot across the western sky. The increasing wind and stinging rain chased Kautz onto the porch of the house.

The following morning the effects of the rain flowed over the riverbanks. Several of Kautz's men later arrived with an irate Dr. Wormley. Wormley's anger and his problems perhaps increased upon the nearby discovery of a ferry boat, a twenty-five ton sloop, and nine other boats cleverly hidden by downed trees and brush in a small creek. "The Dr. when he was brought down was very violent," noted Kautz. The doctor's shouts provided more fodder for his incarceration when he "boasted of being an original Secessionist and that he had raised the first Secession Flag in Virginia in Dec. — 60."[19]

Kautz led his men back to the Cavalry Reserve camp, and they turned their prisoner over to the provost marshal. The nearly constant movement since arriving at Fort Monroe two months before had exhausted the men and their mounts. The chronic wet weather and swampy terrain had created hoof problems for many horses. Yet "a scarcity of horseshoes and nails, little or no coal" and only one anvil meant the regiment's blacksmiths and farriers would have to improvise.[20]

Union cavalry units remained busy during the first two weeks of June as they provided showpiece guards for headquarters' duty, and they maintained road and flank reconnaissance. Some of the horsemen guarded the supply line from White House Landing. These troopers on the Union right flank near the Pamunkey River went on frequent scouts with their haversacks filled with two days' rations. One soldier noted they "rarely managed to return to camp within three or four days, and consequently these extensions of time were very exacting upon our stomachs." In addition to creating a burdensome toll on the men, these efforts proved a drain on horseflesh too.[21]

August Kautz probably did not enjoy bivouac duty under the command of Lawrence Williams. Williams was only two weeks removed from a career-threatening stay in the guardhouse thanks to his fondness for the bottle and his habit of disappearing for lengthy periods from regimental headquarters. Some of these rumors alleged that Williams met with Confederates behind their lines.

Brigadier General George Stoneman had heard these rumors, and he ordered Major Williams' arrest. Kautz happily obliged the order when Williams returned from one of his midnight vanishing acts. The irate Williams soon found himself confined to his tent as four carbine-wielding troopers guarded the outside. Two other issues added to the suspicion directed against Williams. His younger brother had resigned his commission in the U. S. Army and sided with the Confederacy, and Williams was kin to the Lee family.[22]

On May 16, Williams had met with George McClellan at White House and proclaimed his innocence. The next day, Williams wrote a letter to Stoneman's assistant adjutant-general demanding "a Board of Examination be appointed by the General Commanding to investigate the circumstance." Several days later, an amazed Kautz watched Williams arrive back at regimental headquarters restored to command. Kautz caustically observed, the men "had no faith in his [Williams'] judgement and were rapidly doubting his loyalty."[23]

Captain August V. Kautz. Image taken after he had been promoted to brigadier general. Library of Congress.

However, Williams' good performance "in battle with his regiment should have precluded suspicion as to his loyalty." A subsequent defense for Williams came in a letter from the 1st Virginia's colonel Fitzhugh Lee. Lee recalled firing at Williams when he recognized him riding at the head of his regiment during the Peninsula fighting. The Confederate officer also noted that Robert E. Lee's wife and daughter were in the White House landing area at the time, and "[i]t is possible that Williams attempted to communicate with them in some way for social purposes. I am quite satisfied that he was not a traitor."[24]

On June 4, a short time after Lawrence Williams was restored to command of the 6th U. S. Cavalry, McClellan telegraphed his concerns about the right flank to President Lincoln, and again

the flooded Chickahominy played a role. "I have taken every possible step to insure the security of the corps on the right bank,
but I cannot reinforce them from here until my bridges are all
safe as my force is too small to insure my right and rear should
the enemy attack in that direction, as they may probably attempt."
The rains continued to play havoc with military operations and
McClellan informed the War Department three days later that "the
Chickahominy River has risen so as to flood the entire bottoms to
the depth of 3 or 4 feet. The whole face of the country is a perfect
bog, entirely impassable for artillery, or even cavalry, except directly
in the narrow roads, which renders any general movement either
of this or the rebel army entirely out of the question until we have
more favorable weather."[25]

A New York newspaper correspondent signaled his apprehension upon setting foot on Virginia soil at White House. Having
heard all his life that Virginia was "sacred" due to its history and its
natural beauty, he used his pen to deflate the idea. He stated that
"Virginians were guilty of a horrible joke when they pronounced it
'sacred'. If sacred things are the things mostly damned by profane
lips, then the soil of Virginia may be entitled to the name and all
the honors. Certainly, there is nothing about it deserving of reli-
gious, or even gentlemanly, consideration." The amount of mud
which he had to tromp through and then scrape off his clothes and
boots he described with a circus analogy: "Take Barnum's whale
tank, fill it half full of water, dump in several barrels of soil, stir it
up, and call the whole a road, and even then your illustration of
the thing will fall short of the dread reality."[26]

On June 10, McClellan would again apologize for his stalled
army. "I am completely checked by the weather. The roads and fields
are literally impassable for artillery; almost so for infantry." This
message neglected to mention cavalry, which reflected the little
importance he gave to his horsemen. McClellan's unimaginative
utilization of his cavalry coupled with the arm's weak command
structure would soon reap dire consequences for the Army of the
Potomac. The tarnished reputation of the Union cavalry would
take nearly a year to repair.[27]

Robert E. Lee, undaunted by the roads and the weather, would soon send a large body of cavalry to reconnoiter the Union right flank on the south bank of the Pamunkey River. This mission would be led by an unknown brigadier general of cavalry named James Ewell Brown Stuart.

CHAPTER 6

What Is On the Union Right Flank?

EARLY JUNE 1862

J EB STUART'S FAMILIARITY with Robert E. Lee prompted him to write a letter to the new army commander on June 4 in which he outlined what he thought needed to be done to oust the enemy from Richmond's doorstep. Stuart believed that Lee should launch a massive attack against the Union left flank south of the Chickahominy, which was where the Battle of Seven Pines had ground to a stalemate after two days of fighting.[1]

However, Lee had a different plan. He noted in his report written nine months later, "[t]he strength of his [Union] left wing rendered a direct assault injudicious, if not impracticable. It was therefore determined to construct defensive lines, so as to enable a part of the army to defend the city and leave the other part free to cross the Chickahominy and operate on the north bank. By sweeping down the river on that side and threatening his communications with York River it was thought that the enemy would be compelled to retreat or give battle out of his intrenchements."[2]

Over the next several days, Stuart must have mulled over his strategy letter that he sent to Lee. Did he overstep his bounds? Although Lee did not officially respond to Stuart in writing, he must have indicated to the cavalry officer his interest in probing the enemy right flank because on June 8, Stuart rode into the darkness to scout central Hanover County. The following night Stuart would send John Mosby on a dangerous reconnaissance mission into the same area. If Stuart himself still believed an attack against the Union left flank viable, then why would he not send a group of scouts in that direction too?

On the morning of June 9, a weary Jeb Stuart requested a breakfast meeting with a small wiry Virginian named John Singleton Mosby. Earlier, just after sunup, the cavalry commander had returned from a peek behind Union lines east of Ashland. His new aide, Prussian captain Heros von Borcke, had accompanied the general. Stuart probably wanted to familiarize the foreign officer with the area and determine the man's capabilities. More importantly, Stuart had arranged a midnight meeting with one of his spies. The spy failed to show up and after a long wait, the pair rode off deeper into enemy lines to the man's house. When they arrived they discovered that the place stood only a short distance from a Union camp. They found the spy confined to bed with an illness, which explained his earlier absence from the prearranged meeting. Stuart gleaned some important information from the man; then he and a relieved von Borcke hopped back onto their horses and side-stepped enemy patrols on their return to cavalry headquarters.[3]

The midnight ride increased Stuart's interest in the area for future military operations, but he also seemed impressed with the way the large von Borcke handled himself. Born into an aristocratic Prussian family in 1835, Heros von Borcke had received a commission into the Prussian army in 1853. The fascination of combat from across the Atlantic Ocean attracted Captain von Borcke, who took a leave of absence from his army. He sailed to American soil and walked off the deck of a blockade runner in Charleston harbor on May 24, 1862. Less than a week later, he arrived in Richmond, where he met with the Confederate secretary of war, George Wythe Randolph. Impressed with what he saw, Randolph wrote a letter of introduction and sent the young

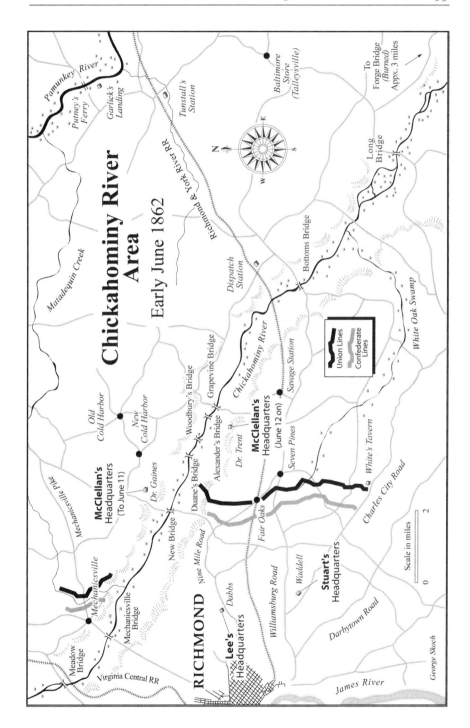

Chickahominy River Area

Early June 1862

Pamunkey River

Putney's Ferry

Garlick's Landing

Tunstall's Station

Baltimore Store (Talleysville)

To Forge Bridge (Burned) Appx. 3 miles

Long Bridge

Richmond & York River RR

Bottoms Bridge

White Oak Swamp

Matadequin Creek

Dispatch Station

Grapevine Bridge

Chickahominy River

Savage Station

Woodbury's Bridge

McClellan's Headquarters (June 12 on)

Seven Pines

White's Tavern

Old Cold Harbor

New Cold Harbor

Dr. Gaines

Alexander's Bridge

Dr. Trent

Charles City Road

Mechanicsville Pike

McClellan's Headquarters (To June 11)

Duane's Bridge

Union Lines

Confederate Lines

New Bridge

Fair Oaks

Scale in miles

0   2

Mechanicsville

Nine Mile Road

Dabbs

Wadell

Stuart's Headquarters

Darbytown Road

Mechanicsville Bridge

RICHMOND

Lee's Headquarters

Williamsburg Road

Meadow Bridge

Virginia Central RR

James River

George Skoch

Captain Heros von Borcke. The Prussian would be wounded a year later at the Battle of Middleburg and his wounds prevented him from returning to full field service for the Confederacy. Image from *Zwei Jahre Im Sattel Und Am Feinde* by Heros von Borcke.

Prussian to find Jeb Stuart on cavalry duty east of Richmond. Von Borcke located Stuart on the eve of the Battle of Seven Pines, and the cavalry general soon found the foreigner worthy of membership to the cavalry staff.[4]

The rapport between the two men would grow into a close relationship developed by sharing dangerous experiences in the upcoming battles. Von Borcke liked Stuart's fancy uniform, "which consisted of a small grey jacket, trousers of the same stuff, and over them high military boots, a yellow silk sash, and a grey slouch hat, surmounted by a sweeping black ostrich plume." He found that the clothes fit well over Stuart's stout build, and he noted that Stuart's "whole person seemed instinct with vitality, his movements were alert, his observation keen and rapid, and altogether he was to me the model of a dashing cavalry leader."[5]

Though von Borcke's initial command of English was poor, he soon acquired adequate speaking skills. Colonel G. Moxley Sorrel recalled that what he remembered most about his initial meeting with the huge blonde-haired foreigner was "[h]e was an ambulating arsenal." Von Borcke attracted much attention and discussion amongst the Southerners because of his six-foot-four-inch frame, which carried a solid two hundred and fifty pounds. As if size wasn't enough, the Prussian also garnered second looks because of the number of weapons that he carried. Sorrel observed:

> A double-barreled rifle was strapped across his back, a Winchester carbine hung by his hip, heavy revolvers were in his belt, right and left side; an enormous straight double-edged sharp-pointed cuirassier's saber hung together with sabertasche to his left thigh, and a short 'couteau de chasse' finished up his right. Besides, his English army saddle bore two large holsters, one for his field-glasses, the other for still another revolver, bigger and deadlier than all the others.[6]

These qualities ensured that those who met Captain von Borcke did not soon forget him. Captain William Willis Blackford became friends with von Borcke and considered him an asset to the staff as he "was a thoroughly educated cavalry officer, a gentleman by birth and breeding, and of extremely frank and polished manners." Von Borcke also had a "curious habit of filing his fingernails to points."[7]

A short time later, Sorrel observed that von Borcke's initial experience with Stuart had caused the German to shed most of his weaponry. Von Borcke's horse certainly appreciated the lighter load since by the second week of June, the large man only carried a pair of revolvers, the huge saber and a blunderbuss.[8]

Upon their safe return to camp from the meeting with the spy, von Borcke probably lay down to rest. Meanwhile, Stuart breakfasted with John Mosby. They sat at a table by themselves away from any staff members as the general carried on some small talk. Campfire smoke, mixed with the smell of bacon and coffee, floated by as both men ate. Mosby waited for the real reason he had been summoned. Stuart, tired from his all-night reconnaissance with his new Prussian friend, unfolded a map and finally gave the scout his mission. An excited Mosby shoveled the rest of the food into his mouth, for he later noted this was the "opportunity for which I had pined." Moments later he jumped on his horse and raced to the camp of his old cavalry company to pick three friends from Abingdon, Virginia for the mission. The cavalry commander wanted Mosby to reconnoiter the enemy's extreme right flank and to find out if McClellan had fortified his line along the ridge above Totopotomoy Creek, which flowed northeast and emptied into the Pamunkey River.[9]

Mosby was born in 1833, and he had attended the University of Virginia. As a youth some acquaintances had considered him "very delicate" and had wagered that he would not live to adulthood. While at school in Charlottesville, he shot and seriously wounded a much larger fellow student who had threatened him. He was convicted, fined and sentenced to jail. However the fine was later remitted, and Mosby received a pardon by the governor. No doubt the reputation of Mosby's victim as a violent man garnered legal and political sympathy. During his brief stint in jail, he became interested in the law profession, which guided him to his prewar work as a lawyer in Bristol.[10]

When war came, Mosby shuttered his law office and joined with fellow members of Company D, 1st Virginia Cavalry. He stood about five-foot-seven inches tall and weighed no more than one-hundred-thirty pounds, yet his contrarian nature ensured an unpredictability that made him a most dangerous adversary. His earlier student experience with a larger assailant had also convinced the young lawyer that firearms proficiency would always be a great equalizer.[11]

Mosby came to Jeb Stuart's attention when Stuart commanded the 1st Virginia Cavalry. Private Mosby then became the regimental adjutant when Stuart later moved to brigadier general, and Captain William E. "Grumble" Jones became

John Mosby dressed in a captain's uniform in 1863. Image from *The Memoirs of Colonel John S. Mosby* edited by Charles Wells Russell, p. 150.

a colonel and the 1st Virginia Cavalry's new commander. Fate soon played a trick on the twenty-eight-year-old Mosby. The new Confederate government ordered elections of officers in early 1862. The men elected twenty-six-year-old Fitzhugh Lee, Robert E. Lee's nephew, to replace the taskmaster Grumble Jones. Fitzhugh Lee wanted another adjutant so Mosby submitted his resignation. Amiable relations between Mosby and Fitz Lee would never flourish after that. Stripped of his lieutenancy, an irritated Mosby went back to Company D. However, his success on several scouting missions brought his name to Stuart's attention again. Mosby's fortune soon changed as Stuart requested that Mosby join the cavalry brigade staff as a scout. Mosby later cited this move as "the origin of my partisan life, that was far more congenial to me than the dull, routine work of an adjutant." Mosby considered Stuart "a man of original genius."[12]

When Stuart commanded the 1st Virginia, the staff members quickly learned to be ready for his pranks. Devoid of typical officer's decorum, Stuart would jest with privates and captains alike. However, underneath his veneer of comedy stood a serious military mind whose own unpredictability made him dangerous to any opposing force. "Stuart was not only an educated, but a heaven-born soldier, whose natural genius had not been stifled by red tape and the narrow rules of the schools," John Mosby wrote and then added, "as a chief of cavalry he is without peer. He cared little for formulas, and knew when to follow and when to disregard precedents.[13]

Colonel Fitzhugh Lee, 1st Virginia Cavalry commander and nephew of General R. E. Lee. Library of Congress.

As the morning sun climbed into the sky on June 9, Mosby led his three friends from Company D, 1st Virginia: Corporal Morgan M. Pendleton, Private A. M. Crockett and either Private John J. Williams or Private Rufus Chapman Williams. They rode toward the northeast as the mild temperature climbed to around seventy degrees by noon. When the group neared the closest road that led directly to central Hanover County and Totopotomoy Creek, they learned that there was a nearby truce meeting underway. They veered their mounts to the left and headed north toward Hanover Court House. As darkness approached, they bivouacked for the night south of the town. At first light the next morning, the group rode southeast. They talked with numerous citizens, most of whom seemed happy to give helpful information to the Confederate soldiers.[14]

Mosby used the fresh foliage for concealment as he and his men approached the Totopotomoy Creek area. Thick vines snaked through the brush along both sides of the creek. At several spots they tethered their horses and inched forward. The scouts looked through their glasses and saw only Union cavalry videttes and sparse numbers at that. The Southerners crept northeast toward the Pamunkey River. Surely the farthest right outpost would be strongly defended. As they approached the junction of the creek and river, all they could see on the creek's east bank was more of the same — a few blue-clad cavalrymen with their horses tethered in the trees nearby. Mosby estimated that "six to eight miles of McClellan's front was a mere shroud of cavalry pickets." The York Railroad main supply line stood only about ten miles away. The absence of Federal infantry or fortifications in such a vulnerable area amazed the scouts.[15]

The foursome quietly made their way back toward their waiting horses, but they passed too closely to some enemy soldiers, who yelled out an alert. The Southern troopers vaulted onto their mounts and raced off through the woods. After a short distance, they veered toward a road but had to stop to let a Federal cavalry patrol pass. The fear of being captured and not delivering the momentous information to Stuart certainly worried John Mosby. When the enemy patrol departed in a trail of dust, the gray-clad cavalrymen found another road that led west.[16]

They soon came upon some more Hanover County civilians who hailed their approach. During the conversation the citizens confirmed the lack of Union infantrymen, and they stated that "only a thin veil of cavalry" protected McClellan's railroad supply line from White House. Mosby could not believe his army's good fortune. "I saw now that I had discovered McClellan's vulnerable point — the heel of Achilles." The day had warmed again, and several men pulled out handkerchiefs to mop their brows. The group soon bid the citizens farewell and trotted off to the west. Once out of sight they sped to a gallop and headed for Stuart's headquarters at the Waddell house on the Charles City Road east of Richmond.[17]

Mosby's arrival carried additional excitement to Stuart's jubilant staff because word had already arrived of Stonewall Jackson's

Dabbs House, headquarters for General Lee. Numerous additions have enlarged this house since the war. When Lee and Stuart met here on June 10 to plan the cavalry raid, the front entry door stood on the left end of the building while the two windows to the right represented the width of this small two-story place. The wings on both ends were postwar additions. Photo by Randall Flynn.

dual victories at Cross Keys and Port Republic in the Shenandoah Valley. Stuart stood up from his camp chair in the tree shade as the sweat-stained Mosby dismounted. The tired scout sank into the cool grass and lay on his back. The general displayed no hostility toward Mosby for his unmilitary bearing but instead became more enthralled with Mosby's information. Quick to see the decisive opportunity, Stuart told Mosby: "Write down what you have said." As Mosby strode to the adjutant's tent to gather paper and pen, Stuart turned and ordered a nearby courier to saddle up the horses.[18]

Mosby sat down at a camp table in front of the tent and scribbled out his brief report. Finished, he returned to Stuart and handed him the unsigned memorandum. Stuart scanned the lines with his piercing blue eyes and then glanced at Mosby. A report of this magnitude destined for the commanding general needed a signature. Mosby carried the paper back to the adjutant's tent and signed it. He returned and handed the sheet to Stuart, who vaulted onto his horse and raced off with the staff escort toward General Lee's headquarters.[19]

Puffs of dust broke from the hooves of the horses as they moved down Nine Mile Road past several camps. Finally the roads seemed to be drying out. The riders stopped at the Dabbs House, located two miles east of Richmond. General Stuart, anxious to divulge his amazing news, slid off his horse in front of the white-washed brick house and handed the reins to his courier. He returned the salute of the sentry, as he bounded up several steps and entered the front door. Robert E. Lee had moved his staff into this place called High Meadows, which was owned by a widow named Mary C. Dabbs. Probably the last time Stuart had seen Lee, the commanding general had sported only a salt-and-pepper moustache. Now Lee's closely cropped thick gray beard covered most of his face.[20]

The two professional soldiers, former commandant and student, greeted each other and sat down. If either mentioned Stuart's previous letter suggesting strategy, it was not noted. Stuart talked about the porous Union right flank, withdrew Mosby's report from his pocket and handed it to the snowy haired Lee. Both officers certainly wondered how such an elemental military formula could be overlooked by George McClellan, especially when that flank stood in close proximity to the main supply depot. Somehow, the Union commander had again allowed his army to be split by a river with White House Landing a short distance behind the most vulnerable wing.

Lee adjusted his spectacles as he read the information that dovetailed with his plans. He knew that he could not afford to make a mistake when confronted by a larger well-supplied army, which stood so close to Richmond. Because the commanding general was not familiar with the scouting talents of John Mosby, he wanted additional confirmation that the Union right flank remained exposed.

Stuart's mind churned at the possibilities when Lee said that he wanted a cavalry expedition to probe the Federal right flank further and even to create some havoc in the rear. The two men glanced at a nearby map as Stuart's eyes settled on the boldest of schemes — a ride all the way around the Army of the Potomac — a trek over 100 miles! Lee's eyebrows must have arched at the idea, as he noted the numerous hazards involved with Stuart's proposed enhancement to the reconnaissance mission. However, Lee did not outright forbid the dangerous ride, which would more than double the miles and the time spent behind enemy lines.

What Lee proposed stirred Stuart, for it was what every lead actor craved — a starring role in an exciting and dangerous drama.

CHAPTER 7

The Battles of George McClellan

G EORGE McCLELLAN wanted to instill confidence in his men after their long, arduous journey to the outskirts of Richmond and their potential disaster at Seven Pines. On June 2 he issued a proclamation addressed to his men:

> Soldiers of the Army of the Potomac,
>
> I have fulfilled at least a part of my promise to you. You are now face to face with the rebels, who are at bay in front of their capital. The final and decisive battle is at hand. Unless you belie your past history the result cannot be for a moment doubtful.[1]

However, there was doubt about McClellan's effort on the east side of Richmond during the first weeks of June, and much of that doubt came out of Washington D.C. George McClellan continued to use the weather and his perceived manpower shortage to thwart queries from Washington for a timeline when he would attack Richmond.

A June 5 telegram from Secretary of War Edwin Stanton informed McClellan that five regiments were headed to the Peninsula by boat from Baltimore. The following day, Stanton ordered Brigadier General George McCall's 10,000-man Pennsylvania division detached from McDowell's force at Fredericksburg to move by boat toward McClellan. McCall's men began to arrive at

White House Landing on June 10, around the same time that Jeb Stuart delivered the information to Lee about the weakness on the Federal right flank. McClellan then informed Stanton, "I shall be in perfect readiness to move forward and take Richmond the moment McCall reaches here and the ground will admit the passage of artillery."[2]

George McCall, at age sixty, was one of the oldest soldiers on the field. He had graduated from West Point in 1822 and then served in the old army in Louisiana and Florida before he saw combat in the Mexican War. He retired from the army in 1853 to become a farmer in Chester County, Pennsylvania. When war came he rejoined the Union army. In late June 1862, less than three weeks after his men arrived at White House Landing and joined the Army of the Potomac, he would be wounded and captured at Glendale [Frayser's Farm] midway through the Seven Days' battles. He would then spend some time at Richmond's Libby Prison. After his prison release, ill health caused him to resign a year later.[3]

A sobering view greeted McCall's Pennsylvanians as they walked off their boats at White House Landing. Stacked on the wharf in plain view sat numerous rough-hewn pine coffins — not empty, but full, awaiting transport north. The Chickahominy fever had reaped its toll. At least some officer might have had the good sense to drape a tarp over the macabre scene.[4]

Soon after their arrival, McCall's men heard the murmurs of frustration amongst some soldiers in the Army of the Potomac. Grumbling about George McClellan was not confined to politicians. Brigadier General Philip Kearny, commanding a division, wrote about his army commander: "He has not the remotest aptitude for war. I sometimes fear, from his management of this war, that he regards it more in a political than a military point of view." A competent and brave combat leader, Kearny had lost an arm in the Mexican War fifteen years before. The frustrated officer noted that McClellan's best chance to capture Richmond was just after the Battle of Seven Pines. He believed that the constant delays only allowed the Confederates to gather more men and strengthen their defenses.[5]

Brigadier General Joseph Hooker held similar sentiments. He highlighted McClellan's multiple mistakes: the failure to attack at Yorktown and then McClellan "permitted the flower of their army to escape" at Williamsburg which ensured that the enemy "had time to create an army to place his Capital in an almost impregnable position." Disgusted with the eventual Union retreat from Richmond, Hooker added, "I only regret that I ever saw the Army of the Potomac."[6]

Another festering problem for McClellan in the spring of 1862 was President Lincoln's obsession with protecting Washington D.C. The correspondence between Washington and McClellan's headquarters in mid-May created confusion and irritation. A letter from Secretary of War Stanton on May 18 established hazy lines of command authority between McClellan's Army of the Potomac and McDowell's troops at Fredericksburg. While McDowell was to begin moving toward the south, McClellan received orders to extend his right flank to the north to connect with McDowell. However, McDowell's main mission as dictated by Lincoln was to "always [be] in position to save the capital [Washington D.C.] from all possible attack" despite being sent to aid McClellan in attacking Richmond. What infuriated McClellan and led to a correspondence tug-of-war between Washington, Fredericksburg and McClellan's headquarters was Stanton's urging that McClellan not give McDowell any orders "either before or after your junction, which can put him out of position to cover this city [Washington]." McDowell would also "retain the command of the Department of the Rappahannock and of the forces with which he moves forward."[7]

McClellan believed that Lincoln's fears of an attack against Washington were unfounded, and he later cited the May 18 order as the reason he had to maintain supply depots on the Pamunkey and thus maintain a line that extended from the Pamunkey south to the James River, a distance of some twenty-seven miles. The Chickahominy River compounded his problems because it split his forces in the middle. He wrote, "[h]ad General McDowell joined me by water I could have approached Richmond by the James, and thus avoided the delays and losses incurred in bridging the

Chickahominy, and would have had the army massed in one body, instead of being necessarily divided by that stream." However,

Major General George B. McClellan, commander of the Army of the Potomac. National Archives.

he cited these excuses to explain his difficulties on the Peninsula in his official report that he wrote on August 4, 1863 from New York after he had been sacked by Lincoln.[8]

McClellan also pleaded in his post-campaign defense that the proposed link up with McDowell by land "obliged me to expose my right in order to secure the junction, and as the order for General McDowell's march was soon countermanded, I incurred the great risk, of which the enemy finally took advantage, and frustrated the plan of campaign." Of course, this plea discounts the basic military necessity to properly defend the flanks, which he failed to do along the Pamunkey River.[9]

British army observer Lieutenant Colonel Garnet Joseph Wolseley indicted McClellan over this exact failure. The foreign officer stated: "McClellan can never be excused, under the shelter of Government orders, for placing his army in the false, and therefore dangerous position it was in when attacked on the Chickahominy. It was the gravest of errors, for which he had to pay in reputation, and his army in blood."[10]

President Lincoln obsessed about the safety of Washington, D.C. because of Stonewall Jackson's successful forays around three different Union commanders in the Shenandoah Valley. When the president looked at his maps, which was a frequent occurrence, the Blue Ridge Mountain passes at Harper's Ferry, Snicker's Gap and Ashby Gap scared him. He pictured the phantom-like Jackson funneling troops through these passes which could place veteran gray infantry within a few days march of Washington. Lincoln's involvement in Union troop movements and his issuance of orders to various commanders only increased McClellan's agitation as the days of May and then June passed.

Jackson's victories at Cross Keys and Port Republic on June 8–9 near Harrisonburg, Virginia only validated Lincoln's fears. The idea behind Lincoln's words written to McClellan a month before had not changed. "I am still unwilling to take all our force off the direct line between Richmond and here."[11]

In McClellan's defense, he did indicate as early as June 2 his desire to move the corps of Fitz John Porter and William B. Franklin to join the rest of the army south of the Chickahominy River. This move would consolidate the Union army front and not leave a muddy morass, the Chickahominy, to split the army in two. It would also have allowed McClellan to defend both flanks more easily and to move his supply base to the James River.[12]

Correspondence between George McClellan and his wife Mary Ellen revealed the fertile discontent between Washington and army headquarters. A letter written to his wife on May 26, just after Major General Nathaniel Banks' loss to Jackson at Winchester, showed McClellan's blistering feelings toward Lincoln. "Some of the Presdt's dispatches for the last two days have been amazing in the extreme. I cannot do justice to them so I shall not attempt to describe them. I feared last night that I would be ordered back for the defense of Washington!"[13]

On June 8, McClellan received a telegram from McDowell stating that he had been ordered again to move his troops from Fredericksburg south to link up and to aid the attack on Richmond. McClellan indicated to his wife that he believed the telegram was self-serving because McDowell stated he "received the order with great satisfaction." McClellan then turned his pen on McDowell stating, "I have not replied to it, nor shall I — the animal probably sees that the tide is changing & that I am not entirely without friends in the world."[14]

McClellan scanned his maps and realized that the muddy roads and burned bridges that confronted McDowell would result in immeasurable delay. He urged that McDowell's men be moved via boat due to security, speed and less confusion. Plus, McClellan did not want to pull front line troops to extend and reinforce his right flank to meet McDowell. The irritated army commander wrote back to Stanton: "An extension of my right wing to meet him [McDowell] may involve serious hazard to my flank and my line of communications and may not suffice to rescue him from any peril in which a strong movement of the enemy may involve him." However, Jackson's success at Cross Keys and Port Republic again cancelled McDowell's move toward McClellan. Military historians now are left to wonder how a reinforcement by McDowell's 30,000 troops on the Union right might have upset future Confederate plans and thus the outcome of the Peninsula Campaign.[15]

On June 11, McClellan announced in a letter to his wife that he hoped to take a tour by horseback along his front. He doubted he could ride the entire length of his lines because the rain again threatened; plus, he had not been on horseback since about June 1 thanks to his malarial flare ups. "I must be careful for it would be utter destruction to the army were I to be disabled so as not to be able to take command — [General Edwin V.] Sumner would ruin things in about two days ..." He also noted that reinforcements from McCall's command had reached White House Landing.[16]

However, McClellan still hesitated to take the initiative. The reporter George Townsend recorded a common sentiment amongst the Union troops when he recalled a conversation with one irritated soldier: "I volunteered to fight. To fight, sir! not to dig and drive team. Here we air, sir, stuck in the mud, burnin' with fever, livin' on hardtack. And thair's Richmond! Just their! You can chuck a stone at it, if you mind to." This soldier then told Townsend what he feared: "A'ter a while them rebbils'll pop out and fix us." Soon, this soldier's fears would become reality.[17]

CHAPTER 8

Planning for the Great
Chickahominy Raid

JUNE 10–11, 1862

J EB STUART AND HIS STAFF spent the cold rainy evening of
June 10 preparing for the proposed cavalry expedition although
Stuart had kept the specifics to himself as ordered by General
Lee. He thought about the best troops and subordinate commanders
needed for the mission. He needed aggressive fighters, but he also
wanted men with navigation skills who were familiar with Hanover
County. Then as he thought of circling the Army of the Potomac,
he realized that he needed troopers who knew all the back roads
of New Kent and Charles City counties too. No doubt such a move
would bring on a collision with his estranged father-in-law, who had
failed Virginia in her time of need. He would especially relish the
opportunity to embarrass Brigadier General Philip St. George Cooke.

A courier arrived at Stuart's headquarters before noon on
June 11. He saluted the general and then handed him paperwork
from Lee. Stuart opened the envelope and unfolded the paper.
His mouth must have smiled under his thick brown beard as he
read the orders: "You are desired to make a secret movement to
the rear of the enemy, now posted on the Chickahominy, with a
view of gaining intelligence of his operations, communications,
&c." The missive also urged him "to destroy his wagon trains" that
moved laden with supplies from Piping Tree Ferry.[1]

69

General Lee's order recommended taking only men and horses fit enough to "stand the expedition" while leaving enough gray-uniformed cavalrymen behind to protect the main army. Lee also urged keeping enough flanking scouts out ahead to rake in information while preventing any enemy surprises. This mission was not intended for just a handful of men; instead, it was to be a reconnaissance in force to probe well behind the right flank with enough offensive firepower to protect the raiders and to reveal the enemy's troop deployment.[2]

Probably due to Stuart's impulsive suggestion to circle McClellan's army, Lee added a caution in his order. Buried in the text, Lee urged, "return as soon as the object of your expedition is accomplished …" and do "not hazard unnecessarily your command or to attempt what your judgment may not approve; but be content to accomplish all the good you can without feeling it necessary to obtain all that might be desired."[3]

Intelligence had reached Lee's headquarters that perhaps the enemy's right flank had been strengthened, and the commander passed this on in his order too. "A large body of infantry, as well as cavalry, was reported near the Central Railroad." This news probably represented the arrival at White House Landing of George McCall's 10,000-man reinforcing division from Fredericksburg. Lee also reiterated, "remember that one of the chief objects of your expedition is to gain intelligence for the guidance of future operations." Although Lee had left the details of the mission for Stuart to plan, the warning of the strengthened right flank might have cemented in Stuart's mind that he needed a large force.[4]

On the same day that Stuart received his reconnaissance orders, Lee moved forward with his future plans. Brigadier General Alexander Lawton's brigade comprised of six large regiments rode by train from Savannah, Georgia toward a Shenandoah Valley rendezvous with Jackson's men. Brigadier General William H.C. Whiting's division moved from Richmond with eight regiments to aid Stonewall Jackson too. General Lee noted that this plan "at the expense of weakening this army" was an unorthodox move in the face of a superior enemy, but it was really an elaborate ruse.

Jackson would merge these reinforcements with his Valley troops and "move rapidly to Ashland by rail or otherwise, as you may find most advantageous, and sweep down between the Chickahominy and Pamunkey, cutting up the enemy's communications, &c., while this army attacks McClellan in front."[5]

Robert E. Lee needed Stuart to uncover the answers to three questions while on his mission. Where was McClellan's right wing deployed? How far to the north did the wing extend? Would there be room for Stonewall Jackson's troops to maneuver and to slice into this wing? With these questions answered, Lee believed his bold plan to consolidate his troops and then use a turning movement would force McClellan's men out of their lines to fight on ground of Lee's choosing.

On June 12, McClellan moved his headquarters from Dr. William Gaines' plantation near New Bridge across the river to the yard of Dr. Trent on the Grapevine Bridge Road near the south bank of the Chickahominy. Before he moved, he indicated in a letter to his wife that he had "to take a farewell ride some 7 or 8 miles up this side of the river to look again at the ground & give the last instructions to [Fitz John] Porter & [William] Franklin for their guidance on this side of the river." This move seemed to require much attention from the army commander; thus, the next day when reports arrived of Rebel cavalry behind the right flank, he delegated the pursuit to Fitz John Porter.[6]

Several days before, word had reached McClellan of the Confederate effort to reinforce Jackson in the Valley with Richmond troops. This chess play by Lee certainly reinforced for McClellan the inaccurate idea that Lee must have superior numbers. The Union commander also wondered when he would have access to McDowell's troops.[7]

On June 7, McClellan's chief of staff and father-in-law, Brigadier General Randolph B. Marcy, had sent instructions to Philip St. George Cooke to "extend your patrols well in the direction of Hanover Court House and towards the Pamunky also up the

Chickahominy three or four miles above the Central Rail Road."
This order emphasized McClellan's concern for an attack against
his right flank. During this period Cooke had apparently moved
his cavalry headquarters to an area between Old Cold Harbor and
Gaines' Mill.[8]

Meanwhile, the cavalrymen from the 6th Pennsylvania, Rush's
Lancers, still waited in their camps near Old Church for more
exciting duty. Corporal Thomas W. Smith, discouraged by idleness,
noted to his sister, "this laying around Camp with nothing to do
but take care of one Horse is a very Lazy life." He also believed
that Richmond would eventually be taken, but "it will not be taken
so soon, nor so easy, as some People think it will." During his days
spent scouting the heavily wooded land on the Peninsula he realized the impotence of his regiment's nonsensical weapons. Smith
wrote, "I don't think our Lances will ever be of any use in this
war unless we should get a chance to charge in an open Field." It
would be another year before the limits of the lances uselessness
would be realized. Regimental chaplain Samuel Gracey noted his
men finally received Sharps carbines and turned in their lances
on May 26, 1863.[9]

1862 Sketch of 6th Pennsylvania Cavalry. *Battles and Leaders of the Civil War*, edited
by Johnston and Buel, vol. 2, p. 319

Despite a lack of real usefulness on the battlefield, the lances did invoke psychological advantage against those Rebels the Pennsylvanians faced. While Confederate captain William Blackford credits the Lancers for their natty uniforms, he does admit to some concern when he faced them in line of battle at the end of June. "I must confess I felt a little creeping of the flesh when I saw this splendid looking body of men, about seven hundred strong, drawn up in line of battle in a large open field two or three hundred yards off, armed with long poles with glittering steel points. To think of one of these being run through a fellow was not at all pleasant."[10]

Before sunup on June 11, bugle calls awakened the Lancers. Fifteen minutes later they swung into their saddles and hoisted their lances to go on a forage expedition. The column slogged across swamps and creeks as the sun rose and heated the day. Several miles later they turned off the road and approached a large two-story white framed house that sat on a red-brick foundation. Mrs. Willoughby Newton owned this place, which was named Summer Hill. The return of Yankee troops placed the women, children and slaves on alert as previous visits had been unpleasant. This encounter would be no different.[11]

Several Lancers circled the house as they looked for hidden food or enemy soldiers; then they turned their attention on the nearby barn. The Pennsylvanians dismounted and stared for a moment at the padlocked door. The overseer ran up, but he was too slow in removing the lock. The siding splintered and snapped as soldiers kicked, pulled and pried at the wood. Corn rocketed through a hole in one wall and piled onto the ground. Several horses nuzzled their way forward and ate. Some soldiers scooped the corn into saddle bags while others shoveled the grain onto wagons.[12]

Many of the Lancers cared little for Southern civilians especially when Union soldiers suffered "injustices" caused by Confederates. Lieutenant Theodore Sage captured a "beautiful mare" while on patrol near the Pamunkey river on May 24. He wondered whether he could keep the animal, as he feared "some bloody Rebel will come and claim him and if that is the case he will have to be given up as the Rebels are treated as if they had never done anything wrong in their lives." Sage then ranted about a nearby civilian who complained to Union authorities about his fence rails being taken by a cavalryman to fuel a cooking fire. The offending trooper then spent some time in the guardhouse. The same civilian had earlier refused to provide enough boards and nails to provide a coffin for

a deceased Federal trooper until coerced by the arrival at his house of the Lancers. Sage lamented the leniency shown to "the bloody cutthroats." He insisted that they "ought to be hung from the nearest tree."[13]

Other Lancers rode to nearby Westwood, owned by Mrs. William S. Brockenbrough, sister-in-law to Mrs. Newton. There the troopers raided the barn and filled several wagons with the family's provisions while other Lancers chased down sheep. Mrs. Newton later indicated that she felt lucky because the four officers who "went over every part of the house ... were moderate in their robberies" at Summer Hill. The frustrated woman then wrote, "This robbery now goes on every day. The worst part of

Lt. Theodore Sage, Company F, 6th Pennsylvania Cavalry. Sage later became the regimental quartermaster, and he was killed on November 4, 1863 while escorting a supply wagon after an encounter with Mosby's Rangers. D. Scott Hartzell Collection, USAHEC.

our thralldom is, that we hear nothing from our own army." Mrs. Brockenbrough expressed her resentment toward the Pennsylvanians when she wrote, "The truth is, my contact with the Yankees has resulted in all the little good that ever belonged to me being laid on the shelf, and all the worst feelings of which I was capable being kept in the most lively active exercise."[14]

When Lancer's corporal Thomas Smith later returned with his squadron to their camp, he probably cared nothing about the anger of the local population. That night he "parched" some corn "in a mess pan, and had a first rate supper."[15]

The outraged ladies of Summer Hill and Westwood did not know that within two days they would hear from their own army. They would also play a sad, but poignant part in the unfolding Confederate drama behind Union lines.

CHAPTER 9

The Raid Begins

JUNE 12, 1862

2 AM

ONE MUST WONDER how much sleep, if any, Jeb Stuart had before the he walked out of his tent to awaken his staff at 2 AM, on June 12. This mission signaled the first large use of Confederate cavalry in Virginia. Certainly the portent of the expedition and its many unknowns had to weigh on his mind. If Jeb Stuart harbored any anxiety about his task, he concealed it well from his staff and men. Anxiety would perhaps need to wait until he led his men into a tight spot. For now, only a confident bearing would do, as all soldiers had a right to expect from their generals. Not one to take counsel of his own fears, he certainly did not lack faith or confidence in his own command abilities.

Stuart had made careful calculations of the strengths and weaknesses of his cavalry regiments, their commanders, and his own staff as he decided who to include on the ride. The orders from Robert E. Lee stated, "I recommend that you take only such men and horses as can stand the expedition, and that you take every means in your power to save and cherish those you take." By the spring of 1862, nine of the fourteen Confederate cavalry regiments available for duty in Virginia hailed from the Old Dominion State. Stuart would ensure that the Virginia regiments handpicked for the expedition contained soldiers who came from the various counties that the mission might traverse.[1]

"Gentlemen, in ten minutes every man must be in his saddle!" Stuart's voice boomed out. Staff orderlies, sergeants, and officers dressed and rushed in different directions gathering equipment, feeding horses and stuffing dried food into their own mouths. At the ten-minute mark, Stuart swung into the saddle as the moonlight bathed the area. Lieutenant John Esten Cooke, Flora Stuart's first cousin, sat atop his own horse and watched Stuart with awe. By the war's beginning, Cooke had written three novels, and his pen could flourish any scene. During the initial battle at Manassas in 1861, Cooke had served as a sergeant in charge of a Richmond Howitzers' cannon crew. By early 1862, he became a volunteer aide for Stuart. He received a commission in May 1862 and became a staff ordnance officer. Cooke described Stuart in the saddle: "The gray coat buttoned to the chin; the light French sabre balanced by the pistol in its black holster; the cavalry boots above the knee, and the brown hat with its black plume floating above the bearded features, the brilliant eyes, and the huge moustache, which curled with laughter at the slightest provocation."[2]

However, only six months earlier, Stuart had expressed reservations about his wife's cousin. He had indicated to Flora: " Jno Esten [Cooke] is a case & I am afraid I cant like him. He is like your Pa in some peculiarities." Stuart used harsh words against the young writer, but the general finally seemed to accept Cooke.[3]

The immense thick beard was signature Stuart, and he knew it. Perhaps to hide his small chin and unhandsome features, which had garnered the misnomer of "Beauty" while at West Point, Stuart had shunned the razor since his Indian fighting days with the 1st Cavalry on the Midwest plains. Like the biblical Samson, who found strength in his hair, Stuart had written to Flora in December 1861 describing "this abominable beard of mine for I have'n't touched a hair of it with a razor for 7 years No[r] do I ever intend to."[4]

John Mosby sat ready atop his horse in the darkness too, as he was excited about an adventure created by his previous reconnaissance. When the staff began to ride away, an officer remaining behind asked the general when he would return. "It may be for years, it may be forever," Stuart answered.[5]

Meanwhile, well ahead of Stuart's staff rode Colonel Fitzhugh Lee at the head of his regiment, the 1st Virginia Cavalry. Fitz Lee was known as an excellent rider despite being short and stout. One of his soldiers described his heavy, long, dark beard as being "of unusual length."[6]

Fitz Lee was General Lee's nephew and was the third man to command the regiment after Stuart and Grumble Jones. The younger Lee had graduated from West Point in 1856 despite a lengthy demerit record. Twice superintendent Robert E. Lee, not wishing to show favoritism, had recommended his nephew's dismissal for leading other cadets on night-time tavern visits. The current U. S. Secretary of War Jefferson Davis overruled the senior Lee both times.[7]

The twenty-six-year-old Fitz Lee had somehow survived these early military missteps to become an excellent cavalry officer in the U. S. Army. He gained experience with assignments to both Carlisle, Pennsylvania and then west Texas to fight Indians with the 2nd U.S. Cavalry. Then on the eve of war he returned to his alma mater to serve as a cavalry instructor.

The 1st Virginia Cavalry preceded the staff into Richmond, and the column rode through the darkened streets of the city's north side. Skittish cats parted the way ahead of the riders as nearby dogs barked at the moan of leather and the clop of hooves. Once out of the capital city, the horsemen joined Brook Road and moved north as scouts rode ahead and toward the flanks for security.

At around 5 AM, the smell of wood smoke greeted the group when they arrived at the Mordecai and Young farm area. Here the bivouac of the 9th Virginia Cavalry spread along the rolling hills. Staff and company officers took care of a myriad of details to prepare the expedition, now comprised of almost 1,200 riders, for what would become a big adventure.[8]

Mrs. Mordecai's property stood four miles north of Richmond between Brook Road to the east and the Richmond, Fredericksburg & Potomac Railroad on the west. Seven companies of the 9th

Virginia Cavalry Regiment stood eager to ride while companies A, H and I would miss the mission because of their detached service. Two companies led by Captain William Beverly Wooldridge from the 4th Virginia Cavalry stood ready to ride with the 9th Virginia.[9]

The 9th Virginia's commander was General Lee's second son, twenty-five-year-old Colonel William H. F. Lee, called "Rooney" by friends. Rooney Lee had entered Harvard in 1854 and then left three years later after an unimpressive academic performance. His father had intervened and successfully sought a lieutenant's commission for the young man. In early 1859, Rooney resigned from the army and returned to Virginia. He married and moved to the family property at White House Landing to farm the land until the war intervened.[10]

Colonel William H. F. "Rooney" Lee, commander of 9th Virginia Cavalry and son of R. E. Lee. Library of Congress.

Four other 4th Virginia Cavalry companies led by Captain Robert E. Utterback were attached to Fitz Lee's 1st Virginia. Colonel Williams C. Wickham commanded the 4th regiment, but he was convalescing at his home near Ashland after being wounded at Williamsburg the previous month. A number of men in this regiment's Company G, Hanover Light Dragoons, rode along because of their knowledge of Hanover County. Stuart also included several men from the 3rd Virginia Cavalry's Company G. These New Kent County horsemen would later prove invaluable because of their local knowledge.[11]

Part of Jeb Stuart's handpicked party included three cavalry companies from Lieutenant Colonel William T. Martin's Jefferson Davis Legion, nicknamed "The Little Jeff." Martin's men had earlier departed their camp on the Charles City Road east of Richmond and joined the route of Stuart's staff and the 1st Virginia. Each man carried three days' rations that consisted of hard bread and dried bacon. The thirty-nine-year-old Martin had worked before the war as a district attorney in Natchez, Mississippi. Company C, nicknamed the Southern Guards, hailed from Mississippi. Company E, known as the Canebrake Legion, came from Alabama while Company F, the Georgia Hussars, came from that state. Rounding out the 250 men under Martin's control rode some South Carolina troopers known as the Boykin Rangers, led by Lieutenant John Chesnut.[12]

Two cannons commanded by twenty-four-year-old Lieutenant James Breathed from the Stuart Horse Artillery arrived. When the war began, the Maryland-born Breathed had abandoned his medical practice in Missouri and travelled east to join the Confederate effort. One of his cannons was a twelve-pound howitzer while the

Lieutenant Colonel William T. Martin, commander of the Jefferson Davis Legion. Martin later was promoted to brigadier general. Postwar image. MOLLUS, USAHEC.

Lieutenant James Breathed, Stuart Horse Artillery. The Marylander had moved to Missouri to practice medicine before the war. After the war he served as a doctor in Hancock, Maryland. He died in 1870 at age thirty-two, and his death was possibly caused by complications relating to an old war wound suffered in June 1864. *Confederate Veteran*, vol. vii, 1899, p. 168.

other was a rifled piece. Lieutenant William Morrell McGregor rode along to assist Breathed. McGregor, an Alabama native, had left college to enlist in the 10th Alabama before being coaxed by John Pelham to join the Stuart Horse Artillery.[13]

As the column turned onto Brook Road and headed north, most of the men wondered about their destination. Private Joseph Dunbar Shields probably just hoped the rain wouldn't begin falling — again. The Mississippian noted, "I believe it rains more here than any place in the Confederate states." Shields described himself as "a truly back side rebel" because he had spent so much time in the saddle during operations on the Peninsula that he had worn out the seat of his pants.[14]

The adjutant of the 9th Virginia Cavalry remembered the "surmises and conjectures as to our destination" began the day before when the orders arrived for the men "to prepare three days' rations, and the ordnance officers to issue sixty rounds of ammunition to each man." Nineteen-year-old Sergeant George William Beale recalled the electric excitement that surged amongst his fellow cavalrymen as they checked and rechecked their horse accouterments and then their own personal equipment.[15]

When Rooney Lee's men pulled out of camp, an excited trooper yelled back to some glum-looking soldiers left behind: "Goodbye, boys; we are going to help old Jack drive the Yanks into the Potomac." Those soldiers who rode in the middle of the column tasted grit stirred up by the many horses ahead. Numerous men sang out with excitement as Stuart galloped by. Exhilaration no doubt swelled the general's chest too as he led these 1,200 men toward the unknown.[16]

John Mosby saw some of his 1st Virginia Cavalry friends, and he pulled on his reins to join them. They pestered him for news about their destination, but he remained mum. The only information the men really had sat in their haversacks and saddle bags — three days' rations. They all knew that a horse could go a long way in three days.[17]

Another energized soldier, Private Charles R. Chewning, recorded, "I have never seen so many troopers at once, we must

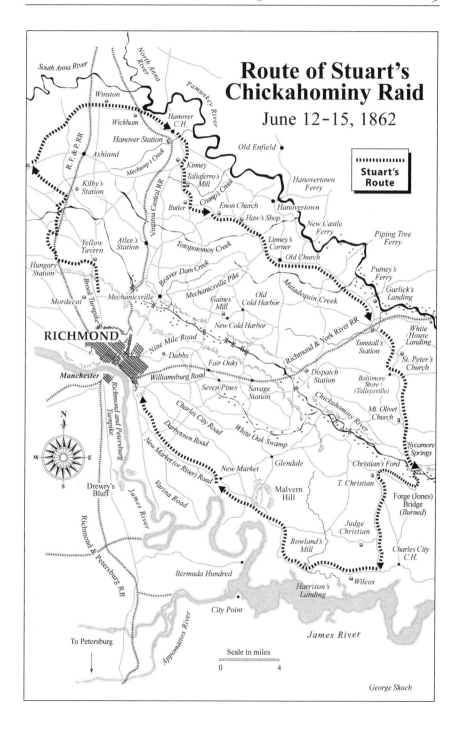

Route of Stuart's Chickahominy Raid

June 12–15, 1862

Stuart's Route

South Anna River
North Anna River
Pamunkey River
Winston
Wickham
Hanover C.H.
Hanover Station
Old Enfield
Ashland
R. F. & P. RR
Kinney
Taliaferro's Mill
Hanovertown Ferry
Mechump's Creek
Kilby's Station
Crump's Creek
Butler
Enon Church
Hanovertown
Virginia Central RR
Haw's Shop
New Castle Ferry
Piping Tree Ferry
Yellow Tavern
Atlee's Station
Totopotomoy Creek
Linney's Corner
Old Church
Hungary Station
Beaver Dam Creek
Brook Turnpike
Mechanicsville Pike
Old Cold Harbor
Matadequin Creek
Putney's Ferry
Garlick's Landing
Mordecai
Mechanicsville
Gaines' Mill
White House Landing
RICHMOND
New Cold Harbor
Nine Mile Road
Richmond & York River RR
Tunstall's Station
Dabbs
Fair Oaks
Dispatch Station
St. Peter's Church
Manchester
Williamsburg Road
Seven Pines
Savage Station
Baltimore Store (Talleysville)
Richmond and Petersburg Turnpike
Charles City Road
Darbytown Road
White Oak Swamp
Chickahominy River
Mt. Olivet Church
New Market (or River) Road
New Market
Glendale
Christian's Ford
Sycamore Springs
Drewry's Bluff
Varina Road
Malvern Hill
T. Christian
Forge (Jones) Bridge (Burned)
James River
Richmond & Petersburg RR
Judge Christian
Rowland's Mill
Charles City C.H.
Bermuda Hundred
Harrison's Landing
Wilcox
City Point
Appomattox River
James River

To Petersburg

Scale in miles
0   4

George Skoch

make a grand sight." His elation soared when Rooney Lee cantered the 9th Virginia Cavalry forward to lead the parade. Forgotten were the words he scribbled in his journal on the previous day: "We came here to fight but we just muddle around in these thick woods."[18]

Old men, women and children waved as they crowded the porches of houses near the road. The sight of so many Confederate soldiers bolstered most civilian spirits this close to Richmond. Several times troopers recognized friends or family and pulled out of the column for a hug or handshake.[19]

Those who had bet that the destination was the Shenandoah Valley overconfidently imagined counting their money when the column turned left off Brook Road just before Yellow Tavern, and headed west toward Hungary Station and Louisa Court House. They crossed the track of the Richmond, Fredericksburg and Potomac Railroad [RF&P] at Hungary Station and turned north. Their path paralleled the railroad toward Kilby Station.[20]

Kilby's Station known as Elmont today. Looking south along the Richmond, Fredericksburg & Potomac R.R. tracks. On June 12, 1862, a contingent of Confederate cavalrymen waited here to join Stuart's main column as it passed by a short distance to the west. Note historical marker on left. Randall Flynn photo.

By mid-afternoon the greens and yellows of distant trees and fields shimmered as the temperature passed eighty degrees and climbed higher. The mixed sounds of cicadas and grasshoppers hammered the ears and drowned out all else. Soldiers scanned the rare blue sky for rain clouds, but only sunshine beat down on the backs of the animals and the men as the column twisted and turned on the numerous back roads. As the dust rose, caking eyes and mouths, it made the ride especially difficult for Lieutenant Colonel Martin's horsemen and Lieutenant Breathed's artillerists, who carried the tail of the column.

The troopers skirted west of Ashland and then guided on the right bank of the South Anna River as it flowed east. The shadows grew long as the sun, a huge flaming ball, began to disappear behind the trees. They crossed the RF&P Railroad again, and most men were relieved when Stuart led the column into a large field located on the Winston farm. There they bivouacked for the

Winston Farm today. This area is located several miles north of Ashland. Stuart's men bedded down along the rolling terrain here at sundown on June 12, the first night of the ride. The farmhouse is barely visible in the trees in center background. Randall Flynn photo.

night. The farm stood near the community of Taylorsville, close to the burned railroad bridge over the river. However, the change in the column's direction created more speculation amongst the men because they now moved east away from the Shenandoah Valley.

The tired, sunburned soldiers dropped off of their mounts. Some of the men who had departed camps east of Richmond had covered about thirty miles that day while those camped on Brook Road had ridden about twenty-two miles. Corn dodgers and dried bacon, scraped out of haversacks, served as a cold supper since Stuart had ordered no fires and no noise. The men fed their horses and unhitched their bedrolls. The fortunate ones who did not have picket or guard duty soon hit the ground fast asleep.[21]

Several contingents of scouts had earlier moved to the east during the gathering twilight. One of these groups comprised the 4th Virginia Cavalry's private Frank Stringfellow along with two members of Stuart's staff, Lieutenant Redmond Burke and Captain William D. Farley.[22]

Both Burke and Farley had served Stuart well, and he enjoyed not only their company, but more importantly, he valued the various skills they each brought to military operations. In December 1861, the cavalry leader had written to his wife about Burke: "Redmond Burke rode up & reported for duty yesterday — we have made a great glorification over him. He had many narrow escapes & has a wonderful set of yarns to tell." Before the war, the Irish-born Burke had lived in Shepherdstown, (West) Virginia and had worked as a stone cutter there and at Harper's Ferry. Burke, at forty-six-years of age, represented one of the oldest faces on the staff.[23]

The twenty-six-year-old Farley hailed from South Carolina and had graduated from the University of Virginia. When the war began he initially enlisted in the 1st South Carolina. He stood medium height with a muscular frame and dark brown hair. His innate scouting skills combined with bravado attracted the attention of several Confederate leaders including Jeb Stuart. He had led several reckless undermanned charges, one of which resulted in his capture. Farley was released in a prisoner exchange in the spring of 1862, and Stuart offered him a place on staff as an aide and scout. The general praised Farley's performance in the fight at Williamsburg in May. "I will, however, mention the fearless daring and cool and determined courage always so conspicuous in Capt. W. D. Farley, attached as volunteer aide. He manages to get into every fight, and is always conspicuously gallant. He is a young man of rare modesty, merit, and worth, who can scarcely be replaced." Stuart would not regret these words.[24]

Farley probably raised some staff eyebrows when he claimed to have killed more than thirty enemy soldiers. These same staff members must have been surprised when they saw this brown-haired warrior open a book of poetry or scribble some of his own verse during spare moments. John Esten Cooke also noted that Farley was "passionately fond of Shakespeare."[25]

Earlier when the main body had neared Ashland, a Mississippi private named Jesse R. Sparkman reported that he and fourteen other horsemen had left with a lieutenant, probably Hanover County native David A. Timberlake from the 4th Virginia Cavalry. They scouted until darkness when the officer took five men and pushed into enemy lines while the rest of the group bivouacked. About 2 AM, on June 13, Lieutenant Timberlake and his small group returned, and they sat down and drank some buttermilk that a local woman had presented to them.[26]

Confident that his scouts would intercept any Union patrols, Stuart decided to go on another midnight ride. Rooney Lee joined his commander, and they rode four miles to a nearby estate named Hickory Hill. They climbed the steps of the mansion house and rapped on the door, which awakened the residents. Stuart wanted to visit with the owner, Colonel Williams Wickham, the wounded and convalescing commander of the 4th Virginia Cavalry. Wickham was also a first cousin to Rooney's wife, Charlotte. At some point during the visit, Stuart slumped asleep in his chair, which was not surprising since he had been awake for almost twenty-four hours. Some reports have Lee and Stuart breakfasting at Hickory Hill. The pair then headed before sunup back to the Winston farm, and they might have had a close call on their return, as John E. Cooke recorded they "narrowly escaped capture from the enemy near." However, no reports from Stuart, Lee or any other staff member reported a close encounter with the enemy.[27]

At some time early on the morning of Friday, June 13, the tired threesome of Burke, Farley and Stringfellow returned and reported good news to Stuart. They had queried numerous Hanover civilians and all reported that the nearest Yankees were at Old Church, some twenty miles away. This news seemed to be momentous.[28]

The pale outline of a new day began to grow in the eastern sky as the gray-clad troopers rolled up their blankets, fed their horses and then themselves. Suddenly some bright lights shot into the sky "making a whizzing noise and bursting into fiery flashes above the tree-tops." Several witnesses confirmed the launch of these signal flares or rockets, yet they seemed to negate Stuart's desire for secrecy. One historian surmised that the launch may have been a prearranged signal to General Lee that the great cavalry expedition was headed east. The 1st Virginia Cavalry's private William Z. Mead recalled the rockets being launched around midnight and the sky to the south toward Richmond briefly illuminated from a corresponding rocket launch there.[29]

The men mounted their steeds without a bugle call. Scouts Burke, Farley and Stingfellow and probably John Mosby moved out ahead of a small detachment of 9th Virginia cavalrymen led by Adjutant William Todd Robins. Robins was a twenty-six-year-old Virginia Military Institute graduate, who would later become colonel of the 24th Virginia Cavalry. Robins' group formed the advance guard, and they entered the road and turned east toward Hanover Court House. Just behind came a squadron of companies B and C led by Captain Samuel Amery Swann. Another squadron composed of companies E and F commanded by Captain William Latane followed. The enthusiasm grew for most of the men, as they realized the direction of the ride seemed headed toward the enemy's right flank.[30]

Sergeant George W. Beale rode next to Latane for several miles and he later noted that the twenty-nine-year-old Essex County physician "seemed serious and reflective." As Latane looked back over his shoulder at his younger brother, John, and at the faces of the men in his squadron, perhaps the gravity of his responsibility affected him. William Latane had received a promotion from lieutenant to captain a month before. He now had only a few hours left to live.[31]

CHAPTER 10

First Contact at Hanover Court House

FRIDAY, JUNE 13, 1862

6 AM–9 AM

A RECONNAISSANCE PATROL from the 6th U. S. Cavalry trotted into Hanover Court House. The beautiful ride that morning surrounded by fresh leaves and blossoms "would have driven the soul of an artist wild with delight" noted Private Sidney M. Davis. This serenity continued but for a short while longer. As the 6th Regulars reached the town, and possibly rode past the court house toward St. Paul's Church, they saw a line of about thirty enemy horsemen blocking the road ahead. The column of Regulars halted about a quarter-mile away and sent three men forward to investigate the enemy group which was probably an advance scout led by Confederate John Mosby.[1]

The three Union troopers rode cautiously forward and halted some fifty yards away. One of the Rebels hollered, "'What do you all want?'" The three Unionists held a hasty conference and soon turned their horses and returned to their waiting group which soon raced away south and probably veered onto the Pole Green Church Road. Private Davis gave several glances over his shoulder to the west where the enemy column still stood its ground on the road. Suddenly, he noticed something else — "a cloud of dust rising above the tree-tops in the distance." Several of his fellow troopers had earlier teased Davis because of his nervous glances and the chastisement grew stronger when he pointed out the dust.[2]

Earlier that morning, as the Confederate column rode east from their bivouac at Winston farm, the growing light revealed a narrow road bounded by steep banks, thick trees and brush. The 9th Virginia's lieutenant William T. Robins, leading the advance guard, peered ahead for trouble. There was no place to maneuver, and the route looked ripe for an ambush. Finally, a field opened on the right, and a large white house, the front porch guarded by six columns, stood on a steep hill. Built by Hill Carter in 1835, this place was known as South Wales. After another mile they passed the road to Hickory Hill, the Wickham house, where Jeb Stuart and Rooney Lee had spent the early morning hours. The road sank downhill and disappeared to the right. Robins and his men rode into the fringe of the woods and peered ahead toward the crossing of the Virginia Central Railroad. The tracks and the ribbon of dirt road appeared clear.

Stuart had earlier gathered his regimental commanders and informed them of his plans "so as to secure an intelligent action and co-operation in whatever might occur." He remained confident because the scouts had returned with information that "no serious obstacles" existed on the way to Old Church, almost twenty miles away from Winston farm.[3]

The gray column clopped across the tracks and continued on past woods and fields. A light breeze carried the sweet scents of spring buds. Stands of green corn pointed skyward. Troopers mopped the sweat from their foreheads as the sun rose. Two miles later they approached Hanover Court House from the west. The main body halted to await word from John Mosby and his scouts, who had earlier ridden cautiously toward town.

Mosby recalled that "just as we got in sight of the village, a squadron of the enemy came, reconnoitered us, and as we simply

Virginia Central Railroad crossing known as Wickham Crossing. Looking northwest along Hickory Hill Road [Rt. 647] that runs between Winston farm and Hanover Courthouse. Hickory Hill formerly owned by the Wickham family stands just west of here. Randall Flynn photo.

halted and did not run away, rightly concluded that a support was behind us and left in a hurry." He sent Frank Stringfellow back to find Stuart. The young scout galloped past Robins' advance and soon located Stuart. He informed the general that they had found the first obstacle — an unknown-size enemy force in town. The time was about 9 AM, as Stuart led the column forward from the west. They next stopped behind a wooded hill near the white-frame St. Paul's Episcopal Church, built in the 1840s. Stuart moved forward and saw numerous horses saddled on the village road while blue-clad troopers milled about. He turned and uttered some instructions to Fitz Lee, who soon led his 1st Virginia Cavalry into the woods to the south to block the enemy's escape route. The tail of Fitz Lee's troopers soon disappeared.[4]

Stuart waited for the trap to be set, but suddenly shots rang out from the Unionists. The green lawn in front of the court house

St. Paul's Episcopal Church. Stuart's men passed in front of this historic church that still stands on the west side of Hanover Court House. Randall Flynn photo.

coursed with confusion as men grabbed at bridles and vaulted onto their horses. The 150 troopers from the 6th U. S. Cavalry patrol, led by Captain J. Irvin Gregg, raced south. If they escaped, word would soon reach Union army headquarters of the Confederate cavalry presence. Stuart hoped that Fitz Lee would be in his blocking position, so he gave the signal for his column to continue into town.[5]

Lieutenant John E. Cooke watched with glee as the "startled bluebirds" left a cloud of dust in their wake. Some of the Yankee troopers swiveled their upper bodies and fired parting shots from their carbines. Stuart saw no reason to pursue close as he kept expecting to hear a blast of small arm's fire ahead signaling that the fugitives had been cut off by the 1st Virginia.[6]

Lieutenant John Esten Cooke. Cooke was a novelist who was born in Winchester in 1830. He served on Stuart's staff for two years. He also was Flora Cooke's cousin. After the war he wrote *The Wearing of the Gray* along with several other books that highlighted his war experiences. John Walter Wayland Papers, Stewart Bell, Jr., Archives Room, Handley Regional Library, Winchester, Va.

What the Southern cavalry chieftain did not know was that the glue-like dark mud of Mechump's Creek had almost devoured the horses and men of Fitz Lee's regiment. By the time the 1st Virginia Cavalry dragged themselves out of the swamp onto the Mechanicsville Road, the 6th Regulars had already thundered past. After the dust cleared, Stuart's cavalry had only one captive, a sergeant from the 6th Regulars. Several soldiers escorted the prisoner to see General Stuart, who inquired about the prisoner's unit. After several more questions, Stuart ordered the sergeant released, but told him to carry word back to the regiment's commander, Major Lawrence Williams, that Stuart looked forward to meeting the 6th U. S. Cavalry in "a fair hand-to-hand fight, some day."[7]

Hanover Court House modern view. This famous building sits across the road from Hanover Tavern. Author photo.

Hanover Tavern modern view. When Stuart's men passed this place several troopers threatened to hang tavern keeper Clevars Chisholm because of his Union sympathies. This historic building has been restored and highlights a museum, restaurant and repertory theatre. Author photo.

Hanover Tavern circa 1890. Hanover Tavern Foundation.

When the Rebel column rode into Hanover Court House, the red brick court building stood on the east side of the road. This small t-shaped structure had entry doors guarded by an open-ended portico fronted by tall keyhole-like openings. In 1763 in that same building, Patrick Henry had won a famous case in which he chastised the British king for attempting to set prices on tobacco paid to ministers. The two-story Hanover Tavern stood across the road. A long, open porch ran the length of the L-shaped wooden travel spot.

Some of the local Hanover troopers muttered harsh words about the tavern owner, Clevars S. Chisholm. Two of Chisholm's sons had enlisted in the Confederate service, yet the outspoken Clevars had made known his support for the Union. His political sympathies had not waned despite losing 750 bushels of "partly shelled and partly in the ear" corn to Union cavalrymen led by Brigadier General William Emory several weeks earlier. One Hanover resident later overheard some Virginia troopers "cursing" the elder Chisholm as "they regretted they had not strung him to a tree."[8]

The rooster tail of dust to the south of Hanover Court House marked the way Stuart could not go, but worse, the escaping "bluebirds" carried word of the "secret" gray presence on the Union right flank. However, luck would combine with negligence to benefit Stuart because the officer leading the 6th Regular's patrol either failed to send word of the Rebel presence to Cavalry Reserve headquarters or the courier never arrived. Nearly six more hours would pass before Brigadier General Philip St. George Cooke would discover the huge problem on his right flank.[9]

CHAPTER 11

Haw's Shop to Totopotomoy Creek: A Running Fight

FRIDAY, JUNE 13, 1862

11 AM–2:30 PM

L IEUTENANT ROBINS trotted south with the Confederate advance guard away from Hanover Court House. The 1st Virginia Cavalry had returned to their place in the column with the horses' forelegs and bellies dripping water and mud from Mechump's Creek. Near the back of the column came Lieutenant James Breathed's two cannons, followed by Lieutenant Colonel Will Martin's Jeff Davis Legion, who guarded the rear.

Trees shaded both sides of the road as Robins' advance climbed uphill from the swamp bottom. They rounded a gentle curve and approached an intersection with the Hanovertown or River Road, about a mile south of Hanover Court House. Then, Robins spotted more horsemen just ahead. This discovery signaled another Union patrol led by the 5th U. S. Cavalry's lieutenant Edward H. Leib. These Union troopers had been on the road since 6 AM.

Earlier that morning, Lieutenant Leib had received last-minute instructions from Captain William Royall before departing Old Church with Company F to patrol northwest toward Hanover Court House. A sergeant accompanied by eight men galloped on ahead to act as an advance guard. Leib wrote that his column moved "cautiously," and near 11 AM, they approached to "within a half mile of Hanover Court-House." Leib did not indicate that he expected enemy contact, yet the glacial pace suggests otherwise because it took five hours for his cavalry company to cover about eleven miles.[1]

Leib seemed unaware that Confederate cavalry had chased Captain Gregg's 6th U. S. Cavalry patrol out of Hanover Court House earlier. Gregg's troopers had fled Hanover Court House headed south toward Mechanicsville while Leib's men approached the village from the southeast.

At about the same time that Leib's men neared Hanover Court House, Captain George F. Cornog's patrol from White House

Lieutenant Edward H. Leib, Company F, 5th United States Cavalry. Leib led the second Union cavalry patrol that bumped into Stuart's men near Hanover Court House on Friday, June 13. This image shows Leib later in the war as a brevet lieutenant colonel. MOLLUS, USAHEC.

Landing sauntered into Royall's Old Church camp. Cornog, who commanded Company B, 11th Pennsylvania Cavalry, had discovered nothing out of the ordinary during the ten-mile scout. Royall indicated "all was quiet along his front" as well. Cornog and his company soon turned back toward White House Landing. Neither officer could have envisioned how the situation in their area would soon change.[2]

Meanwhile, just southeast of Hanover Court House, one of Leib's scouts reined to a halt. He saw horsemen ahead. They looked like enemy cavalry, so he galloped back to tell Leib. The lieutenant urged caution as he knew that a friendly patrol from the 6th Regulars might be in the area. Leib moved his men for cover in the woods and then advanced alone to determine what force lay ahead. He discovered about two squadrons of cavalry with about fifteen troopers in the advance guard, but he was still too far away to determine whether they were friend or foe. Advancing still farther through the woods and still alone, Leib reported that he came "to the banks of a small stream, upon the opposite side of which I could still see the horsemen in line. As I approached the stream an officer and 6 or 8 men came down the opposite side. Immediately upon seeing me they turned about and joined the main body. I then knew them to be the enemy."[3]

However, an irritated 5th Regular trooper disputed Leib's version. Private John McCormick stated that Leib sent a sergeant and ten men ahead to investigate the mysterious assembly of troops. Leib ordered McCormick to go with the group and get close enough "to inquire what troops they were and what their business was." McCormick muttered that they were obviously the enemy as he could tell the rank of the officers. Leib snapped at McCormick to "obey orders."[4]

McCormick rode forward with the group and crossed a wooded ravine. The young private then moved on ahead by himself to within seventy-five yards of the Rebel troopers. He discovered a "heavy black-oak gatepost at the roadside the hight of my breast when on horseback." He swung his Sharp's carbine around and rested it on top of the post and fired at a group of enemy officers. Moments later McCormick raced back to his ten colleagues, and they galloped back to Lieutenant Leib and the waiting column. Like kicking over a yellow jacket nest, McCormick's rash action brought about 100 Confederates "at full gallop" with guns blazing. When the wide-eyed McCormick neared Leib, the officer said, "'Did you ask those troops who they were?'" McCormick's response was, "'Lieutenant, here they come; ask them yourself.'"[5]

Amidst the scattered shots, Leib saw he was outmanned, and he reversed his company "by fours" and raced back southeast along the River or Hanovertown Road, sometimes referred as the Hanover Court House — Old Church Road. A courier sped off to advise Captain Royall about the encounter with an estimated two enemy squadrons. This report would not have drawn too much concern as small Confederate cavalry patrols frequently probed the area. However, Leib had failed to discover the more than 1,000 gray cavalrymen screened by the trees and terrain.

He told his sergeant at the head of the column "to retire slowly and in order, regulating his gait by mine." Leib returned to the rear and selected a competent man "to keep the enemy in sight." The officer then noted that he selected six men to keep their eyes on this man, and then he sent several other troopers racing off ahead to gather the various guards earlier left at the road intersections. Satisfied with his decisions, he joined the middle of his column as they galloped away. When he glanced over his shoulder, he happily reported, "The enemy did not immediately follow."[6]

Jeb Stuart elected not to chase this enemy patrol either. He nodded to Lieutenant Robins to turn right at the road intersection, which was probably at Dr. Lycien B. Price's house. They continued about two more miles south to a Dr. Kinney's house. The Kinney place, a two-story white frame house flanked by brick chimneys at each end, stood just right of the road

Jeb Stuart assumed that each Union patrol would sound the alarm, so he elected to turn left near the Kinney house and move on a less-traveled road toward Taliaferro's Mill. Thick woods soon flanked this narrow road as it snaked and dropped toward the mill on Crump's Creek, another potential ambush spot. The throaty bark of frogs rose up from the swamp. The overarching tree limbs provided welcome shade as the temperature approached ninety degrees.

Robins and his advance, with eyes wide and guns ready, approached the creek bridge. Close behind followed a 9th Virginia Cavalry squadron commanded by thirty-one-year-old Caroline County native Samuel Amery Swann. Captain Latane's squadron trailed Swann's men. One of Captain Swann's companies rode forward and dismounted as skirmishers. They fanned out into the woods on each side of the road. Once several men crossed the bridge, the area seemed clear, and Robins rode past the wooden

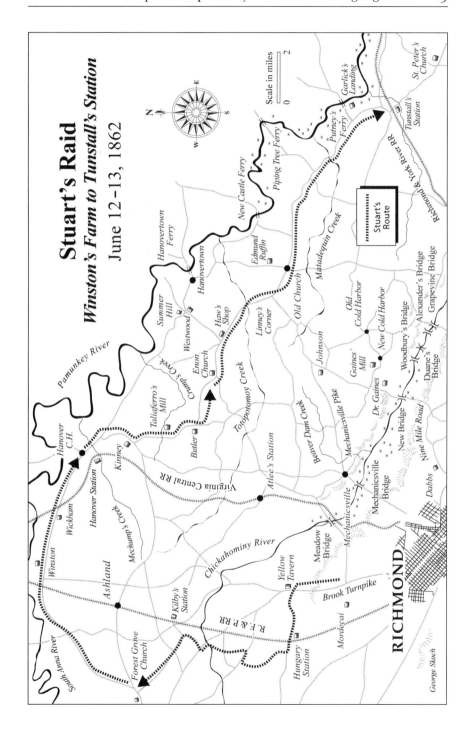

Stuart's Raid
Winston's Farm to Tunstall's Station
June 12–13, 1862

Scale in miles
0   2

Stuart's Route

St. Peter's Church

Garlick's Landing

Tunstall's Station

Putney's Ferry

Piping Tree Ferry

New Castle Ferry

Richmond & York River RR

Matadequin Creek

Grapevine Bridge

Alexander's Bridge

Hanovertown Ferry

Hanovertown

Edmund Ruffin

Old Church

Old Cold Harbor

New Cold Harbor

Woodbury's Bridge

Pamunkey River

Summer Hill

Westwood

Haw's Shop

Limney's Corner

Johnson

Gaines' Mill

Duane's Bridge

Enon Church

Crump's Creek

Taliaferro's Mill

Totopotomoy Creek

Beaver Dam Creek

Mechanicsville Pike

Dr. Gaines

New Bridge

Nine Mile Road

Hanover C.H.

Butler

Atlee's Station

Mechanicsville Bridge

Mechanicsville

Dabbs

Kinney

Wickham

Hanover Station

Mechump's Creek

Virginia Central RR

Chickahominy River

Meadow Bridge

Winston

Ashland

Kilby's Station

Yellow Tavern

Brook Turnpike

RICHMOND

R.F.&P. RR

Mordecai

Hungary Station

South Anna River

Forest Grove Church

George Skoch

mill on the left. He sent a rider back to bring the rest of the column forward.[7]

Nearing the bridge, many troopers eased their mounts toward
the cool water, and the beasts leaned down and slurped their fill.
Some men dismounted and submerged their canteens. It seemed
to take forever for the thirsty column to cross the rickety wooden
bridge. The group finally moved ahead at a good trot while officers
and sergeants urged their men to close up the column.

As Robins and his men topped the rise from Crump's Creek,
the trees gave way to cornfields. The blistering heat danced over
everything in the shimmering bright light. Robins stopped and
raised his field glasses to scope the fields and road. He did not see
any blue-uniformed soldiers.

———— ◦ ————

The 5th Regular's lieutenant Leib had left a single trooper behind on
a hill to watch for the Confederate pursuit. Leib had urged the man
to wait no longer than twenty minutes and if there was no threat in
sight, to catch up with the blue column. The 5th Regulars reined to
a dusty halt at the crossroads village of Haw's Shop, some five miles
west of their headquarters camp at Old Church. Leib might have
expected to find Captain Royall with reinforcements, but instead
he found only a few pickets who guarded the intersection that was
sprinkled with several houses and the foundation of a dismantled
machine shop. Leib deployed his men into a defensive position. A
short time later the trailing lone scout arrived. He reported that
he had waited twenty minutes, and the enemy had not appeared
out of the Crump's Creek bottom along River Road. Yet, this scout
had failed to see Stuart's troopers because they were on a different
road. Leib hailed another courier and sent him to Old Church to
report the apparent good news to Captain Royall that the enemy
had not followed. He then sent his rear guard west about one-and-
a-half miles to discover where the Confederate cavalry had gone.[8]

Captain William B. Royall sat under a tent fly in the Old
Church campsite of his two 5th U. S. Cavalry squadrons. The thirty-
seven-year-old Royall had seen action in the Mexican War prior

to graduation from West Point at age thirty. He was probably the oldest cadet in his 1855 class.

Royall had spent two weeks at the Old Church site, which had enabled him to make his headquarters area into somewhat of a spartan home. While welcomed by some soldiers, this lengthy time spent in one place also reflected just how mired George McClellan's army was as it waited for more troops. The time had also allowed Royall to become familiar with the smoky smell from the nearby blacksmith shop at the western edge of the village. He stared at some paperwork piled on his flimsy camp desk.

An unusual looking building, almost hidden by trees, stood just across the road from Royall's camp. Additions to the place appeared to have been made at different times. A three-story red brick façade occupied the western half of the establishment's footprint. Framed boards walled in the eastern section, which was fronted by a two-story porch. A wooden post rose out of the ground near the southeast porch corner. The small sign atop the ten-foot pole announced to passersby that the Old Church Hotel was owned by J. A. Lipscomb. Several mature trees guarded the road front and obscured the hotel roof and second floor from the cavalry camp. Another hotel, Rockett's, stood to the east. The village derived its name from a long-gone church originally built at the road intersection in 1753.[9]

The replacement for the original old church now stood just east of Royall's cavalry camp. A short,

Captain William B. Royall, 5th United States Cavalry. Royall was in charge of two squadrons detached to the Old Church area to patrol from the Pamunkey River to Hanover Court House. He was severely wounded in the fight at Linney's Corner on Friday, June 13 and he would not see combat again during this war. Later he served out west and retired as a brigadier general in 1887. This postwar image shows him dressed as a colonel. MOLLUS-Pa., USAHEC.

curved brick wall beckoned even Yankee horsemen into the narrow drive of Immanuel Episcopal Church. Built in 1853, white-painted brick covered the façade of the small building, but the four turrets at the entrance added a Gothic look. Glass cut in diamond patterns covered the windows. No doubt, soldiers wearing 5th Regular cavalry boots had walked down the plank floors past the ten pine pews to view the brilliant stained glass window behind the altar. Somehow, despite the fifteen-mile distance between Hanover Court House's St. Paul's Episcopal Church and Old Church's Immanuel Episcopal Church, Reverend George S. Carraway managed to lead both congregations. Little did he realize how difficult Union authorities would make his job over the next three years of war.[10]

A courier from Lieutenant Leib rode up on a lathered horse to Royall's tent at about 2 PM. He dismounted and snapped a salute and then handed Leib's dispatch to the captain. Royall and a

Old Church Hotel today. This building sits on Old Church Road [Rt. 606]. Stuart's raiders rode past this place when they attacked the 5th U. S. Cavalry camp across the road. Union cavalry later arrested the hotel's owner for his Confederate sympathies. Randall Flynn photo.

Old Church Hotel circa 1864. This photo by Timothy O'Sullivan and Alexander Gardner shows the hotel on June 4, 1864 when it served as Phil Sheridan's Union cavalry headquarters during the Overland Campaign. Library of Congress.

nearby officer tried to decipher the scrawled message. Royall then listened as the rider told of the "enemy advancing in force from the direction of Hanover Court-House" and the rest of Leib's company was "returning slowly toward camp." This message must have been carried by the first courier dispatched by Leib from the Hanover Court House area at about 11:30 AM. The second courier bound for Old Church from Haw's Shop had not yet arrived.[11]

Royall called over Lieutenant William McLean who was only a year removed from West Point's 1861 class. Minutes later, McLean and about thirty men from Company H tore across the field and headed west on the road. Royall certainly wished he had more men right then, but he had no more reinforcements at hand. Most of Captain James E. Harrison's Company A had been dispatched earlier by a direct order from General McClellan to escort a flag of truce. Their presence would have been helpful. Royall knew that Company C should return soon from picket duty.[12]

Meanwhile, Lieutenant Leib guarded the crossroads at Haw's Shop. A dark outline soaked the brim of his hat as the thermometer edged north of ninety degrees. He waited and wished Captain Royall would arrive quickly with help, yet he knew the one-way distance between Haw's Shop and Old Church was more than five miles. "After remaining at the crossroads about an hour," Leib recalled seeing a trooper riding up from the east. The courier pulled up and handed him an order from Captain Royall "to return to camp." Leib cautioned the Haw's Shop cavalry pickets to be vigilant, and he led his patrol east toward Old Church.[13]

After about a mile, Leib saw a small column of friendly cavalry coming their way from the direction of Totopotomoy Creek and Old Church. It was Lieutenant McLean with about thirty men. When the two companies met, Leib told McLean about the two enemy squadrons near Hanover Court House, but after an hour of waiting at Haw's Shop, they had not reappeared. He did not know where the Southerners had gone. McLean then repeated for Leib the order from Royall to return to Old Church. McLean, the senior officer, then reversed his direction and led his company toward the swampy morass of Totopotomoy Creek. Leib and his men followed.[14]

Back at Old Church, Lieutenant Richard Byrnes and his Company C arrived from their picket duty. Royall motioned for Byrnes, and the lieutenant listened to his captain's instructions. Royall then mounted his horse and galloped alone westward as he passed Lipscomb's hotel and the smelly blacksmith shop.

Byrnes' troopers ran to and fro as they resaddled their mounts. Teamsters pushed wagons into position while others harnessed horse teams. Lieutenant Byrnes then yelled some instructions, and he led the company about three hundred yards away where they formed a line facing west across the road intersection next to the blacksmith shop. Six other troopers took off north on the road toward Hanovertown to scout for the enemy.[15]

Clear of Old Church, Royall slapped the reins across his horse's broad back. He hoped for more speed as he raced toward Lieutenant Leib and Lieutenant McLean. He wondered what lay ahead. The sound of the wind mixed with the thud of the horse's hooves and the squeak of leather as the beast carried him past the open fields and then into the arch of trees that led to Totopotomoy Creek. What he did not hear was the distant rip of guns, which meant that Leib and McLean must be all right. Besides, Royall certainly figured that no enemy force would be foolish enough to strike so far behind their lines.

Leib's men continued behind McLean's company for about a half-mile when several excited riders from Haw's Shop came up from behind. The beleaguered men shouted out "the enemy were about a quarter of a mile back, advancing rapidly." These pickets had been at Haw's Shop and had been overwhelmed by a large Confederate force. The Rebels had appeared so rapidly that several of the pickets and their horses could not escape. Leib hustled a courier forward to alert McLean and then to continue on to inform Royall. He next scanned for a defensive position.[16]

Midway back in the parade of Confederate horses and men, the 9th Virginia's Dandridge William Cockrell pulled on the strap for his canteen. Cockrell, at age forty-two, was one of the older horsemen in his regiment. The heat and the dust from "the long columns of horses on the dry road" bothered all the men except those in the vanguard. Two weeks earlier, Cockrell had complained to his wife about the scarcity of sugar, coffee, rice and molasses. Little did he know how his fortune was about to change.[17]

Frank Stringfellow and Redmond Burke passed Enon Church as they scouted ahead of Lieutenant Robins' advance. Two miles later, the pair approached the five-road intersection that comprised Haw's Shop. Both soldiers halted their mounts as they spotted movement ahead — enemy pickets standing along the road and a field. The scouts realized that they had been spotted too. Several enemy troopers mounted their horses and charged the pair. Stringfellow and Burke fired several shots before retreating toward the approaching Lieutenant Robins with the vanguard.[18]

The two Confederate scouts rounded a bend with the 5th U. S. Cavalry troopers close behind. The scene that unfolded caused the blue-clad cavalrymen to yank hard on their horses' reins. All the way down the road as far as the Union pursuers could see stood a dust cloud that hovered over a long line of Rebel horsemen. Now the chase reversed direction as Lieutenant Robins ordered a charge, and Stringfellow and Burke joined the advance guard as they raced toward the small hamlet of Haw's Shop. Captain Swann's squadron, led by the 9th Virginia's Company B, spurred ahead just behind the advance.[19]

Citizens near Haw's Shop heard the commotion and yelled their support from the nearby fields and homes. "Their constant cheers were soon drowned in the earth shaking noise of squadrons thundering along the road, and the jar and jingle and rush of flying artillery dashing forward with ten-horse teams!"[20]

Robins and his men galloped into the village intersection past the old machine shop and the forge. Union pickets scattered like quail. Despite the warning of Lieutenant Leib, some of the Union horsemen seemed to have been surprised. A handful of fugitives bolted away amidst sporadic gunfire and a clatter of hooves and dust. The rest of Rooney Lee's men soon arrived. They helped to disarm the prisoners and then hand them over to the provost guard.[21]

Jeb Stuart noted that Robins' lightning strike at Haw's Shop rendered such a "wholesome terror" on the Union vedettes that those who escaped "never paused to take a second look" before bolting east. Robins then spurred his advance guard after the escapees while Stuart urged Heros von Borcke to catch up with Robins and join the chase. The excited Prussian made an excellent first impression on his Confederate colleagues as he drew "immense saber" and spurred his horse forward after the Yankees.[22]

The men from the Jeff Davis Legion heard firing ahead from their rear guard position. They quickened their pace, and as they passed a roadside house, Mississippi private Robert S. Young spotted an old lady whom he would always remember. The old lady was "praying for us as we were passing and the skirmish was going on at the other end of the line." Others along the road ran out of their houses and shouted Christian encouragement while expressing disdain for the invading Yankees. As Young reflected on the ride several days later, he noted: "The ladies beyond hanover court house received us with more enthusiasm than I have ever seen."[23]

———

Lieutenant Leib's patrol had stopped a short distance to the east of Haw's Shop, but because of the trees and a ninety-degree bend in the road, they could not see the Confederate pursuers. However, they could hear the approaching gallop of horses. Leib looked east for McLean's company, but they had trotted out of sight. The young officer's mind raced as he looked around for some defensible terrain and a tactical solution to his approaching problem. The brow of a low hill stood to the left of the road. He realized that if he lined up his men at the base of the hill, the shadows might mask his soldiers long enough to get a jump on his pursuers and possibly charge them. However, Leib admitted that he had no idea "if my force was sufficient." If he was outnumbered, he hoped to at least buy some time keeping "them in check with the pistol … to show a bold front and conceal as long as possible the small numbers of my command."[24]

The crescendo of horses grew louder as Leib waited with his men in front of the hill. He urged them to be steady. Then suddenly the lead Rebel troopers rode into view. Leib waited for them to come closer and then gave the order to shoot. The rip of pistol fire shredded the humid air.

Horses squealed as they went down sending their gray-clad riders tumbling through the air and across the ground. Lieutenant Robins swung his mount around and urged his men to withdraw. Colonel Rooney Lee heard the gunfire around the bend in the road, and he shouted for Captain Swann's men "to charge with the saber."[25]

Their swords glinted in the sunlight as Swann led his squadron forward at a trot. When he came around the corner he saw the enemy troopers about two hundred yards away firing at Robins' men. Swann hollered, "Charge!" and his squadron thundered into action with a Rebel yell. Heros von Borcke piled into the fray amidst "blinding clouds of dust" and no doubt frightening anybody, friend or foe, who was within swinging radius of his huge blade.[26]

The 9th Virginia's nineteen-year-old Sergeant George William Beale observed a cluster of Leib's men close to the road. He then saw another group, probably some of the scattered Haw's Shop pickets, in a field on the left of the road near a wood line. A fence skirted the field. Several Confederate troopers jumped off their horses to tear down the obstacle. More gunfire erupted, and a company B trooper went down as a "bullet cut an ugly gash in the flesh." Beale realized this soldier represented "the first blood drawn on our side." The other Virginians twisted and kicked a large hole in the fence, and some of the squadron galloped into the muddy field.[27]

Instead of heading back to the road, Sergeant Beale and several of his men galloped across the sloped field. Suddenly, his horse's forelegs sank "deep in the mire." Like a missile, Beale flew over the animal's head and landed in the mud. Several other troopers also became dismounted in the same embarrassing way. Covered in smelly muck, the Southerners struggled to their feet, but not before their mounts bounded up, and wild with excitement, dashed into the road and riderless "followed the flying steeds of the Federals."[28]

Lieutenant Leib believed that his men emptied ten Southern saddles yet the poor footing in the field probably upended many of the Confederate horses and men, not the inaccurate Union pistol fire. Leib lamented his men's lack of carbines as the enemy's rifles and shotguns gave his own troopers a hot time. With emptied pistols and no time to reload, Leib ordered a charge with drawn sabers, but his 6th Regulars only surged ahead mere yards before a terrifying spectacle appeared. Around the bend galloped Swann's men, and when they saw the Yankees, they bellowed that hair-raising yell again.[29]

The combination of the Rebel yell and the large gray numbers "broke and scattered in confusion" the rest of Leib's men. Swann's Confederates captured several more Union troopers and chased the rest through the woods and back onto the road that dropped downhill toward Totopotomoy Creek. Beale described the enemy's departure as "a confused mass, galloping for the bridge which spanned the creek." Von Borcke credited the enemy escape to their "fresher animals."[30]

Lieutenant Leib acquitted his Union horsemen as he believed that they "held them in check at least twenty minutes," yet his time piece might have been overly generous based on the overwhelming Confederate numbers that Captain Swann's squadron added to the fray. Heros von Borcke recalled that the scrap lasted "a very few minutes" before the chase was on again.[31]

Leib soon "wheeled short about, and went back at full speed." The rest of his line then melted, and they all high-tailed it east to find help. The narrow road funneled the panicked horsemen onto an even narrower bridge across Totopotomoy Creek. This bottleneck enabled several energetic Southerners who had raced ahead in pursuit to capture several more enemy riders in the confusion crossing the creek.[32]

Sergeant Beale stood up in the field and slung the mud off his hands. He watched in frustration as his "young and fiery mare" named Sally Payton joined the enemy stampede and disappeared around the road bend. Sally Payton reached the logjam of screaming Federal troopers and rearing horses at the narrow bridge. She panicked and "leaped down the bank into the river!" Unfortunately, this move sealed the horse's doom.[33]

Either Leib's courier or the gunfire had alerted Lieutenant McLean's thirty men to the problem behind them. McLean ordered his men to turn around, and they deployed on the east side of Totopotomoy Creek in the thick woods on either side of the road. The anxious troopers heard hoofbeats echo across the span as they raised their weapons and wondered who would appear. Thankfully, they saw the blue uniforms of Leib's panicked riders.

Leib shouted for his men to join McLean's line; then, he sent another courier, the fourth one, to inform Royall of the situation. The thick woods and thirty-foot wide chest-deep creek flanked by steep banks made a good defensive position for even these two small Union cavalry companies.[34]

Meanwhile, Captain Swann's enthusiastic horsemen had roared past Lieutenant Robins' group in pursuit of the Federal refugees. Robins reassembled his 9th Virginia advance guard, and they gathered up a handful of prisoners. Swann's chase continued for about a mile-and-a-half when the captain became suspicious. Most of Leib's Federal troopers had disappeared, and "the road became very narrow, and the brush on either side was a place favorable for an ambuscade." Swann drew back on his reins and ordered his bugler "to recall his men," some of whom had ridden well ahead.[35]

Jeb Stuart soon arrived and conferred with Swann. He agreed that they needed to exercise caution, but he knew that it would take time to clear the creek bottom safely. With word of his force behind the Union right flank, time was not on his side. Lieutenant Robins' advance guard rode up and passed Swann as the captain reformed his squadron. Robins' men neared the bridge and saw skid marks in the road, which pointed to the bodies of several blue-clad troopers and their horses. The advance troopers soon dismounted and peeled off into the woods to scout for the anticipated trap.[36]

Colonel Fitzhugh Lee recognized some of the 5th U. S. Cavalry prisoners. This unit had been the pre-war 2nd U. S. Cavalry, where he had served as a lieutenant. A number of these men reached out to shake Lee's hand and addressed him as "lieutenant" despite the Confederate colonel's stars on his collar. Lee took great pleasure in the banter as he asked about certain old friends. John Cooke witnessed the interviews, and he noted the friendly demeanor that the captured enemy troopers extended toward Colonel Lee.[37]

Meanwhile, a small number of Union soldiers held the bridge and the far creek bank for a short time, but they soon noticed that dismounted Southerners began to wade across the creek "above and below the bridge." Lieutenant Leib ordered his men to fall back again, and they probably followed McLean's troopers toward Old Church. His men retreated about one mile disputing ground until the enemy pressure disappeared. The road climbed uphill and then leveled out with fields on both sides. Near an intersection with another road that headed southwest toward Mechanicsville and then Richmond, Leib decided "to hold my position at all hazard, deeming it certain re-enforcements must soon come up." Locals called the strategic spot Linney's Corner. A short time later Captain Royall finally appeared and a relieved Leib turned command of the small force over to him.[38]

Leib told Royall of the large number of Confederate troopers swarming across Totopotomoy Creek and certain to be heading their way. Royall sent Lieutenant Louis D. Watkins to ride six long miles to Cavalry Reserve headquarters east of Gaines' Mill to inform Brigadier General Philip St. George Cooke of the "enemy in force" on the right flank. Amazingly, Watkins appeared to be the first rider sent to alert any senior Union commander to the problem. John Mosby later defended Royall's slow response: "He [Royall] had no cause to suspect the numbers he was meeting, for McClellan had never even considered the possibility of a force breaking through his lines and passing around him." Next, Royall sent another courier back to Old Church to hustle Lieutenant Byrnes forward with the rest of the 5th U. S. Cavalry's Company C. When Byrnes received the order, he sent a man back to the Old Church camp to make sure the teamsters had loaded the wagons with supplies and were ready to make their escape. He then led his men at a gallop toward Royall's position just over a mile west from Old Church.[39]

The arrival of Byrnes' men combined with the soldiers led by Leib and McLean raised Captain Royall's force to only 100 troopers. This small number would have to attempt to slow Stuart's 1,200-member juggernaut that now clattered across the Totopotomoy Creek Bridge headed their way.

CHAPTER 12

Collision Near Linney's Corner

FRIDAY, JUNE 13, 1862

3 PM

CAPTAIN SWANN reassembled the members of his squadron after the brief melee and chase near the Totopotomoy Creek Bridge. Rooney Lee then ordered Swann's men to dismount and to fan out into the woods before they waded into the marshy area to collapse the flanks of the Union defenders on the far bank. Some discussion ensued as to why the Union troopers had not torched the bridge. Perhaps it was an ambush.

The 9th Virginia's private Eustace Conway Moncure carefully stepped into the swampy muck that he estimated was one hundred yards wide. When the twenty-five-year-old Caroline County soldier and his colleagues reached the actual creek bed, they found that the Union troopers had fled their position.[1]

Lieutenant William Robins next crossed Totopotomoy Creek and confirmed that the enemy had vanished. He sent a rider back to bring the rest of Stuart's column forward. Lieutenant John E. Cooke expressed surprise that "the stream was entirely unde-fended by works," and "the enemy's right wing was unprotected." This discovery was precisely the reason that General Lee had sent Stuart and his men on their expedition. Jeb Stuart echoed Cooke's observation when he noted that the enemy's failure to occupy such a "strong position of defense" showed "a weakness" or was perhaps a trap. The Confederate cavalry chieftain next believed that the enemy would defend the high ground closer toward Old Church, which stood on a main wagon supply route. A ride deeper into enemy territory would test this theory.[2]

The unseated Sergeant George Beale soon arrived at the creek and found his frantic horse trying to climb the steep bank, but she kept dropping back into the churned, muddy water. Downed trees prevented her from moving up or down the stream. Trapped, he climbed down to her and took a pistol and a haversack of food from the saddle. He then latched onto some vines and pulled himself back up the near vertical bank. Sadly, he had to abandon Sally Payton to her fate, for there was no time to extricate the animal out of the creek bed.[3]

The rest of Lieutenant Robins' van came across the bridge in order to "advance in skirmish line on both sides of the road" with Swann's flankers. Colonel Rooney Lee called for Captain William Latane to move forward his fresh squadron composed of companies E and F. Latane's men bunched four columns together because of the narrow road and then trotted onto the bridge. The horses' hooves echoed loudly on the planks. Once across the bridge and past Swann's dismounted men, four flankers formed pairs and moved into the woods on each side of the road. Two of these flankers were Private William Campbell and Corporal Stephen Winbourne Mitchell. Campbell was born in King and Queen County but had moved to Iowa in 1858 only to return to enlist in Company F some four years later. The twenty-four-year-old Campbell guided his horse to the left as he zigged around trees and ducked to avoid low-hanging limbs and vines. Mitchell was twenty-eight-years-old and had been a pre-war mechanic in Essex County. Flies and mosquitoes descended on the young men. They waved gloved hands to defend themselves, but then encountered sticky spider webs that lurked in the branches. The going was slow, as the horses clopped through the crunchy leaves piled on the ground.[4]

Lieutenant Robins' men moved ahead as the narrow road climbed up from the creek bottom. Trees lined both sides of the

Totopotomoy Creek Bridge. This is Studley Road [Rt. 606] looking southeast in direction Stuart's men traveled. Lieutenants Leib and McLean defended the far bank with a contingent of 5th U. S. Cavalry troopers for only a short time before retreating up the Totopotomoy Creek ridge. Randall Flynn photo.

Totopotomoy Creek. On June 13, 1862 much of the creek was beyond its banks in a swampy morass. Randall Flynn photo.

road and masked the daylight. As the ground flattened out, Robins saw open fields ahead, and his men dismounted and crept into the woods. Moments later, Robins observed "a force of Federal cavalry drawn up in column of fours and ready to charge." He ordered his men to drop back, and he sent a man back downhill to notify General Stuart.[5]

This scout reached Jeb Stuart and Rooney Lee near the creek bridge and passed the word of the enemy stand. Captain Latane then received an order "to move forward and clear the road." Jeb Stuart did not know the strength of the force that lay ahead, but he "preferred to oppose the enemy with one squadron at a time, remembering that he who brings on the field the last cavalry reserve wins the day." He then urged Fitzhugh Lee's 1st Virginia Cavalry to follow up Latane's men while Captain Swann's skirmishers remounted.[6]

Soon a clatter of hooves passed on the road, and Private Campbell, the flanker, was surprised to see his fellow troopers ride by him as they trotted uphill in response to Robins' summons. The 9th Virginia Cavalry's Company E from Spotsylvania County, known as the Mercer Cavalry, led the way, and Company F's Essex Light Dragoons followed.[7]

Meanwhile, Captain William Royall's curiosity had taken over as he waited at Linney's Corner. He had yet to see any enemy cavalry, but Lieutenant Leib insisted that they were coming. "Wishing to satisfy myself from personal observation as to the strength and character of the enemy," Royall led Lieutenant McLean's men forward followed by Leib and Byrnes' horsemen. After riding a short distance, he spied Robins' handful of dismounted Confederate scouts in the tree line. Royall bellowed out the order "to draw saber" and led his column ahead, which sent the Confederates tumbling back downhill through the woods to their waiting horses.[8]

Royall wisely elected not to follow Robins' dismounted vanguard very far. The Union cavalry captain believed a "few minutes" passed when he heard an unpleasant noise — the sounds of hundreds of

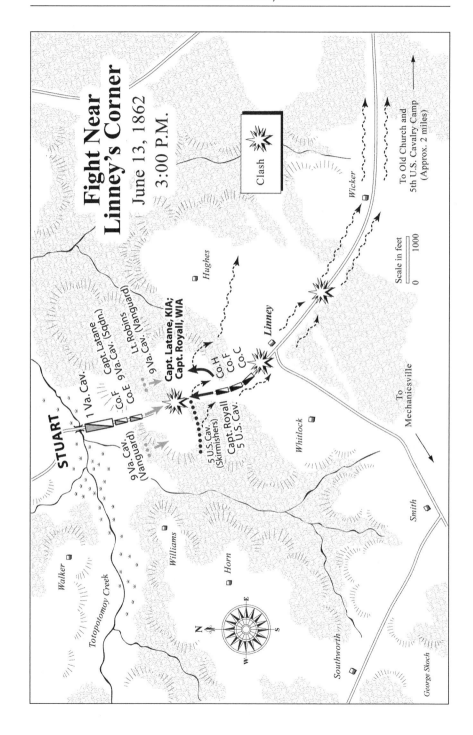

Fight Near Linney's Corner
June 13, 1862
3:00 P.M.

STUART

1 Va. Cav.

Capt. Latane 9 Va. Cav. (Sqdn.)

Co.F Co.E 9 Va. Cav.

Lt. Robins 9 Va. Cav. (Vanguard)

Capt. Latane, KIA; Capt. Royall, WIA

Co.H Co.F Co.C

9 Va. Cav. (Vanguard)

5 U.S. Cav. (Skirmishers)

Capt. Royall 5 U.S. Cav.

Hughes

Linney

Wicker

Clash

To Old Church and 5th U.S. Cavalry Camp (Approx. 2 miles)

To Mechanicsville

Whitlock

Smith

Williams

Horn

Walker

Totopotomoy Creek

Southworth

George Skoch

Scale in feet
0   1000

N
E
S
W

horses coming his way from the Totopotomoy Creek bottom. He knew they could not be friendly.[9]

The time was about 3 PM as Captain Latane at the head of his squadron crested the hilltop, still in columns of fours, and broke into daylight. A large field stood on the left while a smaller field with a thin tree line lay to the right. When he saw Royall's blue-clad troopers ahead in the road, he ordered a charge. Astride his half-Arabian horse, named The Colonel, William Latane soared ahead of his men. However, Latane failed to notice a Union skirmish line that waited in the woods to the west of the road. An excited Lieutenant Robins and his advance men jumped back on their mounts to join the clash.[10]

The terrain and trees hid most of the approaching Rebels from Royall's view; thus, he did not realize that he was heavily out-numbered. Despite what his ears must have told him, he ordered a charge too. Bugles blared along the ridge. Guidons snapped as the two columns galloped toward a head-on collision. Royall spurred his horse directly toward Captain Latane, the man lead-ing the Confederate charge. However, Royall soon saw he had a major problem as large numbers of enemy riders flared into the fields with their horses straining to flank his men on both sides. As the adrenaline surged, Royall believed that he faced about "six or seven squadrons of cavalry."[11]

Only a short distance separated the heads of the charging columns. Latane still might not have seen the danger on his right flank as he, saber in hand, bore down on the threat in the road straight ahead. Suddenly, from the tree line to the right, the Union skirmishers, stampeded by other Rebels in the woods, side-swiped into the midst of Latane's group. A wild melee of sabers, pistols and fists ensued, and then the front end of Royall's column piled into the mess.[12]

Latane focused on the leader of the Union column and sped toward him. He swung his saber at Captain Royall and struck flesh. Royall's hat, sliced in half, fell to the ground. Royall tried to maintain his balance in the saddle as he leveled his revolver and fired point blank twice into Latane's torso as their horses passed.

Neighing and swirling horses mixed with the growing dust cloud. Men yelled, first to bolster their courage and then from wounds. The smell of gunpowder and dirt hung thick in the air.[13]

Just behind Latane rode twenty-nine-year-old private Lewis Alexander Ashton. He swung his saber at a flash of blue uniform and struck something solid. Flecks of blood and sweat flew. The Yankee went down, but then Ashton found himself sailing through the air, after which he landed hard on the roadside. "Disentangling himself from riding gear," the Spotsylvania County soldier bounced to his feet only to face another deadly challenge. A 5th U. S. Cavalry bugler leaned out of the saddle and swished his blade inches away from Ashton. However, the move sent the bugler tumbling off his mount, and as he looked up, Ashton stood over him, "sabre drawn above his head." The bugler dropped his weapon and surrendered. Ashton would later try to serve for ten more months before being discharged for back injuries incurred during his fall.[14]

William Robins watched Latane slump from his horse after being the target of multiple gunshots while he "rode some paces in front of his men." No Confederate who witnessed the clash could confirm that Captain Royall shot Captain Latane while legend credits Latane with striking the Union officer several times about the head and shoulders with his saber.[15]

Lieutenant Byrnes brought up the rear of the Union column, and he remembered hearing Royall yell "draw saber." Several of Byrnes' men ripped apart a fence that protected a field on the right side of the road. Dirt clods flew as his horsemen followed him into the field to parallel Royall's "column of fours along the road."[16]

Several 9th Virginia troopers waited in the wood line at the west end of the field that stood east of the road. They watched as the head of each column approached for a head-on collision. Then, the tail end of the Union column, Byrnes' men, raced into the field just to their front. These 9th Virginians swung their weapons and fired at the Yankees. This fire hit Byrnes' men before they could pull even with Royall and flank Latane's charge. Now Byrnes feared that he might be flanked, so he sent Corporal Benjamin Evans with six men to the right and rear to investigate. Byrne's men fired their

Cavalry Collision. The view is northwest along this road and field where Captain Latane's 9th Virginia Cavalry squadron and Captain Royall's three companies from the 5th U. S. Cavalry collided. Latane died in the road close to this location. This is Studley Road [Rt. 606] between Totopotomoy Creek and Linney's Corner. Randall Flynn photo.

Linney's Corner and Fields. View looks northwest toward Totopotomoy Creek bottom. This is intersection of Studley Road and Bethesda Road [Rt. 606 and Rt. 634]. Randall Flynn photo.

pistols toward the smoke that floated along the tree line, but the range was too great to be more than a nuisance to the Southerners. The Federal lieutenant glanced over his right shoulder to check on Corporal Evans' progress. What he saw stunned him. A bunch of gray-clad cavalrymen had moved out of the woods to cut off Evans. With his right and rear threatened, Byrnes ordered the rest of his men to ride toward Royall's position on the road. However, before he could get close to help, the gray and blue columns smashed into each other amidst swinging sabers, gunfire, smoke, the screams of men and the squeals of horses.[17]

The 9th Virginia's private Campbell watched from his flanker position as Captain Latane's squadron raced past. Campbell recalled, "I suddenly heard the command to charge, and then the clash of arms, with rapid pistol shots." The young soldier kicked the spurs to his mount. "I was in a perfect tremor of excitement and pushed my horse up the hill thru the timber until I came out on top of the hill."[18]

When Campbell reached the edge of the woods, he saw his squadron fighting in the road as the clash began to spill into the field closest to where he sat. He recognized Lieutenant William A. Oliver, also from Company F, a pre-war physician, who was "urging his men to charge" the enemy troops, probably Byrnes' men, forming in the field. Campbell drew his saber and raced to join his lieutenant when the blue line in the field broke, and he joined the chase. Near a tree line he rode down a lieutenant on a wounded horse. "I called to him to surrender," remembered Campbell, "but he turned with sword for a fight. We crossed sabres and went at it, but my men began to close in and he soon surrendered." Blood streamed out of several wounds on the prisoner's head. The prisoner turned out to be the 5th U. S. Cavalry's lieutenant William McLean.[19]

Lieutenant Leib heard the collision just ahead. With saber in hand and reins in the other, he prepared to charge into the melee. He could not see much amidst the smoke and dust. However, moments later soldiers in blue came bailing out of the chaos both on foot and on horseback. Leib stared in horror as a disfigured officer, a death grip on his mount, came at him. It was Captain Royall.[20]

Blood poured down the side of Royall's face and head from multiple saber wounds. He slowed near Leib and yelled for them "to fall back." Leib repeated the orders and then a nearby bugler sounded the alarm. He turned and rode to catch up with Royall. When he looked back, he could not see Lieutenant McLean any-where because he was sprawled on the ground with several saber slashes to his head.[21]

Captain William Latane, commander of Company F, 9th Virginia Cavalry. He led companies E and F in the charge against Captain William Royall's 5th U. S. Cavalry troopers near Linney's Corner and he was killed in action. He was buried by the ladies and servants from Summer Hill and Westwood. His death and burial were celebrated throughout the South in both art and prose. For more on burial see appendix. *Virginia Cavalcade*, winter 1979.

Lieutenant Robins had seen Captain Latane fall to the ground, but he now found himself and about twenty-four other Confederates "borne along by the flying Federals" unable to escape from the chaotic momentum of the enemy retreat. A Richmond *Dispatch* writer added a flair to Robins' experience: "Cutting right and left, the Adjutant was hammering away vigorously on Yankee craniums with great ardor and gusto." Robins believed that each of his colleagues suffered wounds as "we were pushed by our foes in our rear into the ranks of those in our front." As the pile of men, beasts and debris swirled south-east for at least a quarter-mile, Robins saw an opportunity to escape. "I leaped my horse over the fence into the field and so got away" somehow unscathed.[22]

Meanwhile, in the field east of the road, Lieutenant Byrnes and his 5th Regulars witnessed "our force withdrawing rapidly" with Confederates in close pursuit. Now surrounded on three

sides, they had problems of their
own. He waved his arm toward the
southeast, and his men spurred
across the field as bullets dusted
the ground around them. At the
far end they leaped a fence into
another open field, turned in their
saddles and sent some inaccurate
pistol fire toward their pursuers.
Byrnes then saw some enemy troopers trying to cut off his escape to
the woods, and he urged his men to
make haste toward the distant trees.
They hustled forward, and he led
them on a "circuitous route" which
brought them out about a mile to
the east on the Hanovertown Ferry
Road.[23]

On the chaotic Union retreat,
Captain Royall, despite his injuries, somehow stayed in the saddle.
Blood dripped out of his right arm
and saber hand from an ugly gash
that extended from his thumb up
the forearm. A four-inch cut on his
head refused to stop bleeding, and

Lieutenant Richard Byrnes, 5th U. S.
Cavalry. He had served in the pre-
war 1st U. S. Cavalry and risen to
sergeant major. Byrnes' inaccurate
report that he and his men spotted
Confederate infantry just north of
Old Church would stifle the Union
cavalry pursuit of Stuart's raiders.
He later would rise to colonel of the
28th Massachusetts Infantry in the
Iron Brigade and would be killed in
action at Cold Harbor in June 1864.
USAHEC.

doctors would later discover that the blade strike had penetrated
into two layers of the skull. The small number of Union reinforcements that arrived enabled the disciplined Regulars to continue to
fight. Royall "thrust his arm through his bridle rein, and, drawing
his pistol with his left," fired while he urged his men on.[24]

"I wheeled my command twice" to slow the attack "emptying
three or four saddles" each time Royall recalled. However, the
overwhelming Confederate numbers that thundered out of the
Totopotomoy Creek bottom to the sounds of battle proved too
much. Nobody was happier than Royall when his exhausted men

skidded into their Old Church camp. He happily noted the Rebel pressure diminished during the final mile to Old Church.[25]

Private William Campbell led his wounded prisoner, Lieutenant McLean, toward the rear when he passed Colonel Fitzhugh Lee. Surprisingly, Lee seemed disinterested in the wounded officer. Campbell then saw his own colonel, Rooney Lee, and steered his prize toward the 9th Virginia commander. The young trooper remembered Rooney Lee "was exceedingly courteous" toward McLean. However, Campbell's emotions sank as Lee told him of Captain Latane's death and then instructed him to hand the prisoner over to a guard in order to assist with moving his captain's body.[26]

Next to the road, Campbell found the corpse surrounded by Latane's younger brother, Sergeant John Latane, Corporal Mitchell, Sergeant Edwin F. Hundley and William L. Waring, They soon decided to leave the body with John Latane and Stephen Mitchell. Sergeant John Latane, a twenty-three-year-old former University of Virginia student, had joined the 9th Virginia the previous year. Because time and men were now of the essence, John would soon find himself excused from duty, but alone as he sought a proper burial spot behind Yankee lines.[27]

The youngest officer on Stuart's staff, seventeen-year-old Lieutenant Chiswell Dabney, dropped off his horse near Latane's body. A bent saber stuck out of the ground nearby, and Dabney retrieved it. The weapon belonged to Latane, and scuffs near the bend showed where it had been struck out of the captain's hand during the close-in fight. Dabney handed the blade to a nearby Essex County trooper with instructions "to send it to his [Latane's] family."[28]

Lieutenant John Cooke approached a group of 9th Virginians who stood in the debris-filled field where the running skirmish had passed. Then, he saw the body of Captain Latane on the ground. He observed that "many a bearded face was wet with tears." John Mosby also rode by the sad scene of John Latane sitting by the road with his dead brother's head cradled in his lap. Mosby lamented, "We could not stay to give him even a hasty burial."[29]

Meanwhile, George Beale had earlier abandoned his trapped mare, Sally Payton, in Totopotomoy Creek. He snagged a captured horse and then spurred across the bridge and uphill toward the fight, but he soon noticed that the gunfire had stopped. Near the crest of the ridge, he came upon several bloody soldiers from Company E headed downhill toward the bridge. Moments later he found "four men, each holding the corner of a blanket." Beale recognized Captain Latane's boots sticking out from beneath the cover.[30]

Private Richard J. Norris overestimated the Yankee numbers at three hundred men. The twenty-six-year-old Lancaster County soldier delighted in later admitting to a family friend that "we drove them before us like sheep."[31]

Jeb Stuart's pursuit now slowed because of a combination of factors: the heat, Latane's death, wounded men in the van and the fog of war. Stuart also overestimated the retreating enemy force at "two squadrons" [four full cavalry companies], but, in fact, Royall had only portions of three companies. Several captured guidons, prisoners, horses and abandoned equipment might have convinced the Confederate general that he had faced a larger force that his men "dispersed in terror and confusion, leaving many dead on the field and blood in quantities in their tracks." Stuart also assigned a premature demise to Captain Royall as he believed him to be "mortally wounded."[32]

With the 9th Virginia dispersed into the fields and the woods on both sides of the road, Stuart ordered the 1st Virginia to come forward. Amidst the settling dust, he wondered what lay ahead, around the next bend and over the distant rise.

CHAPTER 13

A Momentous Decision at Old Church

FRIDAY, JUNE 13, 1862

3 PM–4 PM

O N THE HANOVERTOWN FERRY ROAD, several Union pickets, earlier scattered from Haw's Shop, rode out of the woods to join Lieutenant Richard Byrnes' party. They excitedly told Byrnes about a column of Rebel infantry that they had seen. The lieutenant looked in the northerly direction that the pickets pointed, and he thought he saw enemy troops too. However, Byrnes could not have spent much time scoping this enemy column through field glasses because he would have noted that they had to be dismounted cavalrymen, as there was no Confederate infantry anywhere nearby. His men soon turned south and arrived at Old Church, where they found Lieutenant Leib and the other survivors "drawn up in line near the edge of the woods." Byrnes reported an enemy "column of infantry" about one mile away. This erroneous report would help add further confusion for Union commanders on this Friday, the thirteenth.[1]

What Lieutenant Byrnes really saw has never been determined. Some historians have shrugged off the mistaken report as having come from an inexperienced junior officer, yet the Irish-born Byrnes had served in the pre-war 1st U. S. Cavalry as their sergeant major.

He had received an officer's commission in May 1861 and then transferred to the 5th Regulars. His errant report must not have harmed his standing because he later became the colonel of the 28th Massachusetts in the famous Irish Brigade before he received a fatal wound at Cold Harbor in June 1864. Byrnes' remarkable report would delay later Union decisions, and it would serve as an anchor when the Union cavalry needed to move with speed if they had any hope of catching Jeb Stuart and his men.[2]

Fitzhugh Lee soon arrived at Linney's Corner with his 1st Virginia Cavalry. The colonel had learned from several prisoners about the 5th U. S. Cavalry camp at Old Church. Stuart seemed amused when Fitz Lee "burning with impatience to cross sabres with his old regiment," next "begged" to lead the attack into the enemy camp. "[A] request I readily granted," Stuart admitted. Stuart looked about and noted the lack of Union defense works along the top of the Totopotomoy Creek ridgeline, which had been a question and concern of General Robert E. Lee. Save for a handful of cavalry patrols and pickets, Stuart's expedition revealed that the Union right flank was still in the air.[3]

Private Charles R. Chewning, 9th Virginia Cavalry, poked at the body of a dead enemy soldier sprawled in the field. Chewning confiscated his pistol along with the extra ammunition, caps and powder flask attached to the dead man's waist belt. A nearby dead horse next attracted the young Virginian's attention. He unhitched a blanket and saddlebags and happily noted "now I can throw away my old ripped quilt and sleep warm these chill nites." Chewning's scavenging consumed his attention until the regiment reformed. Then "I heard Bill Latane was killed. He was our healer and will be missed by all."[4]

John Cooke remounted his horse and rode away from Latane's body. He saw a wounded Union cavalryman. Shot through the chest, the poor man "called for water" as he squirmed "biting and tearing up the ground." Cooke, not wanting to stop, hollered to a servant standing on a nearby porch to take water to the man. He then glanced back and saw a Southerner pulling the spurs off the dying man's boots. "War is a hard trade," Cooke recorded.[5]

———◡———

Back at Old Church, Captain Royall, shaky from blood loss, turned command of the 5th U. S. Cavalry detachment over to Lieutenant Leib and he was careful in "instructing him not to risk another attack, but to remain there until the enemy approached, and then retire by the Cold Harbor road." Leib looked over Royall's "very severe" gashes. Royall's horse sported multiple wounds too, yet the duty-bound animal soon carried its rider to a field hospital.[6]

Royall would spend considerable time in the hospital, but he would recover from his injuries. However, he would not fight again in this war, but he would be brevetted to lieutenant colonel for his single-handed leadership in trying to slow Stuart's raiders.[7]

Leib next sent a courier to report to General Cooke. He sent two other troopers to recall the picket at New Castle landing while other riders headed toward White House Landing to alert the west bound supply wagons to the danger. Lastly, he sent an "express" toward Cold Harbor to find the first Union camp and plead for reinforcements. He and Lieutenant Byrnes then waited in line of battle with their men until an advance guard returned from the west with word of approaching Confederates.[8]

Leib estimated that it took an hour for Stuart's men to approach Old Church. As Fitz Lee's enthusiastic troopers neared the village, Leib abandoned the camp, and he led his men south to join the road that led toward Cavalry Reserve headquarters near Cold Harbor. Lieutenant Byrnes glanced at his watch as they left. The timepiece showed 4 PM. Frustrated, Byrnes believed the day might have turned out differently if his men had carried carbine rifles. Leib later recorded the help rendered to him by First Sergeant James T. Baden and sergeants McMahon and Carter. They rendered "valuable services" since he was the only officer left in his own Company F.[9]

The sweaty men of Fitz Lee's 1st Virginia, weapons in hand and bellowing the Rebel yell, thundered into the 5th Regular's camp on the east side of Old Church. They did not find much of a fight; instead the 1st Virginia chased Union cavalrymen into the woods to the south as far as Matadequin Creek. The 9th Virginia's Richard Norris recalled that when the Union troopers saw the horde of Virginians with "their sabers drawn charging on them with great speed they gave way like chaff before the wind."[10]

Fitz Lee's men soon returned from their chase, and they spied some much needed supplies — boxes upon boxes stacked near idle wagons. Numerous new white canvas tents pitched in a field contrasted against the bright green background of the nearby woods. Rebel soldiers flung open tents and tore into stacked crates.[11]

Amidst the sporadic gunfire, the 1st Virginia Cavalry's corporal Gilbert C. Greenway felt a stabbing pain in his foot. He stopped and carefully hobbled off his horse to find a bloody hole in his boot. Lieutenant Nathan Chew Hobbs, who led a company of Marylanders in the regiment, believed that a friendly trooper accidentally shot Greenway from behind. The bullet had struck part of Greenway's spur and pushed it through the boot leather into the foot.[12]

During one of the day's altercations, which probably happened on the approach to Old Church, the 1st Virginia's Private Thomas P. Clapp received accolades for downing a Federal officer. The officer raised his revolver as Clapp charged, but a well-aimed shot from the Virginian's carbine pierced his heart. The Yankee fired his revolver before striking the ground, and the bullet struck Clapp just below his right knee. Fitz Lee later noted that Clapp killed the officer "in personal combat" … "a deed well worthy of emulation." However, the records do not indicate any Union officer killed in the Old Church melee, so Clapp possibly received credit for wounding either Lieutenant McLean or Captain Royall.[13]

One soldier tossed small cardboard boxes of pistol ammunition to anybody nearby while others "took possession of a number of horses." John Cooke watched in glee as his men gathered up "boots, pistols, liquors, and other commodities." John Mosby enjoyed participating in the "festival" atmosphere too.[14]

A short time later, several men torched the tents, and columns of dark smoke soon boiled skyward. However, humor briefly turned to panic as somebody yelled that one of the burning tents contained gunpowder. "[T]he vicinity thereof was evacuated in almost less than no time," Cooke remembered. The flames soon devoured the tent and when the expected explosion failed to occur, the scavenging again continued. Whooping erupted when a trooper pulled the flap cover back from a Federal ambulance wagon. Inside the ambulance there were no wounded soldiers, but there was an even more precious cargo — a keg of whiskey.[15]

Lieutenant Dabney looked into one tent and discovered a cavalry uniform and boots which might fit his body servant. The young officer next found a pair of pants for himself. He happily noted that this find would save him twenty-five dollars. Moments later another trooper let out a whistle as he stared into a box "which held $5000 in Federal bank notes."[16]

Lieutenant Colonel Richard L. T. Beale remembered that a soldier from the 9th Virginia's Company C came forward with an enemy guidon. Beale recorded that this was "the first trophy of the kind that had fallen into our hands," and somebody placed the small swallowtail pennant in a safe place to present later to Virginia governor Letcher. Soon soldiers brought forward four more captured guidons, which brought the total to five.[17]

One remarkable statistic for Jeb Stuart's ride so far was the low casualty count for his men. Luck played a part, albeit a small one, but certainly if Captain William Royall's 5th Regulars had been armed with carbines instead of pistols, the Confederate losses would have been much higher. With Captain Latane as the only dead Confederate, most of those wounded came from the 9th Virginia's Company E. Several of the names on the casualty list were privates Lewis Alexander Ashton, Joseph R. A. Brent, Henry Frank Coleman, Frederick Stephens Herring and Richard T. Herring.[18]

The 5th U. S. Cavalry had four men killed outright. The list included: privates John Curran and William Max both from Company B; Francis Croel, Company C; Richard Mosher, Company H. About twelve more men were wounded while the Rebels captured at least thirty-five others. A number of the captured Union troopers came from Company A, which had manned the Haw's Shop picket line. Royall's assistant surgeon, Adam Trau, probably had remained behind to treat the wounded as his name also appeared on the prisoner list.[19]

Amidst the circus revelry at Old Church, John Mosby realized that some of his colleagues seemed to forget the predicament they really faced. The raiders could not hope to cross the Pamunkey River on the left if pressed. McClellan's headquarters tent stood only eight miles away at Dr. Trent's place, near the Chickahominy River's Grapevine Bridge. Fitz John Porter's Fifth Corps manned the line near Mechanicsville, about eight miles away. The nearest threat was the Old Cold Harbor headquarters for Philip St. George Cooke's Cavalry Reserve, which stood about six miles to the southwest by road.[20]

Jeb Stuart watched the beckoning columns of smoke, and he knew that his men had to depart Old Church soon. Otherwise, overwhelming Federal forces would converge on what now was a growing embarrassment to both George McClellan's army and its Cavalry Reserve led by Cooke.

Behind the enemy's right flank, Stuart had discovered what Robert E. Lee wanted to know; the area was vulnerable to attack. Now he wondered how to get this essential information back to his commanding general. He certainly pondered which way to turn from Old Church as the crossroads village marked the "turning point of the expedition." Stuart knew that a return by way of Hanover Court House, more than fourteen long miles away, would be expected and would now be heavily defended. The cavalry chieftain also realized that following the right bank of the Pamunkey River and attempting to slip north of Hanover Court House would be hazardous too. The recent rains had raised the water levels, which precluded a safe crossing by man or beast, plus the available ferries and bridges had been burned and would certainly be picketed. A northward detour could also bring the raiders into contact with McDowell's enemy troops, moving south from the Fredericksburg area.[21]

Numerous Federal infantry camps lay five miles south of Hanover Court House; therefore, a rapid march might enable numerous blue-clad riflemen to block Stuart's cavalrymen. A more direct route, southwest toward Richmond, would slice diagonally across Union lines, and Stuart refused to even consider this suicidal idea. One Stuart biographer believed that a return via Hanover Court House might expose the real reason for the expedition whereas "the route around McClellan's army might disguise his purpose somewhat, and it would allow Stuart to retain the initiative" plus the opportunity "to generate some havoc with Federal supply lines" would add an element of bold fun to the ride. The path that Stuart selected, what he considered "my favorite scheme," was the plan that had concerned General Robert E. Lee when the pair had met on June 10.[22]

While Stuart surveyed his situation, numerous villagers came forward to welcome the dusty contingent. One Virginia officer remembered being thrilled when "many ladies ran out, and, with waving handkerchiefs and eyes filled with tears, breathed their blessings on us." Lieutenant Robins gave thanks, for the people did not come "empty-handed" but quickly grabbed anything in sight to help the soldiers "allay hunger or thirst." Several ladies handed beautiful bouquets to the officers including General Stuart, who "vowed to preserve it and take it into Richmond."[23]

John Mosby strapped a captured pistol onto his belt. He watched the festive scene amidst the burning Yankee camp. Mosby admitted that he did not want to turn back because they were "on the flank of the enemy but nine miles from the railroad that was his line of communication." However, he feared that Stuart might reverse course and miss "a chance for him to do something that had never been done."[24]

A few feet away, Stuart discussed with Fitzhugh and Rooney Lee the next direction for the raiders. "Stuart was urgent for pressing on to Tunstall's Station," a relieved Mosby recalled, while "[Rooney] Lee of the 9th agreed with Stuart." Fitz Lee must have raised his eye brows as he glanced at his cousin, for he did not agree with the move. Stuart acknowledged that of his officers, "none accorded a full assent" that continuing east into New Kent County — deeper behind enemy lines — was a good idea. Looping around behind McClellan's army, swimming the Chickahominy River, and passing on the other side of the Army of the Potomac to escape back to Richmond strained the essence of military doctrine. Yet, Jeb Stuart loved a bold, audacious plan, one that nobody who wore Union blue would expect. Stuart seemed pleased that his officers finally agreed "a hearty support in whatever I did."[25]

Clear on his direction and "[w]ith an abiding trust in God," Jeb Stuart decided to inject his own subterfuge into the mission. He asked "the citizens the distance and the route back to Hanover Court-House."[26]

CHAPTER 14

Deeper Behind Federal Lines

FRIDAY, JUNE 13, 1862

4 PM–6 PM

JEB STUART MOTIONED TO John Mosby and quietly said, "'I want you to go on some distance ahead,'" as he nodded toward the southeast, the opposite direction from Hanover Court House. Excitedly, Mosby asked for a guide familiar with the area of eastern Hanover County. Soon two 3rd Virginia Cavalry troopers from New Kent County, located east of Hanover, arrived to assist. One of these men was twenty-five-year-old Private Richard E. Frayser. As the trio trotted off toward the York River Railroad, Mosby realized that Stuart's "decision to go on showed that he possessed true military genius." The presence of scouts from New Kent also showed Stuart's forethought for a potential continuance of the raid deeper behind enemy lines.[1]

The absence of any real Union opposition between Hanover Court House and Old Church perhaps helped make Stuart's decision to attempt a ride around the Army of the Potomac easier. If he had encountered significant opposition up to this point, he would have been forced to alter his plans.

The major factor that Stuart needed to consider was what would be the quickest way back to Richmond. One remarkable aspect of his decision was that he would be completely out of communication with General Robert E. Lee for an extra day. The army commander probably anticipated hearing from Stuart by daybreak on Saturday, June 14. Yet, some twenty-four more hours would pass before Lee would know the success or failure of his young cavalry leader and the vital information about the Union deployment north of the Chickahominy River. Doubts about the quickest versus the safest route back must have thrashed about in Stuart's mind. However, he believed that the hazards of returning via Hanover Court House outweighed the dangers of continuing toward the Chickahominy River.

Despite the weight of his decision, Stuart did not forget his sense of humor. According to a *New York Times* article, Stuart discovered a package "of delicacies" at Old Church addressed to his father-in-law from his mother-in-law. The Rebel cavalry leader took off his gloves and scribbled out a "polite message" to Philip St. George Cooke thanking him for the box.[2]

Stuart next turned to John E. Cooke and said, "'Tell Fitz Lee to come along, I'm going to move on with my column.'" Cooke agreed, "'I think the quicker we move now the better.'" The staff officer rode off to find the 1st Virginia Cavalry commander.[3]

Moments later, Stuart led the column away from Old Church at a "rapid trot." John Cooke wondered what lay ahead, and he knew "adventure of some description might safely be counted on. In about twenty-four hours I, for one expected either to be laughing with my friends within the Southern lines, or dead, or captured." The 9th Virginia's lieutenant colonel Richard Beale recalled the excitement as "cheer after cheer rent the air" from the citizens and bolstered the men.[4]

Later, even with the citizens' cheers from Old Church behind him, Jeb Stuart must have still worried about his decision as his column trotted southeast, deeper behind enemy lines. The concerns from his three regimental commanders certainly gnawed at him. If he felt alone, isolated by the responsibility for the safe return of his 1,200 men and the relay of the important reconnaissance information to General Lee, he did not show it.

Tunstall's Station sat on the York River Railroad only nine miles away — less distance than returning fourteen miles to Hanover

Court House. The thought of cutting McClellan's railroad supply route, if only for a short period, represented an opportunity not to be wasted. He wanted to reach the station five miles southwest of the White House supply depot before dark. Stretching the raid all the way to White House presented another tempting target, but he assumed that McClellan would properly guard this large supply operation. Stuart's main wish was "striking a serious blow at a boastful and insolent foe, which would make him tremble in his shoes." He might have been thinking of his father-in-law first and McClellan second as he later put this thought to paper.[5]

The temperature sweltered in the low nineties as the column moved east past homes near the road. More cheering and clapping greeted the passing horsemen as Southern supporters released their pent-up frustration over weeks of Union presence.[6]

Federal lieutenant Louis D. Watkins galloped into Cavalry Reserve headquarters, about half-way between Gaines' Mill and Old Cold Harbor. Drenched in sweat, Watkins anxiously scanned for Brigadier General Philip St. George Cooke. The time stood at about 2:50 PM. A soldier pointed toward Cooke's tent and the lieutenant trotted over and dismounted. Cooke sat at his field desk in front of the tent as he wrote some correspondence.[7]

Nearly six hours after Jeb Stuart's riders had dashed into Hanover Court House, Watkins carried the first warning to reach any senior Union commander about the Confederate raid. Why Captain J. Irvin Gregg's 6th U. S. Cavalry patrol, that Stuart's men had chased out of Hanover Court House just after 9 AM, had never sent any information to Cooke or to George Stoneman demands a big question.[8]

Sweat streamed off the lieutenant's face as he jumped off his fatigued horse. The frantic six-mile ride from Old Church had exhausted both man and beast. The news that Watkins carried would certainly dim any birthday wishes that Cooke might have anticipated on this day, his fifty-third birthday. Watkins advised that Captain Royall's 5th Regulars needed immediate help after the attack from a larger enemy force. The junior officer related his narrow escape through the woods, and his excited manner led Cooke to believe "that the enemy was close upon my camp." Cooke turned and had his bugler sound "To horse." Cooke must have sensed that the attack came from his son-in-law, Jeb Stuart, which made this affront even more bitter. He tallied in his mind the troops at his disposal — six squadrons from the 5th and 6th Regulars plus the 1st Regulars and the 6th Pennsylvania Cavalry regiments. The nearest infantry camp was Brigadier General George Sykes' division some three miles away.[9]

This moment would be Cooke's opportunity to shine. The defeat and or capture of the Rebel cavalry would pluck Jeb Stuart's feather from his cap and add the plume to the hat of the victorious Federal cavalry commander. Such an opportunity must not be missed.

Brigadier General William H. Emory, commander of First Brigade, Union Cavalry Reserve. MOLLUS, USAHEC.

Cooke scribbled an order for Brigadier General William Emory to hustle the six available squadrons from the 5th and 6th U. S. Cavalry to aid Royall. Meanwhile, Emory noted that the "boots and saddles" bugle warning had created excitement and chaos in all the nearby cavalry camps as troopers ran for their mounts. Emory jumped on a horse and galloped toward Cooke's headquarters only to be met by a Cooke aide with the assignment. He scanned the order and then he rode over to Captain Charles J. Whiting, who commanded the 5th Regulars. Whiting yelled some instructions then led his regiment in the direction of Old Church.[10]

Emory then went in search of the 6th Cavalry's commander, Major Lawrence Williams, but discovered that Williams had departed moments earlier with his regiment on a shortcut toward Old Church. Frustrated, the brigade commander then galloped two miles to catch up with Williams and found that the shortcut had placed the 6th Regulars on the road ahead of Whiting's regiment. Emory stopped Williams and conferred on him command of both regiments along with the order "to push on with all possible speed." The time was just after 3 PM as Williams led some 380 horsemen to try to save the day near Old Church. The 6th U. S. Cavalry's captain August Kautz's bright blue eyes must have narrowed to daggers because his rival, Lawrence Williams, recently reinstated to regimental command, now led the cavalry pursuit of the Confederates.[11]

Satisfied for the moment with the response, Cooke sat back down at his camp desk and scribbled a brief note requesting help from Brigadier General George Sykes' infantrymen. After Sykes received the request, he dispatched Colonel Gouverneur K. Warren's brigade composed of the 5th New York Infantry Regiment and the 1st Connecticut Heavy Artillery [infantry] followed by Company I, 5th U. S. Light Artillery commanded by Captain Stephen H. Weed. Warren recalled that orders to be ready to march toward Bethesda Church at "a moment's notice" arrived at his camp at about 5 PM. "The danger said to be so imminent," wrote Warren, "that proper two-days' provisions could not be had."[12]

Captain Kautz admitted that "Stuart startled us by his impudent raid around our army." He considered the enemy move "incredible and impossible" and believed that "with ordinary vigilance on our part," Stuart's party would have faced "disaster." During the ride toward Old Church, Kautz must have wondered what had happened on the right flank.[13]

About an hour after leaving camp, Major Williams' column approached Linney's Corner. The time was 4:30 PM. Williams no doubt was anxious to make amends for his tarnished name. Sporadic gunfire soon rang out as the Union advance traded shots with Confederate pickets from Lieutenant Colonel Will Martin's

Jeff Davis Legion rearguard. The handful of Rebels galloped in the "direction of Hanover Court-House," recalled Williams. In keeping with Stuart's ruse, these rear guard troopers probably high-tailed away from Linney's Corner, initially headed west and then they turned north toward the Pamunkey River before looping east to catch back up with Stuart's rear again.[14]

Kautz recalled, "we found that a large force of Cavalry had passed after having ridden over Capt. Royall's two squadrons on picket at old Church." The big question now was where did Stuart's men go?[15]

Upon interrogation, a civilian told Williams that Confederate cavalry had passed the area a short time before with "3,000 to 5,000 men, with from two to four pieces of artillery." Williams claimed that he recognized the tall tale and more accurately estimated his quarry at "1,000 cavalry and two pieces of artillery." Then Lieutenant Richard Byrnes' report of the phantom five enemy infantry regiments reached Williams. He sent Lieutenant Watkins, the busy courier, off to locate Captain Royall. However, Watkins soon returned with word of the destroyed Old Church camp and even more alarming news — the Rebel force had not headed back to Hanover Court House, but instead "had gone past the Old Church in the direction of the White House." Officials at White House Landing, the supply depot for the entire Union army had to be warned![16]

Wary of the enemy infantry report, Major Williams sent Lieutenant Christian Balder east with a platoon to probe for the Confederate column and to ascertain their strength and direction. A short time later, Balder and his men returned with a report that the enemy cavalry had definitely abandoned Old Church and headed toward the White House. A courier soon raced off to carry this information back to Cavalry Reserve headquarters.[17]

Another rider earlier sent by Cooke to find the commander of the 6th Pennsylvania Cavalry soon returned to Cavalry Reserve headquarters empty handed. Colonel Richard Rush and the Pennsylvania Lancers had earlier bolted along with William Emory, their brigade commander. Acknowledging his own tentative control over the Cavalry Reserve, an irritated Cooke wrote of Emory, "I supposed he had considered himself authorized to take them."[18]

Cooke then rounded up the nearby 1st U. S. Cavalry and led them about a mile north from his headquarters, where he found Emory with Rush and the Lancers in a field next to the road. A rider soon thundered down the road from Linney's Corner with news from Major Williams that "he had found the enemy in great force" between Linney's Corner and Old Church. Next several disgruntled men arrived from Captain Royall's squadron and related their narrow escape from Old Church. As Cooke processed this information, Lieutenant Richard Byrnes brought word of the enemy infantry column he had seen several hours earlier just northwest of Old Church. Moments later, a staff officer carried the news that Colonel Gouverneur K. Warren was marching from the New Bridge area on the Chickahominy with his infantry brigade and an artillery battery, yet the straight-line distance between Warren's camp and Old Church was seven miles. Several hours would pass before Warren's men could arrive to help with any fighting, and then, how effective would they be after a long forced march on one of the hottest days of the year?[19]

Brigadier Generals Cooke or Emory might have been expected to ride with Major Williams to Linney's Corner to ascertain firsthand the fluid situation, yet they did not. Then later, based on Major Williams' report of large enemy numbers to his front near Linney's, one would have expected Cooke and Emory to spur to Williams' aid with the Pennsylvania Lancers and the 1st U. S. Cavalry. Instead, Cooke sent an order to Major Williams "to hold his position, that re-enforcements were coming, [and] to collect information." Now Cooke perceived another potential problem. The suddenness of the alarm had caused the Lancers and the 1st Cavalry to race out of camp without rations or horse forage. Remarkably, Cooke sent both regiments back to their camps to resupply.[20]

The timelier move would have been to send the Lancers and the 1st Cavalry immediately to Linney's followed by quartermaster wagons loaded with provisions. Cooke later ordered the 1st Regulars to move toward the intersection some two hours after returning to camp for provisions. Then incredibly, Cooke wrote that he "returned to my tent to get a cup of coffee, not being well and having had a long ride in the morning since taking food." One thing seemed certain; the lightning enemy raid, laden with unknowns and confusing information, overwhelmed the fifty-three-year-old commander. The oppressive heat of the day perhaps added to the general's woes too. Brigadier General Fitz John Porter later "express[ed] surprise" that neither Cooke or Emory elected to lead from the front.[21]

The 6th Pennsylvania Cavalry's lieutenant Emlen Newbold Carpenter earlier remembered hearing the bugle blow "boots and saddles." Everybody in camp dropped what they were doing and raced for their horses. Carpenter believed that Cooke did not respond quickly enough to word of the raiders because the cavalry

Lt. Emlen N. Carpenter, 6th Pennsylvania Cavalry. The war disrupted Carpenter's plans to enroll at Harvard. He later served as aide-de-camp to Major General George Meade at Gettysburg. He is pictured here with Major General Phil Sheridan and staff. Carpenter is in center rear leaning against the pillar while Sheridan is second from right in front. MOLLUS, USAHEC.[23]

general thought "it was only a foraging party or something of the sort never dreaming in his listlessness that Stuart would have the audacity to attack him." Yet in Cooke's defense, he received the first report of the attack on Captain Royall's men at about 2:50 PM, and he immediately sent Major Williams with nearly 400 horsemen toward Old Church. The seventeen-year-old Carpenter also believed that the fifty-three-year-old Cooke lacked the vim and vigor for active cavalry operations. Before the war, Carpenter had planned to attend Harvard, but the conflict disrupted this idea. Lieutenant Carpenter had first enlisted in Philadelphia's First City Troop and when the three-month enlistment ended, he signed up with the Lancers. Now, despite his youth, he was a senior lieutenant in the regiment.[22]

When the Lancers rushed out of camp, Corporal Thomas Smith had remained behind with the regimental guards to pack equipment and to saddle the remaining horses. Truth soon mixed with confusing rumors, which hurried the men's work for fear of "a retreat in case the Rebs advanced our way."[24]

Shortly after 6 PM, Warren's infantry brigade neared Cavalry Reserve headquarters. The 5th New York Zouaves looked splendid in their bright red-and-blue uniforms. The 1st Connecticut Heavy Artillery followed. Close behind came Captain Weed's artillery battery.[25]

The instructions that soon flowed from Brigadier General Fitz John Porter's 5th Corps headquarters near Mechanicsville did not help Cooke. Porter had heard the

Brigadier General Fitz John Porter, commander for Union Fifth Corps. MOLLUS, USAHEC.

report from Major Williams claiming the possibility that "the enemy was in force (3,000 to 5,000), artillery, infantry, and cavalry." A short time later, Porter received a message from Cooke indicating that he planned to "attack at daylight." Porter then urged Cooke to use caution and to wait for infantry reinforcements. He did not want Cooke to "attack with cavalry alone the combined superior force of the enemy." The corps commander also demanded a meeting with either Cooke or Emory at corps headquarters at 8 PM that evening.[26]

Meanwhile, a stressed Philip Cooke sought invigoration as he sipped his coffee at his headquarters tent. Another courier soon arrived with more instructions from Fitz John Porter. Porter wanted four squadrons of the 6th Pennsylvania Cavalry to report to Brigadier General George Sykes, who commanded the nearby infantry division. Attached to this order was a "copy of a dispatch" from McClellan's headquarters ordering Cooke to obey all orders that emanated from Porter's 5th Corps. This directive represented a huge part of Cooke's problem as Porter on the evening of Friday, June 13, issued multiple confusing orders from his headquarters at Mechanicsville, nine miles west of the action at Old Church.[27]

The next decision dumbfounded all of the Union troopers who stood by their horses at Linney's Corner as they waited to chase after the Rebel marauders. Philip St. George Cooke, handcuffed by conflicting orders and Lieutenant Byrnes' report of "five or six Regts. of rebel infantry nearby," ordered Major Williams to wait at Linney's Corner for infantry reinforcements. A livid Captain Kautz wrote, "Instead of pursuing at once we bivouacked."[28]

CHAPTER 15

Panic on the Pamunkey River

FRIDAY, JUNE 13, 1862

LATE AFTERNOON

S EVERAL MILES EAST of Old Church, John Mosby and his two scouts heard a horse approach from behind. A staff member raced up and said that Stuart wanted them "to go faster and increase the distance between us." Mosby complied and his entourage galloped off although he complained that he was riding a slow horse as his regular mount had broken down several days before on the initial scout expedition on June 9–10.[1]

Two miles ahead of the main body they came around a bend, and just to the front approached a sutler's wagon. The trio drew their weapons, and the sutler raised his hands in the air. The vendor carried more "tempting things" than Mosby had seen for "two years" as he noted, "we felt as if the blockade had been raised." While the three rifled through the wagon, Mosby looked across a large field on the left side of the road. Numerous naked schooner masts poked up from Garlick's Landing next to Putney's Ferry, about a mile away on the Pamunkey River. This location stood upstream from White House and served as a small forage station to offload provisions from boats and to reload them onto wagons to better resupply Fitz John Porter's 5th Corps.[2]

Braxton Garlick owned the property around the landing. He had resided at nearby Waterloo plantation house until the arrival of Union troops. Garlick then escaped to Richmond to prevent his arrest by Union authorities because they knew him as a "very violent Secessionist, and [he] swore vengeance upon all with Union proclivities."[3]

Mosby sent one of the scouts back to inform Stuart of the "prizes" sitting at the nearby dock while he left the other trooper, probably Private Richard Frayser, to guard the sutler. He then rode alone toward Tunstall's Station not oblivious to his discovery of "a novel experiment in cavalry tactics" — "[c]apturing watercraft."[4]

The hardships that Stuart's raid soon brought to numerous Union sutlers certainly did not bother Doctor Charles Stuart Tripler, the medical director of the Army of the Potomac. Tripler did not like the large number of merchants "huckstering" provisions from the back of their wagons. He wanted the items they could sell limited to "[m]ilk, corn, bread, fresh vegetables, and eggs" instead of all the other "improper articles of food" that they sold. Tripler naively suggested that sutler inspections by Union officers would eliminate the "forbidden articles" when in reality these items would either move to the black market or be confiscated for only the inspecting officers to enjoy.[5]

Meanwhile, just five miles east of Old Church, Stuart's main cavalry column clattered across the small Matadequin Creek Bridge and entered New Kent County. The young George Beale began to take notice of evidence that they had ridden into the middle of "a great army." They rode up on numerous wagons, some of which were manned by enemy soldiers or sutlers while others stood abandoned. Most of the vehicles sported fresh canvas covers with the letters U. S. stenciled on the sides. The churned roads "bore marks of vast trains," and he saw where trampled crops showed where some inconsiderate Yankee drivers had cut roads through ripening fields.[6]

John Cooke watched the scouts and flankers return with captured Union soldiers from supply trains "filled with the most tempting stores." Southern troopers let out whoops of joy over one wagon's cargo reportedly bound for a Federal general and filled with champagne and numerous bottles of wine. Cooke happily noted that "[e]verywhere the ride was crowded with incident."[7]

Stuart, surprised that by late afternoon there had been no appearance by Union cavalry, sent John Cooke toward the rear to warn Lieutenant Colonel Will Martin and his Jeff Davis Legion troopers to be wary of an attack and not to hesitate to unlimber the artillery. Cooke galloped rearward to find Martin. He delivered the message and as he turned to head back to the front a sudden warning of "'Yankees in the rear!'" blew in like a stiff wind. The tinny sound of steel carried along the line as the men wielded their sabers, "fours were formed, the men wheeled about." Moments later peals of laughter followed the warning, which signaled that a successful joke had been played out.[8]

A short time later, Jeb Stuart saw one of the scouts sent back by John Mosby. The rider pulled up and informed him of the enemy supply ships at Garlick's Landing. Stuart had heard that Garlick's was lightly defended so he sent two squadrons to destroy whatever they could find there.

Captain Oscar Mansfield Knight from Company G, 9th Virginia led the detached column followed by Company F led by Lieutenant William Oliver along with some men from Company D. The thirty-nine-year-old Knight had graduated from the Virginia Military Institute (VMI) in 1842 and he was another of the regiment's pre-war physicians. Captain George N. Hammond, twenty-nine-years-old and also a VMI graduate, led a second squadron from the 1st Virginia.[9]

Earlier at around 2 PM, the 1st U. S. Cavalry's lieutenant Joseph S. Hoyer had arrived at Garlick's with an escort of nine men and fifteen teamsters, who manned fourteen wagons and one ambulance. His troopers had helped "a gang of Irishmen" unload forage and other supplies from the boats onto the wagons. Now, as the afternoon shadows grew long, Hoyer glanced at his exhausted men and elected to spend the night next to the river. He planned to escort the wagon train toward the cavalry camp near Gaines' Mill the next morning. With their horses unsaddled and fed, the men set up their bivouac a short distance from the dock and lit cooking fires. The time approached 6 PM.[10]

Lieutenant Joseph S. Hoyer, 1st U. S. Cavalry. Hoyer and his men had their supper disrupted when the Confederate raiders attacked the Garlick's Landing supply depot. MOLLUS-PA, USAHEC.

Then suddenly about twenty Rebels in skirmish line popped out of the nearby woods with guns leveled at the Federals. Hoyer and his men stood up from eating and several of them glanced toward the horses, but the animals stood tethered too far away. Now both lines stared at each other for a moment as index fingers looped over triggers. A Confederate voice hollered for Hoyer's men to surrender. The reply was a blast of gunfire and the skirmishers ran back into the woods dragging two wounded comrades. Hoyer's cavalrymen bolted for their mounts.[11]

Waving sabers, more than 100 hollering Confederate troopers

Garlicks Landing/Putney's Ferry area today. This small supply depot stood upstream from White House Landing. Randall Flynn photo.

Garlicks Landing/Putney's Ferry area. View looks northwest upriver. Randall Flynn photo.

roared into the open area around Garlick's Landing, their approach masked by the tree-lined road. Other surprised Union soldiers ran for the woods leaving overturned plates, pots and pans in their wake. The loaded wagons stood nearby as more shots rang out. Several men raced across the dock and jumped onto the nearest of the three schooners while another dove into the river to swim away. Bullets peppered the water and then the swimmer sank from view. The crew of one boat, the *D. A. Berry*, hacked the mooring ropes and slowly floated far enough away from the dock to prevent destruction.[12]

The 9th Virginia's private Richard Norris rode up on the bank and took aim at the men on the deck of the *D. A. Berry*. The butt of the gun kicked against his shoulder, and he waved the smoke away to see a body fall over the gunwale and splash into the water. He did not see the man resurface.[13]

Lieutenant Hoyer's men, now outmanned and outgunned, vaulted onto their horses and spurred "to the underbrush for protection." Two other loaded supply trains from the 17th and 44th

New York Infantry regiments stood nearby while their unarmed escorts raced away. A surprised Hoyer noted "[h]ad they been armed I might have repelled their [enemy] attack with greater effect." The officer stopped some distance away and watched as numerous horses and mules, cut loose by the Southerners, scared by the gunfire and chaos, stampeded all about the open area next to the wharves. Two days later, Hoyer still had not tracked down all of his men. He believed that three troopers had surrendered while eleven still remained missing.[14]

Soon, dense columns of smoke rose skyward as flames ate into the two remaining transport boats, the *Island City* and the *Whitman Phillips*. Bales of hay and the parade of about seventy-five wagons also burned. Captain Knight ordered the "prisoners, horses, and mules" rounded up and they soon returned to the main road to catch up with the main contingent headed toward Tunstall's Station. They left behind the bodies of three other Union soldiers who died in the attack.[15]

Quartermaster Sergeant Drowne Potter, 16th Michigan Infantry, died after he dove into the river to escape. A sergeant from the 83rd Pennsylvania Infantry lay dead on the deck of the *D. A. Berry* as it floated away. The numerous prisoners included three sutlers who obviously had conducted a brisk business as a brief search of the men turned up large sums of money.[16]

The gray-clad cavalrymen apparently captured a Philadelphia merchant named John Laughlin along with his partner, a "Mr. Parker", as the pair attempted to escape from Garlick's Landing to White House. A passenger who later disembarked off the *Nelly Baker* at Fort Monroe, told a Philadelphia *Inquirer* reporter that Laughlin had $15,000 on his person when he was caught.[17]

Late that afternoon, the twenty-one-year-old New York reporter named George Alfred Townsend rode along a road between Garlick's Landing and White House Landing. Suddenly he heard galloping horses, and then a Union officer pounded past on a lathered horse followed by about a dozen other soldiers. Townsend's day and his newspaper story would soon get very exciting. The soldiers "rode as if some foul fiend was at their heels," he remembered. When

George Alfred Townsend. The twenty-one-year-old Delaware native was probably the youngest journalist of the war. He first wrote for the Philadelphia *Inquirer* and in 1861 shifted to the *New York Herald*. His book, *Rustics in Rebellion: A Yankee Reporter on the Road to Richmond, 1861–65*, included his eyewitness account of Stuart's raid. In 1865, Townsend wrote extensively about Lincoln's assassination which resulted in another book, *The Life, Crime, and Capture of John Wilkes Booth*. Mathew Brady took this image. Brady — Handy Collection, Library of Congress.

Townsend yelled out to the "lunatics" what the problem was, one of the troopers hollered over his shoulder, "The Rebels are behind." A forlorn teamster brought up the rear, riding bareback, a broken wagon harness trailing behind in the dusty road. These cavalrymen shouted out a warning to a nearby wagon train stopped at a black-smith shop. Those wagons spun around and raced off behind the horsemen toward White House. Townsend had seen enough and he decided to escape on a side road toward the river. Soon, carbine fire broke out to the rear. He spurred for cover in the woods. Near a creek he hid deep in some underbrush.[18]

The reporter related the scene as he waited and watched:

> A few breathless moments only had intervened, when
> the roadway seemed shaken by a hundred hoofs.
> The imperceptible horsemen yelled like a war-party
> of Comanches, and when they had passed, the
> carbines rang ahead, as if some bloody work was
> being done at every rod.
> I remained a full hour under cover; but as no fresh
> approaches added to my mystery and fear, I sallied forth,
> and kept the route to Garlicks, with ears erect and expectant
> pulses. I had gone but a quarter of a mile, when I
> discerned, through the gathering gloom, a black, misshapen
> object, standing in the middle of the road. As it
> seemed motionless, I ventured closer, when the thing resolved
> to a sutler's wagon, charred and broken, and still
> smoking from the incendiaries' torch. Further on, more of
> these burned wagons littered the way, and in one place
> two slain horses marked the roadside. When I emerged
> upon the Hanover road, sounds of shrieks and shot issued
> from the landing at Garlick's, and, in a moment, flames
> rose from the woody shores and reddened the evening. I
> knew by the gliding blaze that vessels had been fired and
> set adrift, and from my place could see the devouring element
> climbing rope and shroud.[19]

The responsibility for defending the supply points at both Garlick's and White House fell to Union lieutenant colonel Rufus Ingalls. The previous night, he had ordered Captain George F. Cornog's Company B, 11th Pennsylvania Cavalry to ride to Garlick's Landing. Ingalls would have sent more defenders to strengthen the spot if he had "supposed the enemy would make a movement so unaccountable." Earlier that morning, Cornog's cavalry company had departed Garlick's and scouted upstream to Hanovertown Ferry and finding no concerns had returned via Old Church where Captain William Royall indicated that all was well.[20]

Now, as Cornog's men neared Garlick's Landing, he sent Lieutenant J. Dewees Roberts with four men to ride to the nearby mill to arrest the miller, a Rebel sympathizer. While Cornog's patrol waited for the return of Roberts' team, "several of the Fifth Cavalry came rushing in at full speed, horses covered with foam, and almost ready to drop." These men had escaped either from Old Church or the Linney's Corner fight, and they blurted out a warning about the large Confederate force a short distance behind.[21]

Before the Pennsylvanians could react to the news, the two Confederate squadrons led by captains Knight and Hammond swept to attack Garlick's Landing. The Pennsylvanians, vastly outnumbered, turned to relay the warning to Rufus Ingalls at White House. After several minutes, they passed the startled George Townsend. Lieutenant Roberts and his small group soon caught up with the rest of Captain Cornog's men. They next met a westbound wagon train, which Cornog ordered back while his cavalrymen protected the rear giving the impression "that his company was the rear-guard of a large force." At several points the Pennsylvanians formed a line of battle in front of Confederate scouts to buy time for the wagons to escape to White House.[22]

Five miles later, Captain Cornog's 11th Pennsylvania Cavalry patrol and the 5th U. S. Cavalry refugees skidded to a stop at the main Union supply depot. They blurted out news of their encounter to Ingalls. When Cornog counted heads, he discovered that Corporal Harrison Carson was missing.[23]

At the same moment the telegraph office at White House depot hummed to life with a warning from Brigadier General Randolph Marcy, McClellan's chief of staff, telling of the attack against Captain Royall's troops around the Old Church area. Telegraph message in hand, Ingalls now listened to the bad news that "the depredations of the rebels" had moved to Garlick's and likely were "already very near the depot."[24]

In a moment Ingall's mind calculated how he could best defend the place with the small force on hand "not exceeding 600 men of all arms." He would soon roust about 250 convalescents out of hospital beds and issue them rifled muskets. A mix of guards and civilians soon gave him about 900 men for his defense. But first, Ingalls charged back up the steps into his headquarters house to scribble out a telegraph reply to Marcy's warning. At the same time, several miles down the York River Railroad tracks, several Confederates climbed up the spindly splintered telegraph poles near Tunstall's Station and severed the wire that connected White House with the Army of the Potomac headquarters.[25]

When Ingalls handed his message to the telegrapher, the man looked over the words and then began to click out the letters. Seconds later, he glanced up at the officer with a look of concern. The line was dead.

CHAPTER 16

Cutting the Union Supply
Line at Tunstall's Station

FRIDAY, JUNE 13, 1862

LATE AFTERNOON

JOHN MOSBY MOVED AHEAD by himself toward Tunstall's Station after passing the road to Garlick's. He came around another bend and saw a horseman accompanying a teamster driving a wagon loaded with supplies. Both men raised their arms in the face of Mosby's guns, but not before one fumbled for his own pistol which ensured that he got a close-up look into the Virginian's gun barrel.[1]

Mosby disarmed the men when suddenly a bugle blew. Startled, he looked up to see a "body of cavalry" assembled about four hundred yards off. Mosby's contrarian nature now came into play. "My horse was pretty well fagged out. The vedette and sutler surrendered, but I was in a quandary what to do. I thought there would be more danger in trying to run away on a slow horse than to stand still. I concluded to play a game of bluff — I drew my sabre, turned around, and beckoned with it to imaginary followers."[2]

Mosby "put spurs and galloped across the field, at the same time shouting to his imaginary men to follow him." Whether the ruse spooked the 11th Pennsylvania Cavalry troopers or the sight of Lieutenant Robins leading Stuart's vanguard around

Lt. Albert P. Morrow, 6th Pennsylvania Cavalry. Morrow and a fellow officer escorted a supply wagon westbound from White House Landing on Friday, June 13. They failed to heed a retreating teamster's warning that enemy cavalry was near and they became prisoners. D. Scott Hartzell Collection, USAHEC. This image located in Capt. Henry Whelan's file.

the bend was not known, but the Union cavalry company bolted away. Mosby stopped his charge and returned to his prisoners. He dismounted and threw the wagon's canvas covering back. The treasure stacked inside included blankets and lots of leather boots and shoes. However, the biggest prize brought a smile to John Mosby's face. Forty Colt revolvers complete with leather holsters.[3]

The supply wagon that Mosby now searched might have belonged to the 6th Pennsylvania Cavalry Lancers. Earlier that day, Lieutenant Charles B. Davis, acting quartermaster, and Lieutenant Albert P. Morrow had departed White House to escort a wagon full of provisions and equipment back to the regiment's camp near Gaines' Mill. They had earlier delivered some sick soldiers to the hospital at White House Landing.[4]

Southeast of Old Church a worried teamster told Davis and Morrow about the fighting ahead. The lieutenants elected to continue on with the wagon, but they did let their wagon driver head back to White House. The quartermaster wagon never returned to the cavalry camp, and Lancer corporal Thomas Smith speculated that both officers "were taken prisoner or killed." Morrow and Davis would actually spend the next several months in Richmond's Libby Prison certainly wishing they had heeded the teamster's warning and raced back toward the Pamunkey River.[5]

Meanwhile, Private Richard Frayser, whom Mosby had left a little more than a mile behind to guard another captured sutler's wagon, had spurred on to catch up with Mosby. Frayser soon bumped into some Union cavalrymen as he rode toward Tunstall's Station.

At the same time, the 11th Pennsylvania Cavalry's lieutenant J. Dewees Roberts and his four men escorted their prisoner, the arrested miller, along a side road. They saw Frayser ahead. Frayser observed that the enemy sat on horseback "drawn up in line of battle in a field" next to the road. Roberts yelled out to Frayser to inquire "what command he belonged to?" Frayser, bolstered by the proximity of the main Rebel column, replied that he was with the 8th Illinois Cavalry. The officer might have detected Frayser's accent or he might have looked down the road to see the Confederate "column sweeping rapidly down upon him." His suspicions confirmed, he yelled a warning to the advance picket, but it was too late as several Confederates surrounded and captured Corporal Harrison Carson. Lieutenant Roberts and his Union troopers wheeled and took off on the road toward White House, but not before he yelled to Frayser, "to hell with his 8th Illinois Regiment." In the confusion, Roberts "abandoned" his own prisoner to speed their escape.[6]

Nearby, Jeb Stuart gave a cursory glance at his map. Tunstall's Station lay about two miles ahead. He ordered Lieutenant William Robins to take about thirty men and ride southeast to cut all telegraph wires and to "obstruct the railroad." Lieutenants John Mosby and Redmond Burke and Captain Will Farley accompanied the group. Stuart informed Robins that several prisoners had indicated that a company of infantry guarded the rail station. He now hoped that no reinforcements had arrived there yet. Robins realized that Tunstall's "was our point of danger" as "the enemy could easily throw troops along its [rail] line to any given point."[7]

Robins and his advance soon came upon an enemy supply wagon stuck in a mud-hole near an intersection with the road that branched left, to the east, toward White House. The driver had cut the horses away and ridden off to safety while a bold sergeant "stood his ground and was captured." An investigation into the wagon's contents revealed canteens and more Colt revolvers. Robins spied a nearby telegraph wire and he sent a man to cut the cable with an axe. Then a body of enemy cavalry appeared. It was probably the 11th Pennsylvania Cavalry patrol minutes earlier fooled by John Mosby. With sabers drawn, both groups stared at each other across two hundred yards. When the main Confederate body appeared, the Union patrol turned and "retreated down the road to the White House." Robins watched them disappear, but not before a lone rider bolted across a field to carry a warning to Tunstall's Station.[8]

Concerned about the potential danger near the railroad, Stuart had earlier sent John Cooke to hustle Lieutenant James Breathed's two cannons to the front. Whatever Federal force blocked the way ahead would need to be quickly eliminated if Stuart's men had a prayer of cutting through to the Chickahominy River. Any delay now increased the chance that the Southerners would be caught.

However, Cooke soon discovered a problem. Breathed and his men fussed and fumed to move one of the cannons. The rifled piece, which weighed almost 1,000 pounds, had been partially swallowed by a mudhole and buried to the axle. Cooke recalled, "The horses were lashed, and jumped, almost breaking the traces; the drivers swore; the harness cracked — but the guns did not move."[9]

The day's "great heat and rapid marching" showed as sweat rolled off the worn-out artillery horses. The sweet dank smell of the muck permeated the spot as several men glanced anxiously toward Lieutenant Colonel Martin, who approached with his rearguard. Cooke relayed General Stuart's instructions, and Lieutenant Breathed soon rode ahead with the lighter howitzer. Lieutenant William M. McGregor remained behind to figure out how to free the mired gun.[10]

John Cooke laughed at what happened next. He heard a sergeant with a German accent suggest to McGregor that the horses were spent, and it couldn't be done, "'But just put that keg on the gun and tell the men they can have it if they only pull through!'" The sergeant pointed toward a nearby parked ambulance that carried a captured keg of whiskey absconded from the Old Church camp. With the keg soon "perched on the gun" several artillerymen plunged knee-deep into the mud pit to try for the prize. They strained and cursed, but somehow lifted the gun carriage and its caisson by the wheels and slogged with it out of the hole. The keg was soon safely tucked away and each mud-covered hero no doubt longed for the night's bivouac so they might celebrate with the contents. Some of the artillerymen might even have poured some samples from the keg as the column moved on.[11]

However, Stuart's men needed to be discreet about imbibing alcohol as the cavalry general looked askance at the use of spirits. Stuart, a lifelong teetotaler, had written a letter to his lawyer brother in January 1861, noting that he had given a twenty-minute temperance speech at Christmas to his men while stationed in the Kansas Territory. He proudly declared that one-fourth of the men in his old cavalry command belonged to the Sons of Temperance. When he became the Confederate cavalry brigade commander in the fall of 1861, he wrote "My Hd Qrs are distinguished by the *total absence of intoxicating drink*."[12]

Now, Will Martin breathed a sigh of relief as the horses strained in their traces and the cannon began to roll. Globs of mud flew into the air from the wheels and the spokes. He then turned to urge Lieutenant John Chesnut's Boykin Rangers (Co. A, 2nd S.C. Cavalry) from South Carolina to be extra vigilant at the tail-end of the column as the Yankees had "eight to ten hours' notice" from their passage through Hanover Court House." The worn condition of the artillery horses and the mud-churned road, especially near Tunstall's, concerned Martin as he constantly feared a lightning attack from behind.[13]

The difficulty of the Jefferson Davis Legion's mission seemed to grow as the vanguard gathered more prisoners and sent them rearward to be herded by Martin's men. Captured horses and mules added to the entourage plus the abandoned wagons already picked over by those ahead still needed to be searched and then burned. At some point during the afternoon, probably between Matadequin Creek and the Garlick's Landing turnoff, Martin heard a commotion, and he turned to look back as some of his men wheeled their horses and reached for weapons. A grubby cavalry column that numbered twenty-five soldiers dressed in Union blue slowly approached. A sergeant carried a white flag tied to the tip of his saber. These disgruntled 5th U. S. Cavalry troopers surrendered themselves, their horses and their weapons. One of the Federal cavalrymen related that a local woman told them "resistance was useless; that they were surrounded on every side by rebels; and that they had better surrender at once." The ruse had worked.[14]

Lieutenant Colonel Richard Beale remembered that the road near Tunstall's became so congested with abandoned Union wagons that the main body switched from column of fours into column of platoons and trotted into the fields along the road. Hunger, thirst and curiosity lured some men out of the column toward the wagons. He watched as some of the men "became laden with more than could be carried."[15]

Heros von Borcke remembered hearing that one of the captured wagons carried special supplies for General McClellan. A closer inspection revealed "cigars, wines, and other dainties." The German officer insisted that the entire train go up in flames "because we could not be burdened with booty." Yet it would be complete naivete to believe that some of these luxuries did not find their way into Confederate saddle bags and haversacks.[16]

As Stuart's van approached Tunstall's Station from the north-west, debris scattered along the road revealed panic amongst the Union teamsters. "Wagons had turned over, and were abandoned," recalled John Cooke who noted the "'hornets in the hive'" had been disturbed. Some drivers had stopped to toss supplies onto the roadside to enable their mule team to escape faster. Then something caught Cooke's eye. He jumped off his horse and sifted through one pile to find several prizes — "a fine red blanket, and an excellent pair of cavalry pantaloons." Most troopers now bypassed the discarded items not wanting to weigh their horses as word spread that they would probably have to cut their way through the enemy guards at Tunstall's.[17]

Remarkably, the twenty or so Union infantrymen guarding the rail depot at Tunstall's had not received any warning of the approaching gray storm. Then, suddenly out of the orange sunset galloped a panicked rider. Reportedly, he did not slow down, and when a soldier standing near the tracks hollered, "'What's to pay?'", the 11th Pennsylvania trooper yelled back "'Hell's to pay!'", as he raced away. Several of the guards first heard and then saw "Hell" charging their way waving sabers.[18]

William Robins and his men let out a high-pitched Rebel yell, which struck more fear into the guards as "[t]he greater part scattered for cover." The surprise was so complete that Robins reined to a halt in front of a captain with thirteen men. They stood in front of the depot — empty-handed, their needed rifles stacked nearby. One gutsy man bolted from the pack and grabbed a weapon. He pulled at the flap on his cartridge belt as he tried to load the gun, but not before Robins' saber whipped by his ear. The soldier dropped the gun and slid into a ditch as he scuttled along to make a successful escape. Robins did not give chase, but instead turned back

Tunstall's Station on Richmond & York River R.R. This modern view looks southwest toward Richmond and this is the direction that the ill-fated Union train came from. Notice the cut on both sides of the track. Stuart's men lined the top of each embankment as they poured fire into the rail cars as the train sped by. Route 606 [now called Old Church Road] crosses the tracks just northeast of this spot. Randall Flynn photo.

toward the captain, who offered his sword and men as prisoners. This officer probably was the 42nd New York Infantry Regiment's captain James McGrath. McGrath's assistant, Lieutenant John Price, also stood nearby with his hands in the air.[19]

A pipe dangled from the Union captain's mouth. One of Stuart's staff officers had just lost his prized meerschaum in the charge and now leaned down and demanded the Yankee's pipe. Incredulous, the captured officer refused until the staff officer snatched it and thrust it in his own mouth. The shape of the pipe's bowl brought a smile to John Cooke as he noted, "[a]nything more hideous than the carved head upon it I never saw."[20]

The 9th Virginia's William Campbell recalled bumping into "a few yankees" at Tunstall's Station. "I remember getting from one of them a spy glass which is still in my possession," Campbell noted years later.[21]

Several Confederate cavalrymen now raced to cut more telegraph wire while others put axes to the spindly telegraph poles. Some cut down trees and dragged the logs and other heavy debris onto the rails.[22]

The severed telegraph wires bought Stuart some added time. The disruption of the telegraph ensured that accurate information of the raider's whereabouts could not be relayed to Dispatch Station and to Army of the Potomac headquarters. Even better, the next direction of travel by the raiders could not be relayed either.

Lieutenant Redmond Burke and Frank Stringfellow took several men and rode along the single track. About a half-mile northeast, the line crossed Black Creek, and Stuart wanted the bridge burned.[23]

Moments later all ears cocked toward the southwest. A whistle blew followed by the steady beat of a train coming from the Chickahominy River and the center of the Union line. A thin column of smoke soon appeared from around the bend as the engine headed for Tunstall's. Burke's men reined their mounts toward the woods. Robins shouted orders for the prisoners to be hustled away, and then he raced toward a switch to throw the train into a short siding. He fumbled and banged the switch's padlock with no success. Finally, he sprinted away from the track and joined the other troopers for the ambush. Jeb Stuart arrived then with the main body and could not believe that the depot was guarded by only "15 or 20 infantry, [all] captured without their firing a gun." Anticipation grew with the noise of the locomotive. Unknowingly, Stuart's men would soon add themselves to the unofficial cavalry record book for attacks against three different modes of transportation in one day.[24]

The tender preceded the engine, which pulled, according to various accounts, between eight and twenty flat or gondola cars loaded with soldiers, many of them invalids. Engineer Charles Condell manned the engine named *Speedwell*, the letters stenciled across the side of the black cab. Condell eased off the throttle, and the brakes squealed as he slowed for the water tank next to the station. About a quarter-mile away he "saw a number of mounted soldiers cross the track." They appeared to be Federal cavalrymen. But something seemed amiss. The station appeared vacant of soldiers, which was abnormal. Then something caught his eye — a log across the track. The brakes screeched louder as he slowed more, tossing blue-clad soldiers onto the splintery floor of the flatcars. Then came a gunshot from the right. Condell saw more cavalry wearing light-colored uniforms in the wood line. The nearest group of Confederates yelled at the engineer to stop. However, Condell "threw open the throttle valve" and poured on the steam as the tender smashed into the logs catapulting them off to the side. George Beale later insisted that the premature gunshot warned the engineer of trouble.[25]

Somehow the wheels of the train stayed true to the rails. The engine raced past the station belching dark smoke as it entered a railroad cut. Numerous gray-clad troopers had dismounted and assumed a perfect firing position on both banks. Lieutenant Colonel Beale stood with the 9th Virginia Cavalry hidden in a ravine near the tracks. When the shooting began, his men "dashed up the hill, and as the train passed at a fearful speed they sent a shower of buckshot and ball in pursuit, with what effect we never learned." One Union officer riding near the engine likened the sound of bullets hitting the boiler "to gravel suddenly being projected against the sides of a tin vessel." A "thundering volley" tore into the flatcars full of about 300 soldiers, officers and loyal laborers.[26]

Some of the Confederates looked back for James Breathed's cannons. The artillery shells might certainly have ended the train's journey. However, the big guns were nowhere in sight, their arrival delayed by the muddy roads.

Enemy soldiers hugged the railcar floor for cover while others jumped off the speeding train. The 6th New York Artillery's private John Biggs fell dead while the 19th Massachusetts' private William H. O'Neil scurried for cover on the car. He cradled his bloody right arm, which would later be amputated. Lieutenant John Brelsford, 81st Pennsylvania, crawled for cover too, as he sought to protect a painful wound in his leg. White House doctors later cut away his pants and found four fresh bullet holes in the skin. Something struck the hand of an 87th New York drummer, Robert Gilmore, while the 100th New York's William Bradley broke a leg, probably from jumping off the train.[27]

Captain William Farley was known as "a remarkable shot," and General Stuart yelled to him to focus on the engineer. Farley and Heros von Borcke fired into the engine as it snorted past, but the engineer ducked for cover in his iron and steel cab. The poor man made a popular target as the 9th Virginia's private Eustace Conway Moncure "took one good shot at the engineer as he crouched in his cab." Farley then asked for von Borcke's blunderbuss and he raced off spurring his horse to pull even with the engine cab. Farley fired the heavy scatter gun, and the engineer appeared to be hit as he fell to the floor. However, the train built speed as it continued on. Von Borcke climbed his horse onto the embankment and emptied his revolver at the troops on the train. Several Union soldiers returned fire and the Prussian felt his hat jump as a bullet cut two holes through the felt, just missing his scalp.[28]

Lieutenant Cooke watched as "the train rushed by like some frightened monster bent upon escape, and in an instant it had disappeared." General Stuart seemed sure that Farley's "unerring fire" had killed the engineer and that the runaway train would have a catastrophic crash upon its sudden arrival at White House. He would be wrong on both counts. Exuberant Confederate reports of their accurate gunfire creating wholesale slaughter to the train's occupants would prove inaccurate too. The Union casualty count later showed two dead and eight wounded.[29]

The jump from the train injured several Federal soldiers while others bolted for the woods. Confederate troopers chased several of them down, and most surrendered without a fight. A few soldiers had stepped off the train when it slowed for the station and were unable to jump back on. One of these men, Colonel George B. Hall, from the 71st New York, suddenly found himself a prisoner, but in the ensuing confusion, he managed to escape. Meanwhile, a paymaster watched from the station platform as the $125,000 payroll left in his charge sped away. He, too, eluded capture. However, the 55th New York's lieutenant Hibbert B. Masters was not as fortunate as he soon found himself placed with the growing lot of prisoners guarded by Will Martin's men. As the train escaped from the Tunstall's Station chaos, a travelling newspaper correspondent breathed a sigh of relief. He admitted "that the ride, though exciting enough for a thrilling account, was not one he would choose to repeat very frequently."[30]

Now as darkness draped the Tunstall's area, flickering light to the northwest revealed the burning hulks from the large wagon train. Several miles away, the smudge of oily smoke still hung above the trees in the direction of Garlick's Landing, which provided evidence of the destructive work of captains Knight and Hammond. The party began again as John Mosby claimed "[c]hampagne and Rhine wine flowed copiously." Stuart must not have seen the drinking or else he elected to not notice these infractions.[31]

Lieutenant Burke again continued with his group to the railroad bridge across Black Creek. Soon flames, fed by the creosote and tar-soaked timbers, lit the track northeast of Tunstall's. Others managed to pry up one rail near the depot. A short time later, smoke began to boil from a nearby railcar full of corn.[32]

Finally, the rear guard arrived with the unharnessed horse and mule teams from the burning wagon train. Then, about an hour after the train had passed, the two squadrons involved in the wharf-sacking at Garlick's rode up too "with a large number of prisoners, horses, and mules." Several Confederates then herded up the other prisoners and the assorted captured beasts from around the rail depot and turned them over to Will Martin's men. Jeb Stuart glanced at his watch and noted that they had spent too long at Tunstall's. They had to get moving.[33]

Stuart must have looked northeast along the track that beckoned toward White House Landing, only four miles away. The lure of capturing the Army of the Potomac's massive supply base must have been irresistible, but Stuart realized there were too many unknowns. A successful attack against White House Landing would certainly disrupt the timetable for McClellan's move to seize Richmond. While McClellan had left everything else on his right flank poorly guarded, certainly the wharves, boats and mountains of supplies had to be protected by a large force of infantry. Stuart had also just interrogated a prisoner, Corporal Harrison Carson from the 11th Pennsylvania Cavalry. Carson confirmed that at least one infantry brigade, possibly more were still at White House. Some of the captured teamsters corroborated the story. However, Carson and the teamsters did not know that this brigade from McCall's Pennsylvania Reserves had departed early that morning by train for Dispatch Station. In any event, this inaccurate information helped Jeb Stuart make his decision.[34]

Stuart realized that the rail line could bring more riflemen to the scene, which might trap his men against the Pamunkey River at the supply depot. A quick escape along the muddy roads would be difficult. Prudence called for something different, yet the cavalry general later told John Cooke that attacking White House was so tempting that "he could barely resist it." Also, a Confederate attack at White House would not come as a surprise since the shot-up train would carry word of their presence in the area.[35]

The allure of a ride to White House was strong for Rooney Lee too, as he wondered what the Yankees had done to his property. He later wrote his wife, Charlotte, that he wanted "to take a trip to the White House," but he lamented that there was no time for a visit as they needed to leave Tunstall's in an "expeditious" manner.[36]

Lieutenant Robins and his advance led the raiders southeast of Tunstall's Station with Rooney Lee and the rest of the 9th Virginia just behind. Richard Frayser and several 3rd Virginia Cavalry troopers from New Kent County joined Robins to help lead the way. They followed the road over Black Creek and headed up an incline that the locals called Southern Branch Hill. A now familiar sight came into view in the growing darkness — more abandoned wagons.[37]

Meanwhile newspaper reporter George Townsend emerged from his hiding place in the woods west of Tunstall's Station. He looked to the east and noticed another glowing light flickering beyond the trees ahead. He rode in that direction and soon discovered Tunstall's Station in flames. He must have hidden again in the woods to the west of the tracks because the last remnants of Confederate cavalry did not depart the depot until around 11 PM. Townsend scanned the area as he noted "the vicinity was marked by wrecked sutler's stores, the embers of wagons, and toppled steeds."[38]

Jeb Stuart had believed that moving beyond Tunstall's Station would lessen his vulnerability, yet the fires all around the depot that "illuminated the country for miles" increased his worries as he knew that Federal troops could not be far behind. The condition of the road worsened, and the addition of so many prisoners and confiscated horses and mules slowed the column even more.[39]

As William Robins swayed in the saddle, his stomach rumbled from hunger as the advance again bypassed the abandoned supplies to leave them for troopers farther back to search. One of these soldiers was the 9th Virginia's Eustace Moncure. The twenty-five-year-old Caroline County soldier counted about fifty idle wagons. The Union drivers had obviously received word of the approaching trouble and had unharnessed the saddle horse from each wagon's four-horse team before they disappeared into the darkness. Moncure and his colleagues unharnessed the remaining horses and mules while some did a cursory search through the wagons.[40]

Lieutenant John Cooke, a writer and a book lover, rescued "a small volume" of poetry from one wagon. When he thumbed through the fly-leaf he saw the name of a woman from Williamsburg scribbled on the page. He must have wondered whether the book represented a gift from a Union sympathizer or else it represented Union thievery.[41]

Lieutenant Chis Dabney lamented that "I lost my spur my glove & my purse with $200 in it also my commission." He had planned to use the money to buy another horse. However, he soon forgot his missing valuables when Stuart ordered him to gather several men to torch "a large train of Yankee wagons." This job was exciting for any man, especially a seventeen-year-old. When the column moved on, flames roiled the branches and leaves overhead as the wagons burned.[42]

Captain Heros von Borcke's empty canteen clapped against his side as he rode off. He turned his head away from the heat rolling off the wagons as "my parched tongue was cleaving to the roof of my mouth." In the dimness of last light a nearby rider "held out a bottle of champagne" and hailed the Prussian officer. Von Borcke upended the bottle and took a big slug. "Never in my life have I enjoyed a bottle of wine so much," he later wrote.[43]

Just past the newest cluster of abandoned wagons, the main body crossed another frail bridge over a creek. John Cooke remembered then seeing a field that covered acres and acres, all filled with more wagons. "They were all burned," he noted. "The roar of the soaring flames was like the sound of a forest on fire. How they roared and crackled! The sky overhead, when night had descended, was bloody-looking in the glare."[44]

Well ahead of the newest destruction, Lieutenant Robins thought of "the well-filled haversacks with which we started from camp had long since been empty." He recalled the food brought out earlier that day by citizens relieved to see Confederates again in eastern Hanover County, but that had been hours ago. With still no time for his advance men to enjoy the spoils of the bypassed enemy wagons, his exhausted soldiers and horses plodded on along the road. As they moved deeper into enemy territory, shadows seemed poised to strike around each bend, as the full moon, just above the eastern horizon, began its climb.[45]

CHAPTER 17

Chaos at White House Landing

A FRUSTRATED LIEUTENANT COLONEL Rufus Ingalls had begun defensive preparations for an attack against White House Landing as soon as he heard the bad news from the 11th Pennsylvania Cavalry patrol and the 5th U. S. Cavalry refugees. Ingalls' only solace was the belief that George McClellan would send an "overpowering force" to his aid, but he doubted any help would reach him before dark. He did not relish the idea of defending the supply depot from a bunch of Rebels whooping their yell into the darkness.[1]

The next portent of trouble came with the dead telegraph line. Now shortly after 7 PM, the bullet-riddled train full of invalid soldiers screeched to a halt near the White House wharves. The engineer, still very much alive, swung down from the engine cab along with the other military passengers who regaled Ingalls' men with stories about their close encounter with numerous enemy soldiers at Tunstall's Station, only four miles away.

Colonel Josiah Harlan, commanding the 11th Pennsylvania Cavalry, answered the summons of Ingalls. Harlan's men soon discovered that "picnic soldiering at the White House came to an abrupt end." Harlan took three companies [D, I, and K] and raced off to "occupy and reconnoiter the rail and wagon roads toward Tunstall's.

Next, gunners rolled two three-inch ordnance rifles from the 1st New York Artillery [Wilson's Battery] onto the grassy plain that guarded the landside approach to the acres of supplies. Members of the 93rd New York Infantry and two companies from the 3rd U. S. Infantry moved into defensive positions just behind the cannons.[2]

Ingalls then called on 250 walking wounded from the nearby hospital tents and issued the men rifles. Joining them on the line came a handful of civilians who worked at the supply depot as guards, sutlers and shipping company employees. Several loyal local citizens also joined the effort. The U. S. Navy's lieutenant Alexander Murray moved five gunboats close to shore to "sweep the plain of any hostile force." This flotilla included the *U.S.S. Sebago, Marblehead, Corwin, Currituck* and *Chocura*. The navy gunners seemed anxious to drop big shells on any Confederate cavalry that dared to appear. Lieutenant Fred W. Owen rowed ashore from the *U.S.S. Sebago*. Owen, a signal officer from the 38th New York, was temporarily assigned to the navy boat.[3]

Owen talked with Ingalls and then climbed up onto the peak of the White House roof to establish a signal station and to adjust the gunboat fire if needed. There, he leaned against the chimney as he used his glass to scope the railroad track, fields and woods toward the southwest. Several tall smoke columns climbed across the sunset. Owen's boss, chief signal officer Major Albert J. Myer, recorded that "this near approach of the enemy's forces created much alarm at the depot at White House."[4]

Now, Ingalls and his men could only sit and wait as official sunset came at 7:17 PM, followed by darkness. The night would also take away the naval gunboat advantage as neither the roof-top observer nor the naval gunners could acquire and safely fire at enemy targets. Soon the sounds of whippoorwills and cicadas kept the Federal defenders on the White House plain company as the soldiers strained to hear any sign of trouble. These men hoped that gunfire from Harlan's 11th Pennsylvania troopers, blocking the roads ahead, would provide ample warning of an attack.[5]

Reporter George Townsend decided that the safest place to go after witnessing the destruction at Tunstall's was White House

Richmond & York River Railroad Bridge at White House Landing today. This view looks north across the Pamunkey River. The original bridge was burned in May 1862 by Confederate troops. This spot was the center hub of activity as laborers and soldiers offloaded the boats and reloaded supplies onto trains and wagons for the ride to army lines near Richmond. Randall Flynn photo.

Lieutenant Colonel Rufus Ingalls on horseback. Late on the afternoon of Friday, June 13, 1862, Ingalls scrambled to mount a defense of the White House Landing supply depot as he and his men waited for an attack. MOLLUS, USAHEC.

Landing. He luckily approached the nervous pickets in the dark without getting himself shot. When he arrived at the grand depot, he found the "greatest confusion existed" as soldiers, civilians and invalids moved about preparing for the anticipated attack. "Sutlers were taking down their booths," Townsend wrote, "transports were slipping their cables, steamers moving down the stream."[6]

The sudden threat caused Ingalls to realize that he should have pressed for more troops. He reflected several days later: "With the depot stretching from Cumberland to this point, with three hundred ships crowded into so small a river, containing all our supplies, a much larger force would seem necessary to its protection." He admitted that his failure to demand more men to help protect White House and the rail and road network stemmed from the belief that his sparse force was adequate this far behind the main line. He also knew that George McClellan "wishes every good soldier with him in front of Richmond." Thus, an unexpected result of McClellan's zealous demand to the Lincoln administration for more front line troops was that subordinate leaders, especially in the rear areas, decided to make do with what few soldiers they had rather than risk angering the army commander.[7]

What continued to drive George McClellan's request for more reinforcements came from inflated intelligence assessments. Allan Pinkerton and his operatives continued to miscount the number of Southern defenders around Richmond. As late as June 26, Pinkerton issued a report that showed Robert E. Lee harbored 180,000 men to defend Richmond. Pinkerton further clouded the situation when he stated "this number is probably considerably short of the real strength of their army." He would continue to stand by his numbers when he noted in an August 14 report that Lee had 200,000 men available during the Seven Days' Battles that erupted during the last week of June. However, Lee would actually have less than 85,000 men to guard the capital city. These skewed numbers directly contributed to the confusion that erupted behind Union lines on June 13 and ensured that McClellan's right rear flank would be undermanned.[8]

Union Laborers at White House Landing. Library of Congress.

Union Laborers next to Wharf at White House Landing. MOLLUS, USAHEC.

A correspondent for the *New York Times* watched in amazement as "a regular stampede took place" at White House. When the mail boat *Nellie Baker* steamed away from the supply wharves early on June 14, she "was crowded with hangers-on of the army and civilians

Lieutenant Colonel Rufus Ingalls in center. Image probably taken later in war after promotion to Chief Quartermaster for the Army of the Potomac and a brigadier general slot. He is a member of the U. S. Army's Quartermaster Hall of Fame at Ft. Lee, Virginia. MOLLUS, USAHEC.

who thought Fort Monroe to be a more congenial climate." Another newspaperman, stuck amidst the White House chaos, questioned the "unaccountable policy" which left the army's main supply line so "weakly guarded through the twelve miles of the track from White House to the Chickahominy Bridge."[9]

Several hours after darkness swept over the Virginia Peninsula, Ingalls must have wondered why he had heard nothing from Colonel Harlan. He would continue to wonder until daylight the following morning. Meanwhile, the main Union force that could chase Stuart's men still sat in place at Linney's Corner, west of Old Church. Confusing and conflicting orders ensured that Brigadier General Philip St. George Cooke used snail-like caution before deciding what to do. Flames from burning boats and wagons illuminated Garlick's Landing and Tunstall's Station as trigger-happy troops guarded the approaches to White House Landing. Everybody who wore Union blue worried where the raiders would turn up next, yet the Rebel column moved southeast gradually away from White House and the Pamunkey River.

Caution against attacking White House had prevailed over Jeb Stuart. Now his men rode toward another river, the Chickahominy. Some thirteen miles separated Cooke's Union cavalry at Linney's Corner from the head-end of Jeb Stuart's expedition. The decentralized command structure of the Union cavalry, authorized and promoted by George McClellan, helped create the hysteria and confusion as numerous different Federal units and commanders tried to decipher and then respond to Stuart's penetration on the right flank. As the commander of the Army of the Potomac, McClellan owned the blame for the poor response to the enemy raid. However, before Jeb Stuart's forces departed Tunstall's Station, the search was on for a scapegoat at army headquarters. The shadow of dishonor would miss McClellan allies Fitz John Porter and George Stoneman. Instead, the blame would fall on Philip St. George Cooke, who was already disowned and was now embarrassed by his son-in-law Jeb Stuart.

CHAPTER 18

The Fog of War

A S THE SUN BEGAN TO FALL toward the horizon on that hot Friday, June 13, uncertainty soon led to chaos amongst the Union leadership. As Jeb Stuart's horsemen pounded their way east toward White House Landing, confused Union commanders would issue a series of conflicting orders. Facts mixed with rumors. By the time vital information reached Cavalry Reserve and then Fifth Corps headquarters, the Union response would be frozen in place for some six hours. Much of the blame for this delay and for the mounting embarrassment would be shouldered by Philip St. George Cooke.

Fitz John Porter indicated that the first word of the Confederate raid reached his Fifth Corps headquarters near Mechanicsville at about 4:20 PM. This alarming news probably next crossed the Chickahominy River and reached Major General George McClellan's army headquarters at 5 PM. Porter was McClellan's most trusted subordinate; thus, the army commander had complete confidence that Porter's units posted north of the Chickahominy River would be able to handle the problem. Porter also assumed "that General Cooke would pursue with vigor." Both assumptions would prove wrong.[1]

Porter later made clear in his report whom he blamed for the right flank incursion:

> I wish to add that General Cooke seems to have regarded his force as a reserve for the day of battle, and not therefore expected to perform any picket duty; at least no picket duty has been performed by it until ordered by me, except by Captain Royall's command. General Cooke seems to have confined his protection of our flank to scouting with one squadron from Pipingtree Ferry to the point on Pole Creek Church road where rested General Stoneman's pickets.

McClellan demanded an explanation for the breakthrough. Three days later, Porter appointed Major Henry B. Clitz to investigate what happened. Clitz would interview a number of cavalry officers and submit his report on June 18.[2]

Meanwhile, near sundown, Major Lawrence Williams continued to wait near Linney's Corner with nearly 400 anxious troopers from the 5th and 6th U. S. Cavalry. If Cooke or Emory had been at the front with Major Williams, they would have discovered via Lieutenant Balder's reconnaissance that the enemy had departed Old Church. Williams sent this information to Emory, who was sidetracked by riding away from the raid to meet with Fitz John Porter at Mechanicsville. This important piece of intelligence never reached Emory, and it would be several hours later before Cooke would receive the same information. By then, the tail end of Stuart's column was located about nine miles east of Old Church at Tunstall's Station with White House Landing as the next possible target.[3]

As anxious Union troopers stood by at Linney's Corner, the order to continue the chase still did not come. Then, a rider handed Major Williams an order from Emory to hold his position as "the enemy's infantry were in force at the Old Church." Because Emory had never received the earlier information about Lieutenant Balder's reconnaissance to Old Church, the hours' old concern from Lieutenant Richard Byrnes' inaccurate report continued to work its confusion. Williams must have shook his head and laughed when he read Emory's words. Moments later, another rider arrived with similar instructions from General Cooke that infantry reinforcements were en route; furthermore, the order read, "[d]o not advance unless to attack an inferior force." Major Williams and his men would continue to wait.[4]

As darkness descended on the area, General Cooke's health must have improved, or else he knew he needed to ride toward Old Church to determine the situation. Around 8 PM, five hours after receiving word about the attack against Captain Royall, Cooke departed Cavalry Reserve headquarters and moved northeast toward Linney's Corner. When he arrived at Linney's shortly after 10 PM, he found Williams' cavalrymen in line of battle astride the road and fields to block the expected return of the raiders. The possible presence of Confederate infantry still coagulated Cooke's

thinking: "I thought to move in the direction the enemy had taken at Old Church, and could get no reliable information as to the enemy's strength or whether he had infantry."[5]

Around 10:30 PM, Gouverneur Warren's infantry arrived to reinforce Major Williams at Linney's Corner. Warren scoffed at Lieutenant Byrnes' report of having seen "five or six regiments" of Confederate infantry. When told that only "600 cavalry and two pieces of artillery had passed down toward White House," Warren could not believe that the 5th and 6th Regulars had not galloped off in pursuit. He noted, "I never

Colonel Gouverneur K. Warren, commander for Third Brigade, Sykes' Division, Union Fifth Corps. Warren led the first infantry that responded to Philip St. George Cooke's emergency call. On the night of June 13 and June 14, Warren would argue with Cooke over the slow Union cavalry pursuit. MOLLUS, USAHEC.

for a moment believed we had any evidence of an infantry force."
Several days later, Byrnes would still insist "he was positive that
he saw infantry in force" on the Hanovertown Ferry Road, "yet he
admitted that when he first saw them he thought they were some
of our own pickets (cavalry)."[6]

Warren soon joined the discussion with Cooke and other
officers as the full moon climbed above the trees, beckoning the
way toward Old Church. The lengthy meeting must have centered
on the veracity of the enemy infantry reports and then tailed into
what type of terrain existed southeast of Old Church. A short time
later, Warren sent Colonel Robert O. Tyler's infantry regiment,
misnamed the 1st Connecticut Heavy Artillery, to Old Church to
prove that the enemy had departed the village.[7]

He next put his engineering skills to work as he pulled out some
paper and a pencil and sketched a map of New Kent County. He
handed the map to Cooke. Colonel Warren then pleaded with the
cavalry officer that he wanted to march with the 5th New York to
Old Church and if circumstances dictated, to move all his infantry
two miles farther to blockade the New Castle road intersection and
interdict any Rebel return. Cooke finally agreed to this idea and
Warren moved out at midnight under the bright full moon that
made travel "as easy as in daylight."[8]

Then, more doubt fogged over General Cooke. Colonel Warren
soon received word that Cooke wanted the 5th New York Zouaves
to stay with the cavalry at Linney's while one company moved to
barricade the Totopotomoy Creek Bridge. Exasperated, Warren and
his staff continued to Old Church and met with Colonel Tyler, who
informed him that several servants reported that enemy troops held
the New Castle Ferry. This report was erroneous, but whether the
bad intelligence was purposeful or accidental was not known. The
information did cause Colonel Warren to surmise that Jeb Stuart's
raiders might be crossing the Pamunkey River at the ferry, so he
relayed the information back to Cooke. No sooner had this rider
departed than refugees from the Garlick's Landing disaster arrived
with information that "the enemy had gone on to the White House

about sunset." Warren immediately put one of these men from the 1st U. S. Cavalry on a fresh horse and pointed him toward Linney's to find General Cooke to give him the latest news.

This 1st Regular teamster soon located Cooke, and then another escaped teamster arrived too. They both confirmed that the road from Old Church to Tunstall's Station was clear of the raiders. Cooke consulted his map again. He believed that Stuart had to retrace his route; therefore, he felt confident that he would bump into the larger Confederate force. Because the raiders had such a big lead, he saw no reason to hustle his horsemen southeast. Nor did he relish a night encounter with a larger enemy force that might have infantry. Thus, he did not want to stray far from Warren's infantry. For these reasons, Cooke would not set his cavalry on the lukewarm trail for several more hours — between 3 and 4 AM — and when he did, he kept his horsemen at the pace of Warren's marching soldiers, which negated any speed. Cooke defended his thinking: "An officer had seen their infantry. No one was positive he had none."[9]

Earlier, near sunset, William Emory had departed Cavalry Reserve headquarters for the meeting at Fitz John Porters's 5th Corps headquarters at Mechanicsville. This ten-mile round trip took Emory in the opposite direction from Old Church and away from his men *and* the counsel that Philip St. George Cooke sorely needed. Cooke probably had sensed an upbraiding by Porter as to how the cavalry had allowed such a large enemy force to sneak along the right flank. This potential humiliation was likely the reason he sent Emory to make the appearance. During the Mechanicsville meeting, word arrived from army headquarters that the telegraph line toward Tunstall's Station and White House landing was down.[10]

This ominous message broke up the meeting as Porter then ordered Emory to go find Colonel Richard Rush and take four squadrons of Lancers to "go with all speed" to Tunstall's "but to approach cautiously and avoid ambuscade." The corps commander gave this order without consulting with Cooke. This hastily gener-ated order reflected the decentralized Union cavalry command structure that continued to create confusion. Around 10 PM, Emory and Rush led the 6th Pennsylvania Lancers east from Gaines' Mill past Old Cold Harbor on a twelve-mile ride to Tunstall's Station. These troopers would be the first Union cavalrymen to make a sustained move toward Jeb Stuart.[11]

CHAPTER 19

A Brief Respite at Talleysville

8:30 PM, FRIDAY, JUNE 13, 1862
TO 2 AM, SATURDAY, JUNE 14, 1862

LIEUTENANT WILLIAM ROBINS still spearheaded the advance of Jeb Stuart's column. They reached a road intersection near St. Peter's Church. This worship place was built in 1703, and local legend noted that George Washington and Martha Custis married there inside the red brick building surrounded by towering oak trees. The Confederate column turned right, just west of the church, and headed almost due south. This new road extended from White House to Long Bridge over the Chickahominy River, and it was in awful shape. The horses now struggled to make good time as days of heavy Union supply traffic had churned the road to a frothy mess.

Lieutenant Breathed and his artillerists must have wondered how much worse the roads could get. The bright moonlight helped the riders discern some difficult spots, yet the two cannons in the rear still "had much difficulty in passing," requiring mud-covered men and horses to push or pull. The gunners attached more horses into the harnesses, and the double-teams seemed to help. The growing number of prisoners acquired at each stop increased the length of the parade.[1]

Just north of Talleysville, several big tents, silhouetted in the moonlight, stood like large ghosts near the road. Inside this makeshift hospital, some 150 sick and wounded Federal soldiers lay on cots. Jeb Stuart ordered "it proper not to molest the surgeons and patients in charge." However, a Southern newspaper alleged that some Confederate surgeons did replenish their medical boxes "of a sufficient quantity of morphine, opium and quinine to supply them for six months" from Federal hospitals along the route, which probably included the one at Talleysville. A Yankee correspondent vouched that several Rebels took the hospital's supply of quinine. Another source of captured medical supplies might have come from a "magnificent Federal ambulance" driven by a doctor. This encounter might explain how the 5th U. S. Cavalry's assistant surgeon, Adam Trau, became a prisoner.[2]

William Robins rode past the hospital and brought his horsemen to a halt at the four-house crossroads village of Talleysville, about a mile south of St. Peter's Church. The clock stood at 8:30 PM as they waited for the main body to catch up.[3]

Union troops referred to Talleysville as Baltimore Store, which was probably because of a large sutler operation situated next to the road. Colonel Rooney Lee arrived and gave permission for the men to help themselves to the goods. Robins' men needed to hear nothing more as they ripped into boxes and cans to satisfy their gnawing hunger. One dejected sutler tried to protect his wares to no avail as the ravenous Virginians stuffed their mouths with "crackers, cheese, canned fruits, sardines, and many other dainties dear to the cavalryman." Satisfied, Robins recalled "in the brief hour spent with him [sutler] we of the advance were made new men. I fear little was left to cheer and invigorate those in the rear."[4]

Private Eustace C. Moncure seemed to take pleasure in waking "the men in charge and looted the establishment, appropriating everything which we thought we needed." Heros von Borcke, his thirst earlier satiated, enjoyed the "quantity of luxuries, such as pickles, oysters, preserved fruits, oranges, lemons, and cigars."[5]

Their clothes saturated with forty-miles of dust and sweat since the departure from Winston farm early that morning, exhausted troopers ate their fill and then lay down for a welcome nap. However,

St. Peter's Church circa May 1862. At the crossroads near this church, Stuart's column turned south toward the Chickahominy River. This image shows Brigadier General Edwin Vose "Bull" Sumner with his staff. Sumner stands in the middle with the white beard and large hat. He commanded the Union Second Corps during the Peninsula Campaign. MOLLUS, USAHEC.

the 9th Virginia's sergeant George Beale soon regretted his over-indulgence. He tossed and turned on the ground as he could not find a comfortable position because his stomach began to churn. He lamented the "violent upheaval" that soon followed.[6]

St. Peter's Church today. Randall Flynn.

St. Peter's Church, war-era side view. Library of Congress.

Talleysville/Baltimore Store. Historical marker guards approach to this important war-era intersection. So much Union troop and supply traffic passed through this intersection that several sutlers established a large market operation here. Late on the night of Friday, June 13, Confederate raiders sacked the sutlers' buildings and wagons. View looks south on Route 609 to traffic circle. Randall Flynn photo.

John Cooke stood in front of the sutler's store, but he found the place had been "remorselessly ransacked and the edibles consumed." Cooke scrounged enough food to cram into his mouth while his horse rested nearby. A short time later, the staff officer reflected on the changed attitude he saw and heard. Earlier in the day, some Confederates had voiced displeasure in the continued move deeper behind enemy lines. They believed that their general would "get his command destroyed" and that "this movement is mad." Now, with full bellies and a renewed brazenness, perhaps brought on by the mob-like destruction, Cooke noted that some of these same men echoed "the raid as a feat of splendour and judicious daring which could not fail in terminating successfully. Such is the difference in the views of the military machine, unfed and fed."[7]

Cooke, his own belly somewhat satisfied, now had other needs in mind. He found General Stuart and asked if he could ride for a brief visit to a lady who lived several miles away. Stuart refused because

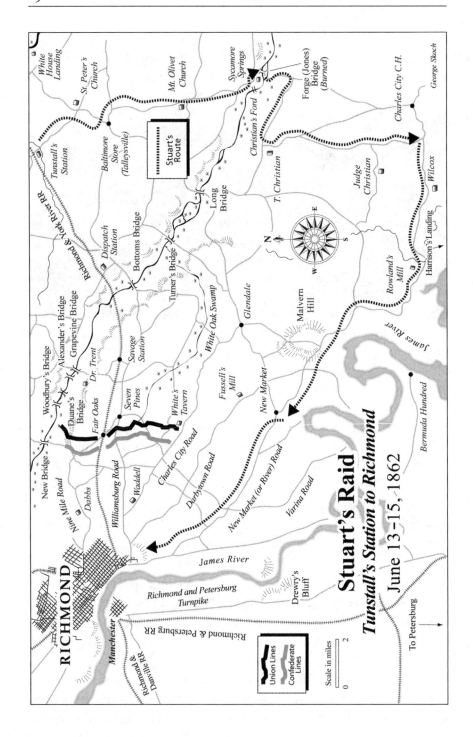

White House Landing

St. Peter's Church

Mt. Olivet Church

Sycamore Springs

Christian's Ford

Forge (Jones) Bridge (Burned)

Charles City C.H.

George Skoch

Tunstall's Station

Baltimore Store (Talleysville)

Stuart's Route

T. Christian

Wilcox

Judge Christian

Harrison's Landing

Richmond & York River RR

Dispatch Station

Bottoms Bridge

Long Bridge

Turner's Bridge

White Oak Swamp

Glendale

Rowland's Mill

James River

Malvern Hill

Alexander's Bridge

Grapevine Bridge

Dr. Trent

Savage Station

Fussell's Mill

New Market

Woodbury's Bridge

Duane's Bridge

Fair Oaks

Seven Pines

White's Tavern

Charles City Road

Bermuda Hundred

New Bridge

Nine Mile Road

Dabbs

Williamsburg Road

Waddell

Darbytown Road

New Market (or River) Road

Varina Road

RICHMOND

Manchester

James River

Richmond and Petersburg Turnpike

Drewry's Bluff

To Petersburg

Richmond & Petersburg RR

Richmond & Danville RR

Stuart's Raid
Tunstall's Station to Richmond
June 13–15, 1862

Union Lines

Confederate Lines

Scale in miles

0   2

he feared that the amorous mission would result in the lieutenant's capture. However, the general indicated that Cooke could take a note for the lady to "Dr. H " — who lived nearby. The thirty-one-year-old bachelor launched himself into the saddle and galloped "through the moonlight for the house, some half a mile distant." The occupant of the house probably was a Dr. Harrison, who lived less than a mile west of Talleysville. Cooke arrived at the darkened house and banged on the front and then back door, but there was no answer. He soon spotted a figure holding a gun and lurking in the dimness of nearby trees. Dr. H and Cooke soon recognized each other, and the owner apologized for mistaking Cooke for a Yankee. They went inside the house and Cooke scribbled out a note for the doctor to deliver to his lady friend. The doctor then wrote a note for Cooke to carry to his own wife, who was stuck behind Confederate lines. Just before the thirty-minute visit ended, the thirsty cavalryman asked for a drink of water, "which was brought from the well by a sleepy, sullen, and insolent negro." The doctor would pay for his loyalty. The next day the servant told a nearby Union picket detail about the doctor aiding a Confederate officer. Blue-clad soldiers later arrested Dr. H, and he would emerge three weeks later from Fort Monroe "looking as thin and white as a ghost."[8]

John Cooke jumped onto his horse and sped back to the crossroads. Near midnight Lieutenant Colonel Martin's rear element finally arrived at Talleysville. After a welcome three-and-a-half-hour break, the advance guard received the order to mount up, and they pushed and pulled their tired limbs back into the saddles. The 3rd Virginia Cavalry's lieutenant Jones Christian joined the lead as they departed the feast at Talleysville. Several of the Talleysville sutlers now found themselves atop mules taunted by their captors "that their destination was Libby Prison."[9]

Around midnight, at about the same time that Stuart's raiders departed Talleysville, an eastbound train from Dispatch Station eased to a stop about a mile before Tunstall's Station. The engine spit out a cloud of steam as Federal infantrymen jumped off the cars. Brigadier General John F. Reynolds' Pennsylvania brigade from Brigadier General George A. McCall's division had earlier boarded the train at Dispatch Station to answer the alarm call about Tunstall's. Reynolds' brigade comprised the 1st, 2nd, 5th, and 8th Pennsylvania Reserve regiments plus six companies from the 13th Pennsylvania Reserves.

Only a few days prior, McCall's division had boarded boats at Fredericksburg and floated to White House to reinforce George McClellan. John Reynolds sent a June 10 letter to his sister, Ellie, denouncing Secretary of War Edwin Stanton's failure to earlier send the reinforcements that McClellan had requested. "It makes me sick," Reynolds wrote, "to think of the absurd ideas people have of military operations — I can't write about them."[10]

McCall's 10,000 men now camped around Dispatch Station, a central spot north of the Chickahominy River on the York River rail line. Shortly after 5 PM, George McCall had tasked John Reynolds to prepare rations and load wagons with extra supplies and ammunition after receiving orders from army headquarters to move "at once" toward White House. Thirty minutes later, another order arrived to signal the brigade to "remain in your present position" but be ready to move immediately.[11]

Then, in the darkness of June 13, word reached McClellan's headquarters of some problem near Tunstall's Station. A one-sentence missive soon arrived for McCall to launch Reynolds' brigade: "Ascertain at once all you can about the disturbance on the Railroad and send a sufficient force to meet them as soon as possible."[12]

Now in the pitch-black next to the tracks, John Reynolds really did not know what he was after. The tall West Pointer had heard varied reports of as many as 5,000 enemy soldiers on horseback, on foot, and accompanied by artillery. The inoperative telegraph line between Tunstall's and McClellan's headquarters had signaled a bad omen.[13]

Reynolds' eyes bore into the darkness as two of his regiments fanned out into the woods on each side of the railway and moved toward a flickering light way down the track near the depot.

The remaining three regiments guided on the rail bed behind the wings. The eerie moonlight, the flames and the snapping of brush put each soldier on edge as their line slowly moved ahead. Those on the track soon saw the dim outline of the water tower. Near the Tunstall's platform, the flames outlined the blackened hulk of a railcar. Several soldiers found a lump along the rail bed and then backed away in revulsion. It was a body, dismembered by a train. The bloody corpse might have belonged to the civilian conductor from the earlier train attack. Somebody hissed for a surgeon. Other soldiers soon discovered another body, with a gunshot wound in the head, lying in the woods.[14]

Brigadier General John F. Reynolds, commander of First Brigade, Third Division [Pennsylvania Reserves] led by Brigadier General George McCall. The Pennsylvania Reserves had arrived at White House Landing via boat during the second week of June 1862. They had established camp near Dispatch Station when Reynolds received an emergency order on the evening of Friday, June 13 to load his brigade onto a train and travel to Tunstall's Station to determine what had happened there. Reynolds would be killed in action a year later at Gettysburg. MOLLUS, USAHEC.

The area seemed clear of any Rebels although several previously captured Union soldiers reported that the Confederate rear guards had abandoned them in haste about an hour prior. A short time later several men brought forward a Confederate they found hiding in the woods. John Reynolds sent men to extinguish the flames in the nearby rail car and on the Black Creek Bridge farther down the track. He realized that his Pennsylvania infantrymen had no hope of catching the Southern horsemen, so with Tunstall's secure again, he awaited orders.[15]

Meanwhile, George McClellan and his staff waited for word on the situation near White House; however, with the telegraph lines broken, they heard nothing. Earlier, at around 9:30 PM, McClellan had sent a query to McCall wanting to know if his Third Brigade was at White House. It was not. Finally in desperation for any news, McClellan send a plea directed to McCall or Reynolds: "Let me know as soon as possible what the trouble is on the Railroad." He also notified them that some 3,000 more troops were en route toward Tunstall's from camps along the Chickahominy.[16]

In the early morning hours of Saturday, June 14, John Reynolds scribbled a message intended for army headquarters and then handed it to a courier. Reynolds noted that his men found the area void of enemy cavalry, and he dismissed the raid as "evidently a dash by a small force most probably a Guerilla one."[17]

At 2 AM, on that morning, Brigadier General William Emory arrived at Tunstall's with Colonel Richard Rush and four squadrons of the 6th Pennsylvania Cavalry. Lieutenant Emlen N. Carpenter remembered the difficult ride from near Gaines' Mill: "We marched all night long over almost impassable roads." He must have ridden near the end of the Lancer column as he thought the time closer to 4 AM when they reached Tunstall's. The still-burning wagons that illuminated the nearby road left little doubt in the minds of the Pennsylvanians that their quarry was close.[18]

CHAPTER 20

Trapped?

SATURDAY, JUNE 14, 1862

1 AM–12 NOON

THE ADDITION TO THE Confederate column of 165 prisoners plus hundreds of captured mules and horses added a dangerous burden to Stuart's men as they departed Talleysville. Some prisoners doubled up on the backs of the animals to improve speed and to close up the column. After several hours of idleness, many of Stuart's men must have worried how close their pursuers might be.

Lieutenants Jones Christian and William Robins rode out with the advance guard. Rooney Lee's 9th Virginia came next followed by Fitz Lee's 1st Virginia. Will Martin's Jeff Davis Legion with Lieutenant Breathed's two cannons again brought up the rear, and their men continued to eat the dust of the Virginia cavalrymen ahead. The time was just past midnight. Forge Mill still lay due south about seven miles. Just beyond the mill stood Lieutenant Christian's antebellum home, Sycamore Springs. Christian had convinced Jeb Stuart that a private river ford on his property would be unknown to Union cavalry and thus undefended.

Bathed again in the bright moonlight, the groan of leather and chatter of cicadas a constant in his ears, John Cooke's slumped body swayed with the steps of his horse as he tried to stay awake. Then he heard the familiar voice of Jeb Stuart in the darkness. Stuart asked Cooke if he knew Rooney Lee's location.

"I think he has moved on, General," Cooke answered.

An agitated Stuart feared that with the column spread out, Lee's 9th Virginia Cavalry might "take the wrong road" and become separated in the darkness. Cooke volunteered to move ahead and search for Lee, and the cavalry chieftain urged him to be careful. Cooke trotted away but suddenly pulled on his reins about two hundred yards later. "[H]oof-strokes in front were heard," Cooke recalled. He pulled out his revolver as he stared at the murky lone figure trotting his way. Then he called out to the horseman, "Halt! Who goes there?"

"Courier, from Colonel William Lee," the figure replied. Relief swept over the staff officer and then Stuart who cantered up seconds later.[1]

Near the rear of the column, Mississippi private Robert S. Young's tired body sagged in the saddle as he tried to remain mounted. His regular horse had earlier become jaded, and not wanting to turn back, he had swapped to another mount that he referred to as "a confederate horse." For most of the day he had to remain vigilant atop the unfamiliar beast, and he recalled: "that was somewhat rough and that tired me more than it would of otherwise done."[2]

William Robins recalled the effect that the moon and exhaustion played on his advance troopers as they tried to keep the horses in the shadows of the roadside trees: "A beautiful full moon lighted our way and cast weird shadows across our path. Expecting each moment to meet the enemy, every bush in the distance looked like a sentinel, and every jagged tree bending over the road like a vidette." John Cooke added a poetic flourish to the scene when he wrote: "The highway lay before us, white in the unclouded splendor of the moon."[3]

Fatigue not only played tricks on the soldiers' eyes, but it also made their eyelids heavy. Cooke remembered seeing whole companies asleep in the saddle, and he felt concern over Jeb Stuart's safety when he pulled alongside and found the general "had thrown one knee over the pommel of his saddle, folded his arms, dropped the bridle, and — chin on breast, his plumed hat drooping over

Olivet Presbyterian Church, built in 1856. Some of Stuart's exhausted troopers probably did not remember passing this building as many of them dozed in their saddles as the column passed. This church still stands on the west side of Olivet Church Road [Rt. 618]. Randall Flynn photo.

his forehead — was sound asleep." As Stuart's body "tottered from side to side" Cooke held onto his arm to keep him from toppling beneath the feet of his horse.[4]

Just over three miles from Talleysville, they passed the moon-bathed walls of Mount Olivet Presbyterian Church, built in 1856. The front of the small wood-framed building faced south. Four tall wooden columns held up the peaked-portico entrance.

The eastern sky began to lighten as they neared the Christian house around 5 AM, on June 14. When Lieutenant Christian had indicated to Stuart that the little-used ford on his family property would enable a safer passage, he had insisted that the well-known crossing at Forge (Jones) Bridge, one mile downstream, would be a likely spot to encounter the enemy.

Jones Christian was correct on one count. His family-owned Christian's Ford stood unguarded by any enemy troops. However, the young lieutenant's face showed concern as he led the column to the north bank of the Chickahominy River. He almost did not recognize the spot because angry brown water roiled along carrying nests of debris. The path that had previously welcomed horses and cattle down to the river's edge had disappeared under a blanket of swirling water. The result was a dangerous ford.[5]

Colonel Richard Rush's Lancers, who had arrived at Tunstall's Station at 2 AM, now represented the nearest Federal cavalry pursuit on Jeb Stuart's trail. However, any serious tactician would place low

wagers on the effectiveness of the Pennsylvanian's primitive lances against Rebel carbines if Rush's men could even catch the dusty tail end of the raider's column. Supposedly, twelve men in each Lancer company carried carbines, which might prove useful on this day.[6]

To track Stuart, Rush's estimated 200 horsemen needed to leave Tunstall's right away. However, because the Pennsylvanians had been in the saddle for eleven hours, Emory and Rush elected to give the men a brief rest until sunrise at

Colonel Richard Rush, commander of 6th Pennsylvania Cavalry. Roger Hunt Collection, USAHEC.

4:45 AM. Eleven miles away, Jeb Stuart and his men were not aware of this decision, which would give them a little more cushion as they stood with their backs against the flooded Chickahominy River.[7]

Finally, between 3 and 4 AM on June 14, Philip Cooke decided to move his cavalry from Linney's Corner to join Gouverneur Warren's infantry at Old Church. Cooke still believed that his son-in-law's Confederates had to return via Old Church, and he thought that his cavalrymen paired with the infantry would be able to stop them. Yet at that exact moment, Stuart's van was only a few miles from the Chickahominy River — a direction that no Federal officer realized or would later be able to fathom.[8]

Warren would soon argue with Cooke about the slow cavalry movement. As far as Cooke knew, the White House Landing supply depot still faced a threat, which made it surprising that he did not move rapidly toward the place? The arguing became stronger when Cooke insisted to Warren that the cavalry would remain with the infantry as they moved east. An amazed Warren shook his head as he knew that this decision would slow the horse pursuit.

When the sun pulled above the horizon that morning, a tall, bearded major named Robert Morris, led a squadron of Pennsylvania Lancers east from Tunstall's on the cold trail of Stuart's men. Morris was a namesake and great grandson of a financier of the American Revolution who had also signed the Declaration of Independence. Before the war, Major Morris had served as the first sergeant from Philadelphia's First City Troop.

Now tired from no more than two hours' sleep, the twenty-six-year-old Morris and his men had heeded their orders to be "fed and saddled" and ready to move out east toward White House and St. Peter's Church to find the enemy trail. Just before the squadron rode off, an angry Colonel Rush urged Morris "to search every house, arrest every white man and send him to General Emory." Once they found the trail he told Morris to send word back to Tunstall's, and he would dispatch reinforcements. Morris' squadron consisted of two companies commanded by captains Henry C. Whelan and James H. Starr.[9]

Captain James H. Starr, 6th Pennsylvania Cavalry. D. Scott Hartzell Collection, USAHEC.

Captain Henry C. Whelan, 6th Pennsylvania Cavalry. D. Scott Hartzell Collection, USAHEC.

Morris and his men rode their horses at a fast walk due to the animals' fatigue. The slowness of the patrol perhaps suited the men too as they had heard rumors of the large enemy numbers and probably feared riding into an ambush. With lances pointed straight up and anchored with a three-foot leather sling over each cavalryman's right shoulder, the Pennsylvanians approached an intersection.[10]

Tracks showed that horses had recently taken the left road toward White House Landing, but Morris noted that the cuts in the soil couldn't have been made by thousands of horses. He detached a lieutenant with a platoon to ride that way to investigate. The rest of the column continued ahead and a short distance later they came to the Rice house. A brief search of the premises revealed nothing suspicious; however, Mrs. Rice said that "she had heard some horses passing up the road in the night." Morris led his men farther south, and they came upon the fresh tracks from numerous horses. The officer and several men approached a nearby house, and the resident indicated that "the enemy, 10,000 strong, had been passing all night." Morris hustled the man with an escort to deliver this ominous news to General Emory at Tunstall's. Confident that he was finally on a warm trail, Morris and the remaining Lancers trotted along toward the main road that stretched between White House and Talleysville. They next came to an intersection that seemed a swampy pond of water.

Several herders stood nearby as a drove of mud-drenched cattle splashed through the obstacle. The man in charge told Major Morris that they had departed White House several hours before and "that none of the enemy were at White House or had been."[11]

With this news, Morris hustled a rider to recall his lieutenant and platoon that he had earlier sent toward White House. He then led the column south again. A short distance later, they came upon a black man beside the road. This man stated that the Rebels numbered about two thousand, and that they had "destroyed" Baltimore Store at Talleysville the night before. Morris looked along his column of just over 100 men and probably wondered what he would do if he caught up with the enemy raiders — or what they might do if they caught up with him. Morris sent another trooper off with the latest news for General Emory. After further questioning of the man, Morris scribbled some additional information on a piece of paper stating that the raiders "had gone toward the Chickahominy," and he wanted another cavalry squadron to "take the Baltimore road direct" toward the river while his own squadron took the main road east toward New Kent Court House and then to the river.[12]

Lieutenant Carpenter grumbled that the Lancers seemed to be the only Federal cavalry making an active pursuit of the enemy as "the 5th and 6th [U. S. Cavalry] had lost the trail." He recalled that following the now warm trail was more difficult because "they [enemy] kept on unfrequented roads cutting across fields, taking to the woods."[13]

Robert Morris then glanced at his watch. The time stood just after 7 AM, and already the sun seemed stifling as he tipped his hat and wiped a bandanna across his brow. His column followed the trail near the red brick façade and cypress-shingled roof of St. Peter's Church, where the swath of horse tracks veered off to the right. Surprisingly, Morris did not follow the tracks, but instead he moved east toward New Kent Court House. His men banged on the doors of several nearby homes, but the citizens did not volunteer any information.[14]

A clatter of hooves soon signaled the arrival of the platoon recalled from White House, and then moments later another squadron arrived. Then a rider approached the major and told him that General Emory wanted the responding cavalry squadrons to stay together. This order prompted Morris' growing group to turn west toward Talleysville. As they neared Baltimore Store and Talleysville, a scouting party rode into the village alert for trouble, but the area seemed clear. Another squadron rode up to boost Morris' force to probably more than 300 horsemen. While several scouts mulled over the tracks of a "considerable force" that headed east, other soldiers toed at the ransacked wares from the sutler's store that littered the ground.[15]

Then, another black man appeared with some useful information. The man claimed that he had just escaped from the Rebel's camp at Forge Mill on the Chickahominy, and that they numbered about 1,500 horsemen. The servant had overheard enemy troopers talking about crossing the river toward Charles City Court House. Major Morris believed it was about 9:30 AM when they left Talleysville headed toward Forge Mill and the burned Forge Bridge. The helpful servant believed that the Confederates might still be on the north bank of the river and vulnerable to attack. However, the frustrated major lamented that the column "could not go faster than a walk, the horses being very tired."[16]

At that very moment, Jeb Stuart and his exhausted raiders seemed trapped on the north bank of the Chickahominy River. If only Major Morris knew the real situation that existed a few miles away to the south.

———

A dejected twenty-seven-year-old Lieutenant Jones Christian realized that his recommendation to General Stuart caused the 1200-man Confederate column to be stranded on the river bank. The delay and the possible demise of the mission could be blamed on him.[17]

Rains west of Richmond during the previous several days had flooded the tributaries that fed the Chickahominy basin. A Union correspondent described the effect of the "freshet" on the nearby James River: "Immense quantities of driftwood, logs, pieces of wreck, etc. have been and are still floated down the stream by the force of the current." Confederate gunners at a fort on the James River had watched in amazement as the current "turned completely around" a sunken paddle boat while her wheels spun water into the air. Another Union writer noted that the push of rainwater hit the Peninsula streams on Friday night. He considered the Chickahominy "the drain of the swamp," which was now a "lake."[18]

Colonel Rooney Lee determined that the threat seemed greater from Yankee guns than from drowning, so he rode his mount to the water's edge and coaxed the animal into the stream. The growing audience watched as the colonel and horse bobbed up and down like a leaf. The current pushed them downstream as they fought to reach the other bank. Then the horse caught its hooves in some underwater snags and went under. The animal's head finally came back up as it kicked its legs free. Unable to climb his horse onto the far bank Lee reversed direction, and they returned to the left bank.[19]

Jeb Stuart rode up and observed the scene as he attempted to conceal his concern over the delay. Private William Z. Mead stood nearby and heard Stuart ask "who will be the first to cross?" Mead joined several other troopers who rushed toward the water. He did not detail whether they swam their horses or just themselves, but he later bragged to his mother: "your son stands with the first three on the other bank."[20]

Christian Ford had an added difficulty. The ford entrance on the Sycamore Springs side sat downstream from the exit spot on the other bank. Lieutenant Robins recorded that "we had to swim against the current." Sergeant George Beale offered to swim over his lieutenant colonel father's horse. The young man mounted the horse named Dan and successfully swam the "compact and handsome bay" and tied him to a tree on the far side. Beale then jumped back in the water and swam back to get his own horse, which had been captured the previous day. He led the animal into the water and "swimming at its head landed it on the opposite shore and saw it go up out of the water. I did not deem it necessary to halter it, but turned to swim back." This decision proved to be a mistake, as he heard "heavy breathing" when he reached midstream. He looked

Christian Ford on Chickahominy River. This little used ford sat on the Sycamore Springs property owned by Lieutenant Jones Christian's family. The Chickahominy River was well out of its banks when Lt. Christian led the Confederate column to the crossing at sunrise on Saturday, June 14. View from Route 618 bridge. Randall Flynn photo.

back and could not believe his effort was for naught, as the horse's dangerous hooves splashed like paddles and threatened to strike him. He quickly swam out of the way and let the wayward mount rejoin the other horses on the north bank.[21]

Peril hovered over several other riders, who tempted the river as they latched onto their mounts. Some men floated free and became swimmers, as man and beast struggled for solid footing or a handhold on the far side. Eustace Moncure clung to the mane of his horse as he urged it onward, and he felt relief when the hooves contacted solid ground. Moncure speculated that some forty 9th Virginia troopers made the hazardous crossing. Several horses also tangled their hooves in submerged tree roots as the current threatened their demise. Soaked, coughing troopers grabbed at the reins to try to pull the animals free.[22]

As more 9th Virginians urged their animals into the water, several men attacked the riverbank trees with axes as they hoped the falling trunks would span the water for a makeshift bridge. However, each tree that splashed into the water was too short and floated away like a torpedo.[23]

Several soldiers led their horses into the water because they thought the animals "would follow each other, and swim the stream." However, this idea proved somewhat unsuccessful when the current carried some of the mounts downstream and out of sight.[24]

Other men tied bridle-reins and halters together and strung them across between two trees. Some troopers gathered fence-rails and lashed them together with vines and rope. About ten men gathered their saddles and climbed onto this flimsy raft. Then, several of the riders hung onto the rope of bridles and pulled the craft into the stream, but their luck ran out in the middle. "The force of the water submerged the lower end of it, sweeping off some of its occupants' saddles, coats and boots, which were hopelessly borne away on the current." One officer noted that this was the one and only voyage of the raft as it became obvious that to cross "twelve hundred horses and a section of artillery here was impossible."[25]

Then Lieutenant Colonel Richard Beale found himself in for a ride, albeit successful, as he pulled himself out on the far bank. The forty-three-year-old officer did not indicate whether he swam, rafted or hung onto a horse.[26]

All open eyes watched Stuart, yet John Cooke recalled that the only hint of nerves that he observed in the general was when he twisted his beard with his fingers. Stuart, a master of his emotions, exuded calmness as he sought a solution. The image of a large enemy force trapping his men against the raging river must have been difficult to erase. Richard Frayser shot glances toward his commander and recalled that Stuart never dismounted as he surveyed the problem.[27]

Other officers gathered around Stuart to discuss alternatives to the dangerous situation. Lieutenant Robins, safe on the far side, observed that "we gave up, for we had crossed over only seventy-five men and horses in two hours," while Lieutenant Colonel Beale believed only thirty-five men had actually crossed.[28]

John Cooke queried Rooney Lee about the situation after the winded colonel had caught his breath from his swim. "I think we are caught," Lee admitted in a low tone. Cooke now had time to think about the unpleasant predicament, as he expected "every instant to hear the crack of carbines from the rear-guard indicating the enemy's approach!" The tired enlisted men seemed to accept their fate, as some slumped asleep in the saddle while others "half-overcome with sleep," stood or sat next to their mounts, with bridles in hand.[29]

The rear guard arrived, and Lieutenant Breathed and his gunners deployed the two cannons a short distance north to blockade the approach to Christian Ford. Jeb Stuart then called over the 4th Virginia Cavalry's corporal Benjamin Turner Doswell. Stuart knew that Robert E. Lee would be anxious to learn of the mission's fate and the essential information that they had discovered. Perhaps an indicator of the tenuous situation, Doswell soon left on his own dangerous mission to weave his way back to find General Robert E. Lee near Richmond. Stuart requested that the army commander launch a diversion south of the Chickahominy River to help mask Stuart's return. Doswell swam the ford with his horse and would later narrowly avoid capture.[30]

Doswell would succeed in reaching General Lee, but he probably arrived after the sun went down that evening. Lee must have feared the worst after receiving no word from his cavalry chief for nearly seventy-two hours. The courier indicated to the army commander that Stuart believed that he would get his men across the Chickahominy River. Lee seemed most interested to hear that Stuart's cavalry had ridden into the rear of McClellan's army, and that they had discovered the right flank and the supply line to be vulnerable. Despite Stuart's request for a diversion along the Charles City Road, Lee would need to wait until the light of the next morning to launch troops to aid their escape.[31]

Rooney Lee now confirmed for Stuart the obvious problems at the ford and the impossibility of crossing the two cannons. Then, some members of the rear guard began a rumor "that a whole division of the enemy was on our track." With time at a premium,

Stuart galloped with his group toward Forge Bridge, one mile downstream. This span had carried the Providence Forge to Charles City road over the swampy river, but Confederates had burned the bridge during the retreat from Williamsburg five weeks earlier. Some of the local 3rd Virginians convinced Stuart that "enough of the debris of the old bridge remained to facilitate the construction of another."[32]

The "stone abutments" of Forge Bridge "remained some thirty or forty feet only apart," recalled John Cooke as he looked across the swift water at the new crossing place. Heros von Borcke estimated that about ninety feet separated the steep banks, but it might as well have been four hundred yards as the splintered and burned bridge beams poked out of the water between the "stone sentinels" of the abutments. Filling this "'aching void'" with a passable bridge would take time, but none of the raiders knew how long before Yankee cavalry would charge down the road from Providence Mill. Stuart's luck again looked like it might be running out with his

Forge Bridge also known as Jones Bridge on the Chickahominy River. View from north bank looking south. This is location of the burned bridge that Stuart's men had to rebuild using wood from a nearby barn. In foreground is trace for war-era road. The Route 155 bridge is in background. Randall Flynn photo.

back still against the flooded river and the expected imminent arrival of Federal troops.[33]

Soldiers walked down along the dirty water's edge to survey their newest predicament. Thick vines with hard green and black thorns covered part of the bank. Brown cypress elbows jutted several feet above the water like cave stalagmites.

Stuart again ordered the rear guard to deploy while Lieutenant Breathed's men unlimbered their two cannons to sweep the road. A nearby building described as a "large warehouse" or barn stood only about one hundred yards away. The structure might provide long boards and beams as troopers kicked, whacked and pulled the walls apart. Then, somebody found a nearby skiff on the bank, and several men dragged it into the water. They soon secured the vessel in mid-stream with ropes as a "movable pier" to aid construction.[34]

Lieutenant Redmond Burke managed the actual bridge building team assisted by forty-one-year-old corporal William H. Hagan. The Richmond *Dispatch* later highlighted "their fatiguing labors"

Chickahominy River at Forge Bridge. View looking east, downstream, from modern Route 155 bridge. In June 1862, the river here was deeper and was about 40 yards wide between each bank. Randall Flynn photo.

in leading the construction effort and referred to Hagan as the "gallant corporal." Early in the war, Stuart had discovered Hagan's talent for scrounging needed equipment and food items and had appointed him to be in charge of the cavalry staff escort, which ensured that he would always be close. The large hairy man would continue to excel and would soon be promoted to a lieutenant's position as the staff commissary and then the quartermaster.[35]

Assistant surgeon John B. Fontaine, 4th Virginia Cavalry, sweated profusely as he carried timbers from the barn. Stuart cheered that so far the doc-

Assistant Surgeon John B. Fontaine, 4th Virginia Cavalry. General Stuart praised Fontaine's skills at scouting and bridge building during the ride. Adele Mitchell Collection, USAHEC.

tor had "little to do in his profession." The general later singled out Fontaine's help with scouting and his exuberance at bridge building.[36]

Richard Frayser watched the bridge grow while Burke and Hagan clambered all over the structure. They made suggestions on board placement and then yanked and kicked on the various parts to ensure strength. Frayser insisted that the energetic duo made the difference in the timely resurrection of the bridge.[37]

Soldiers slid boards from the left bank to the skiff while several men in the skiff extended boards up to the abutment. Finally, a narrow spindly foot bridge stood ready. John Cooke reported that the prisoners crossed the bridge first. Stuart must not have wanted these prizes to be lost in the event of an enemy attack. Once across, escorts mounted the prisoners on captured mules and then led them onward. However, the troopers already across soon discovered a new problem; they were on an island and they still needed to cross the south branch of the Chickahominy.[38]

More 9th Virginia cavalrymen approached the span. "Large numbers of men immediately unsaddled their horses, took their equipments over then returning, drove or rode their horses into the stream, and swam them over." The brave ones who swam alongside their animals held tightly onto the manes while avoiding the hooves. Some men carried their saddles in their right hands while holding their horse's bridles in their left hands as the animals swam along next to the bridge.[39]

Sergeant Beale described his plan for swimming eighteen horses from his company across. "The method was to mount a horse, force it into the water, leap off at once on the lower side and grasping the bridle-bit or halter swim against the current so as not to be swept below the landing-place on the other side." Beale performed his work under the watchful eye of Stuart, who sat on a nearby bridge timber and gave "helpful directions."[40]

The approach for the horses to the water's edge stood upstream of the exit on the other bank. This easier access made the crossing less dangerous than Christian's Ford. To speed the process, the "horses were formed into a column of fours, pushed into the water, and swimming down stream, they easily landed on the other side." Watching the horses in column gave von Borcke an idea, and he claimed that he "took sixty-five horses myself through the angry torrent" to speed things up. He did not indicate how many trips this required, for it would have been too dangerous to tie that many horses together.[41]

Meanwhile, Lieutenant Colonel Richard Beale and the men who had earlier crossed upstream at Christian's Ford headed down the south bank to reconstruct the partly destroyed bridge over the south channel. Beale detailed William Robinson Taylor to head the construction team. They must have found "ample materials," for Taylor's group "soon built a substantial bridge upon the partly-destroyed foundations of the old one." Their work must have been invisible through the foliage to the larger construction team working on Forge Bridge a short distance away to the north. The water here probably flowed fast and deep too because Beale did not send a swimmer across to inform Rooney Lee or even Jeb Stuart of the bridge construction effort over the south channel.[42]

On the north bank, much of the 9th Virginia crossed and some of Fitzhugh Lee's 1st Virginians soon followed. However, Stuart still deemed the process too slow. Plus, he knew there was no way the flimsy swaying structure in its current state could support the weight of the artillery, and he refused to consider abandoning the cannons. The bridge needed to be widened and strengthened with heavier beams, yet he must have wondered if there would be enough time. With half of his men still waiting to cross the bridge, the arrival of large enemy numbers could prove disastrous.

Amidst some "heavier blows," more of the warehouse structure fell to the ground with a crash and a cloud of dust. Then teams of men snaked the long, heavy main pieces toward the river. Miraculously, several of the largest beams just spanned the gap between the bank and the abutments with only inches to spare. The men then laid cross-wise planks between the beams to form a wide secure path for the anxious remaining cavalrymen and artillerists. Cooke watched as General Stuart climbed into the skiff to assist with the work. His humming of songs seemed to become stronger as the reinforced bridge grew. During the lengthy rebuilding process, John Mosby even saw Stuart lying on some grass next to the bank "laughing at the prank he had played on McClellan." Mosby also had spread on the grass a sumptuous array of pilfered foods to fortify the men. He confirmed that Stuart "showed no anxiety and was in as gay a humor as I ever saw him."[43]

Despite Stuart's calm appearance, Mosby noticed that others seemed anxious during the long hours waiting for the bridge to be built, yet "no enemy appeared in sight. That was a mystery nobody could understand." Then several officers discussed a sinister idea. They wondered whether they were being allowed to cross unscathed "in order to entrap us in the fork of the Chickahominy and James."[44]

CHAPTER 21

"Hope To Punish Them"

SATURDAY, JUNE 14, 1862

8:30 AM–3 PM

A 6TH PENNSYLVANIA LANCER courier skidded to a stop at Tunstall's Station in search of Brigadier General William Emory and Colonel Richard Rush. At approximately 8:30 AM, the rider found the two senior officers and gave them the news that Major Robert Morris had located the enemy trail seemingly headed toward the Chickahominy River. Surprised, the officers expressed thankfulness because this information represented the first definitive word on the enemy's movement. They glanced at an available map; then Rush hustled the last Lancer squadron toward Morris.[1]

A short time later, a platoon from the 11th Pennsylvania Cavalry rode up from White House Landing. They confirmed that the main supply depot had remained unmolested. Richard Rush then mounted his horse and led this platoon down the dusty road to find Morris and the rest of the 6th Pennsylvania Cavalry.[2]

Meanwhile, Morris' column departed Baltimore Store/ Talleysville at about 9:30 AM. They covered about four miles toward the Chickahominy River when Morris received a stunning order. Morris recalled that this message instructed him to halt until "Colonel Rush joined me with another squadron." So, in the stifling heat the closest Federal pursuers pulled off the road into

6th Pennsylvania Cavalry known as Rush's Lancers. Note lances stacked on right. MOLLUS, USAHEC.

the shade and waited for Rush's arrival with about another 100 men. Morris' troopers and horses no doubt welcomed the break, but only some four miles ahead, Jeb Stuart's soldiers sweated both physically and mentally to reincarnate the burned Forge Bridge before it was too late. This two hour Union delay would again benefit Jeb Stuart's cavalry.[3]

By mid-morning on June 14, George McClellan still did not know the situation on his Pamunkey River flank or the location of the enemy cavalrymen. At 11 AM, he sent a telegraph to Secretary of War Stanton in Washington that indicated "from 1,000 to

5,000 [Confederates], came around our flank last evening." The message accurately outlined the physical damage wrought by the raiders but indicated that Stuart's riders "ran off" in the face of John Reynolds' infantry arrival at Tunstall's Station. "I have several cavalry detachments out after them and hope to punish them," McClellan noted.[4]

Morris believed that it was about 12:30 PM when Colonel Rush arrived with another Lancer squadron and the 11th Pennsylvania Cavalry platoon. Rush then led the Lancer column toward the Chickahominy with about 500 Federal cavalrymen. They soon received information that the raiders had headed toward Sycamore Springs, and the tracks led that way too. Rush estimated that his men arrived at the area around Christian Ford at 2:45 PM, but his watch must have been fast.[5]

<hr />

At the make-shift Forge Bridge, with sturdier timbers now underfoot, sweat-soaked Confederates grabbed bags and boxes of ammunition from the caissons and lugged these essentials across the span. Horses and mules soon filed onto the bridge, but the real test came next. Several troopers lashed ropes to the front of the caissons and the two heavy gun carriages. A team of men then wrestled the first cannon through the muck and up onto the bridge. The timbers held. Another team moved the second cannon onto the span.[6]

Colonel Rooney Lee then led the rear guard with some of his 9th Virginians toward the bridge. With the artillery, prisoners, animals and men now across, Jeb Stuart must have felt an immense sense of relief. The time was about 1 PM, some eight hours after their arrival at Sycamore Springs. Amazingly, they did not have to cut and shoot their way out.[7]

An exhausted and soggy Sergeant George Beale found his muscles unresponsive when he tried to climb aboard his horse. "The labor of swimming twenty horses across the Chickahominy and exposure for hours to its muddy waters" sapped Beale of energy as a nearby soldier rushed over to give him a push and a pull into the saddle.[8]

The large framed Heros von Borcke acknowledged his own numbing fatigue. The rapid, heavy work on the bridge had elicited no complaints from his muscles, but after crossing the span, he realized he felt soreness "severely in all my limbs." What added to his physical aches was the mental anguish of knowing that they could not stop to rest, but had to keep on riding despite having been in the saddle for most of the previous two days and nights.[9]

When Stuart crossed, he ordered Lieutenant Robins and his vanguard to bring up the rear and to torch the bridge. Stuart then moved on when Lieutenant John Cooke returned after being sent ahead to scout the route. Cooke had earlier moved upstream to the west where he discovered the new problem — they were island-bound faced with another difficult ford. The high water made the new ford deep; plus, it had pushed over the banks "to the depth of about two feet for at least a half-mile." But John Cooke believed the spot would be fordable.[10]

The local troopers should have informed Stuart that Forge Bridge actually led to an island and that a second burned bridge continued across the south channel of the Chickahominy River. If Stuart was aware of the island, then one must wonder why he did not send John Cooke to find the second bridge and see if it, too, could be rebuilt. A short ride due south from Forge Bridge through the swampy woods would have revealed Lieutenant Colonel Richard Beale's bridge-building work there. Then again, one must wonder why Beale had not informed Stuart and Rooney Lee of his efforts. The only explanation that Beale gave was that "before the intelligence of its completion [south bridge] reached the General, he had, after swimming the horses of his command over the northern stream, commenced to ford the southern one from the upper end of the island."[11]

A short time earlier at Sycamore Springs, the Union advance guard had suddenly seen some movement across a field toward the woods. Colonel Rush sent a squadron forward, and they soon dismounted and moved ahead in a skirmish line. The shadowy figures ahead mounted horses and raced away. They wore gray uniforms. Lieutenant Emlen Carpenter then rode forward past the skirmishers with a handful of horsemen to clear the forest. Carpenter found the woods empty of trouble, so he led his men in pursuit. However, after a short distance, he sensed danger when he saw the Rebels race off again. "Fearing they were drawing us into an ambuscade, we waited till more of the regt came up," confessed the young officer.[12]

Downstream a column of smoke topped the distant tree line in the direction where the Confederates had disappeared. Amazingly, Colonel Rush next sent Major Morris with only eight scouts armed with carbines to investigate. Why Rush elected to remain behind with about 500 men at Sycamore Springs while he sent Morris with only a handful of troopers to investigate the fire remains a mystery.[13]

Lieutenant William Robins earlier had supervised several 9th Virginians as they gathered fence rails and other debris. They piled the stuff on the bridge and set it on fire. The flames soon danced above the racing water, and the dark smoke pillar issued a beckoning signal to Major Morris' approaching Lancers. Mesmerized by the scene, the Virginians "lounged about on the ground." Robins found a comfortable seat under a tree on the bank and watched the charred timbers drop into the water with a hiss.[14]

Morris and his men approached the Forge Bridge as its planks and beams spewed smoke and flames. Steam popped as the wood dropped into the swirling water. The shadowy Confederates whom they followed had vanished.[15]

Morris scanned the area. He counted five dismounted graybacks on the other bank. He could not see any other enemy soldiers on his side of the river, so he led the detachment closer to the bridge. One of the Lancers raised his carbine and fired.[16]

The shot zinged over Lieutenant Robins' head and dropped a small limb into his lap. He remembered having "a thankful heart for his bad aim." Robins' men replied with their own gunfire and then hurried into the swamp behind a veil of cypress trees to get their tethered horses. The Confederate officer later wrote, "I at once withdrew the men, and pushed on after the column."[17]

Lancer lieutenant Carpenter recalled that the bullets hit one horse on each side of the river. The time was probably about 1:30 PM, as Major Morris and his men inspected the water's edge to confirm both the bridge's fate and the unwise choice to swim the current and chase the raiders with only nine men. They were perhaps about twenty minutes too late, yet what could Morris have really accomplished with so few soldiers?[18]

Satisfied with this decision, Morris backtracked to Sycamore Springs with their only prize, an inebriated Southern trooper. Apparently, Private John Jacob Schwartz from the 1st Virginia Cavalry had either passed out or wandered away from his colleagues. When the hapless twenty-eight-year-old again opened his eyes, he discovered that he was surrounded by men wearing blue uniforms. The Swiss-born Schwartz, who had enlisted in Abingdon, would spend the next several months at Fort Delaware Prison.[19]

During Robert Morris' absence while chasing the smoke, Colonel Rush had spent the hour investigating the area around Sycamore Springs. Morris' return confirmed in Rush's mind that Jeb Stuart's raiders had crossed the Chickahominy and posed no more threat, at least to Federal troops north of that river. But what about the potential problems the Southern riders might create behind Union lines south of the Chickahominy, on the left flank? Rush failed to indicate in his report whether he sent a courier toward Dispatch Station or Tunstall's Station to alert Union troops south of the Chickahominy to the danger. Remarkably, no evidence seems to exist that troops on the Army of the Potomac's left flank *ever* received any warning about Stuart's men.[20]

Neither Rush or Morris ever mentioned why they did not consider sending some men across the Chickahominy to at least shadow the rear of Stuart's column. Numerous Confederates had already proven that the swollen river, while dangerous, was swimmable. Would not the Union cavalry benefit from knowing the direction of movement for the raiders once across the Chickahominy? A courier could have carried word to Dispatch Station to alert troops near White Oak Swamp to block the roads as Stuart's main column would not pass on the River Road for

more than twelve hours. There was certainly time to have trapped
Stuart's men near the James River.

At around 3 PM, Rush gathered his four Lancer squadrons and
headed back toward Tunstall's Station. They soon met several more
companies from the 11th Pennsylvania Cavalry that had responded
from White House. These additional troopers boosted Rush's
numbers to about 600 men to accost Stuart's 1,200 riders — if the
Union commander wanted to follow.[21]

As Richard Rush led his tired horsemen north, he did not realize that Jeb Stuart's column was bogged down again. The raiders
were not safely across the Chickahominy because the rebuilt Forge
Bridge had deposited them on an island in the middle of the river.
Absent of trees, Major Morris' men would have easily seen the Rebels
who struggled to cross the river at another ford only a half-mile
away on the west side of the island. Yet, the swampy foliage had
obscured another Federal opportunity to disrupt Stuart's plans. A
little more curiosity on the part of Morris or Rush to send several
scouts across the river might have made things more interesting
for the Confederate rearguard.

———— ⌣ ————

Hours earlier, Brigadier General Philip St. George Cooke had
reached Tunstall's Station at about 9 AM, on Saturday, June 14.
Encumbered by fears that he still might stumble across enemy infantry, he ordered the 1st, the 5th and the 6th U. S. Cavalry Regiments
to depart Old Church headed towards Tunstall's at first light —
but to move with Colonel Gouverneur Warren's foot-soldiers. This
remarkable decision by Cooke created much seething and dissension
amongst the Regular cavalrymen and their officers. When Cooke's
slow-moving column had neared Garlick's Landing, they heard that
the enemy had bypassed White House. With little possibility now
of running into any of Stuart's soldiers, either cavalry or infantry,
Cooke ordered his horsemen to spur on ahead of Warren's men
toward Tunstall's Station. Many of Warren's soldiers had emptied
their canteens during the hot march and Cooke told Warren to halt
his men at the first water they found near the railroad. The spent

infantrymen, mud-covered and sweat-drenched, finally arrived at Tunstall's Station around noon only to find that the Confederates had been gone for nearly sixteen hours.[22]

Shortly after Cooke's arrival, Brigadier General William Emory departed Tunstall's with an infantry regiment and a section of artillery that had arrived with Cooke. Emory rode with the cannons to Baltimore Store, where he received word that Stuart's raiders had already escaped across the Chickahominy.[23]

Around 3 PM, Cooke then departed Tunstall's Station with elements from the three Regular cavalry regiments. However, after a brief ride, a courier arrived from the south with word from Emory that the Confederates had escaped. Cooke and his men returned to the rail depot and spent the night there. Emory and Rush later arrived at Tunstall's, where they too bivouacked for the evening.[24]

The following morning Cooke would lead the Cavalry Reserve back to their camp near Gaines' Mill. He wrote a one-page report outlining Union cavalry operations in pursuit of his son-in-law. However, when the repercussions of the raid rolled down from McClellan's headquarters tent, numerous fingers pointed toward Cooke. On June 16, Brigadier General Fitz John Porter demanded a more exact accounting of the cavalry actions, and Cooke seemed astonished to discover that "parts of my conduct" had been called into question. The now embattled fifty-three-year-old cavalry commander wrote back that the lack of nearby support for Captain Royall and his 5th U.S. Cavalry squadrons at Old Church might be blamed on orders that originated "from the Headquarters of the Army." Such a direct shot at Porter's good friend, George McClellan, while true, would not aid Cooke's cause. Then, Cooke ended his reply to Porter: "I will make the report of the march to Captain Royall's relief and the pursuit of the enemy as soon as I have time. Every moment of this day has been occupied by more pressing duties."[25]

A lump must have formed in Cooke's stomach when he next discovered that the 12th U. S. Infantry's major Henry Clitz would conduct a formal and rapid investigation "into the facts connected with the attack upon the cavalry outposts commanded by Captain

Royall, Fifth Cavalry." Clitz's report when finished would go directly to Fitz John Porter.[26]

Philip Cooke probably burned through several candles on the night of June 16 as he labored in his tent to put his defense on paper. His additional report submitted on June 17 was nearly three pages long as he defended his decisions. Cooke's explanations did not change Porter's mind as the 5th Corps commander wrote, "I have seen no energy or spirit in the pursuit by General Cooke of the enemy or exhibited the characteristics of a skillful and active guardian of our flanks." Porter and McClellan had skewered their scapegoat.

One of the most damning indictments of the timid Union cavalry pursuit came from a junior officer. The whole affair left the 6th Pennsylvania Cavalry's lieutenant Emlen Carpenter wishing for some brazen Southern-style leadership in the blue ranks. The young cavalry officer recorded: "The whole affair was as brilliant [a] success on Stewart's part and a disgraceful failure on the part of Cooke to prevent it. Gen Cooke is an old soldier & has not got the *vim* necessary to maneuver against Stewart. We want a man like [Turner] *Ashby* to Command the Cavalry Reserve."

Carpenter insisted that if Captain Royall had been sent proper reinforcements, then "the whole thing would have been nipped in the bud," yet Royall's men had already been overrun near Old Church by the time Cooke received word of the raid. Carpenter correctly realized that Cooke's slow response with inadequate manpower helped Jeb Stuart put distance between the closest Union pursuit. The lieutenant noted that "Every body I have heard condemns him [Cooke] as being most *too slow* to command the cavalry reserve. I hope he will do better next time at all events."[27]

Philip Cooke's handling of the pursuit did not impress Colonel Gouverneur Warren either. Warren later recalled his multiple arguments with Cooke as he urged the cavalry to move ahead of the plodding infantrymen. Instead, Cooke urged Warren's men to continue just behind the cavalry horses. Warren noted his men "bore up pretty well as far as the crossing of the Mattadequin, but the roads were heavy, the men tired, and the sun intensely hot. It was impossible for all to keep up. They fell down exhausted and faint and some were sun-struck." He considered the march "very severe" after hiking more than forty-one miles in the heat in less than forty-eight hours. Warren's report further damned Cooke: "I deem it my duty to say that I do not believe from the way in which General Cooke conducted the operations that the enemy would have been prevented from returning to Hanover Court-House by taking the road along the Pamunkey River. It was impossible for the infantry to overtake him [enemy], and as the cavalry did not move without us it was impossible for them to overtake him." Warren wrote a more blunt letter to his brother on June 16. He called the pursuit "a weary tramp, and an unsuccessful one foolishly managed."[28]

Major Clitz interviewed all the principal officers involved in the June 13–15 Union fiasco, and he submitted his report to 5th Corps headquarters on June 18. Clitz noted that numerous cavalry officers agreed that if Cooke had quickly moved to Linney's Corner and then Old Church with *all* his cavalry assets "and pursued with vigor, leaving his infantry supports to guard the road between Old Church and New Castle Ferry over the Pamunkey River, as he was urged to do by Colonel Warren, the enemy must have been overtaken, perhaps at the Baltimore Store, or at any rate before he could have crossed the Chickahominy." In reality, a vigorous pursuit likely would have brought Cooke's men into contact with Stuart's rear guard near the Talleysville/Baltimore Store area.[29]

Yet Cooke, besieged by confusing orders and mixed up information combined with fatigue and heat, seemed unable to decide whether to push the chase to catch Stuart or head to defend White House. A rapid pursuit could have accomplished both goals, but instead he elected to wait until the next morning.

Major Lawrence Williams' arrival with the 5th and the 6th U.S. Cavalry at Linney's Corner on Friday, June 13, no more than an hour after the passage of Stuart's rearguard, might have been a decisive factor. A determined Union cavalry pursuit that nipped at the tail of Stuart's column would have slowed the Confederates and possibly changed the outcome. This scenario would have complicated Stuart's situation and forced him to detail Lieutenant Colonel Will Martin's rear guard to stand and fight, risking their capture along with the two cannons. Martin summed up the lack of action for his men when he wrote, "As all the fighting was done in front, the Legion had no opportunity to take part in the series of combats and skirmishes."[30]

Philip St. George Cooke's star had reached its zenith.

CHAPTER 22

Headed for Richmond

SATURDAY, JUNE 14, 1862

2 PM–11 PM

J EB STUART'S TRAIL ACROSS the Chickahominy River's Forge Bridge led into an island swamp. The brown waters that swirled around the tree trunks had submerged much of the land. "The water was above our saddle-skirts," noted George Beale. The artillery horses struggled to pull the pair of cannons which disappeared underwater several times. When this happened, only the tops of the trailing caissons and limbers could be seen as they resembled the squared prows of shallow barges. Then, a limber attached to a caisson burrowed into a hole. Men dismounted and slogged through the mess as they reached below for sturdy handholds to push the two-wheeled piece. The horse team strained in their harnesses and then something snapped. The pole had broken. The sunken limber had to be abandoned. It was "the only thing on wheels that we lost," boasted Beale.[1]

The entire column, including the cannons, somehow crossed this new ford, despite its deep water. However, this effort took more precious time. When Lieutenant Robins reached the ford with his bridge burners, the crossing had been deepened by the previous traffic. He and his men had to swim their horses. Once across, they quickly caught up with the rear as the column had again slowed because of more swampy terrain.

The prisoners now rode at the front of the column; in fact, two captives rode on the back of each captured mule. These mules found tough footing in the "treacherous mud-holes" just south of the Chickahominy. When the animals fell, they dumped their Yankee cargo into the ooze, which elicited numerous unkind remarks from the prisoners and was greeted by much Southern laughter. When the escorts led the way into a third swamp, Lieutenant John Cooke overheard one of the prisoners say "'How many d—d Chicken-hominies are there, I wonder in this infernal country!'"[2]

Once across both branches of the river, the column made a right turn onto a small farm road and traveled about two miles before turning south toward the home of Thomas Christian. Jeb Stuart might have briefly stopped there with some staff members before continuing although Richard Frayser insisted that Stuart seemed "much fatigued he did not draw rein" at Thomas Christian's place. The rest of the column headed southward toward Charles City Court House.[3]

John Mosby noted that although they were across the Chickahominy, they were not clear of danger. "We were still thirty-five miles from Richmond and in the rear of McClellan's army, which was five or six miles above us." The multiple swamps they had to cross and the heavy, deep mud left them vulnerable to attack, and the ride to Richmond meant the possibility of danger around each bend in the road.[4]

After about four miles, the raiders reached the area just west of Charles City Court House. Stuart and his staff rode up to the palatial home of Judge Isaac H. Christian. John Tyler, who had served as the tenth president, had built this house in 1815 and named it Woodburn. A pair of chimneys stood at each end of the two-story frame building while a one-story wing guarded each flank of the home. Several soldiers lolled on the lawn as the family entertained the staff "in princely style under some lovely shade trees." The men enjoyed some refreshments before somebody brought a carpet out of the house and spread it onto the grass for the general and his weary staff to lay down to sleep.[5]

The remainder of the command bivouacked nearby in the fields of Buckland, home of Colonel J. M. Wilcox. The time must have been about 4:30 PM. The exhausted men slid off their mounts and found places on the ground to sleep, as they were happy for any rest after thirty-six hours in the saddle. The horses, necks down, munched their fill in the fields of clover. However, not all of the Jeff Davis Legion troopers could relax as they had more than one hundred prisoners plus horses and mules to guard.[6]

After two hours of sleep, Jeb Stuart jumped up off the ground "fresh as a lark" observed John Cooke. Cooke later admitted that the ravenous staff very nearly ate the Christian's "out of house and home."[7]

Stuart knew that his men needed some rest, but he also knew that any senior Union officer who glanced at a map would see that blocking the main roads near the James River with infantry and dismounted cavalry would trap the raiders. Around sunset, Stuart turned command of the expedition over to Fitzhugh Lee with orders to begin the ride toward Richmond again at 11 PM. The cavalry chief then headed west on the thirty-five mile trek with a courier and the 3rd Virginia Cavalry's private Richard E. Frayser to find General Lee and to give him a full report of the Union vulnerabilities. Stuart brought Frayser along because of "his thorough knowledge of the country" already previously displayed on the raid. The general later highlighted Frayser's abilities in his official report, and the private's performance soon vaulted him to a captain's slot on the staff.[8]

Despite the expectation that the James River Road would be picketed by the enemy, no staff member questioned Jeb Stuart's desire to reach Richmond by sneaking through Union lines from the rear with only two other men. The threesome would need to pass through the Union 4th Corps area near White Oak Swamp held by Brigadier General Silas Casey's division. If they cleared this area without trouble, they might next run into patrols from Brigadier General Joseph Hooker's 3rd Corps division.[9]

As the three riders rode toward the disappearing sliver of orange sunset, they began to feel the creeping, overwhelming tentacles of

Richard S. Rowland's house where Stuart and his two scouts stopped for coffee on their thirty-five mile trek to Richmond. The house still stands along Route 5. Randall Flynn photo.

fatigue. After about six miles, they stopped at Richard S. Rowland's house next to Rowland's Mill "to quaff a strong cup of coffee." Frayser had learned that this was the general's favorite drink. They rested for about fifteen minutes; then, a rejuvenated Stuart vaulted into the saddle. The younger men rushed to follow him.[10]

In the darkness the trio trotted along the James River Road and the croak of frogs grew. Each curve in the road harbored hiding spots for Union soldiers. Later, moonlight pried through the tree canopy and reflected off the water beside the road. All three men must have frequently fingered their weapons as their eyes scanned ahead for movement, yet the Federal troops in the area had not received a warning to be vigilant for the Rebel raiders, especially from the rear.

Meanwhile, when darkness slid over the Charles City Court House area, some soldiers lit cooking fires to heat their well-earned rations. When ten o'clock struck, the officers and sergeants moved across the fields at Buckland as they looked to rouse the telltale lumps that revealed the slumbering cavalrymen. The ghostly moon-light helped them with their search. Near 11 PM, the resaddled horses and mules resumed the dusty ride toward Richmond.[11]

Lieutenant William Robins again moved off to lead his advance guard west into the unknown along the James River Road which linked Charles City Court House and the capitol city. The road paralleled the James River which curved like a loose rope only a mile to the south. Federal gunboats on the river might present a potential problem as their big guns could drop large shells into the middle of the column.[12]

The men again knew that their survival might depend on being quiet; thus, the monotonous sound that followed their march came from cicadas and other night bugs. The occasional eerie plea from a whippoorwill echoed from the woods.

Then, out of the darkness in a field stood a number of unnatural-shaped objects that glowed in the moonlight. A brief but nervous investigation revealed a bivouac site of tents — all vacant. The com-mand moved on. "Human endurance had reached its limit on this night's ride," admitted George Beale. Somehow the "weary horses" stayed awake as they carried along their riders, who canted from side to side in "drowsy unconsciousness." Beale found this leg of their journey the most difficult: "If the march of that fourteenth day of June was not the longest we ever had made; it was, including the excitement and labor incident to crossing the Chickahominy, by far the most taxing and exhaustive on our physical powers."[13]

Private Eustace C. Moncure's chin banged against his chest and then snapped up as he tried to stay in the saddle. The 9th Virginia trooper spoke for all when he recorded: "I never experienced such a tiresome and sleepy march, all night long up the river road."[14]

The heat, swampy humidity and dust helped add to the misery of the main column, yet potential danger lurked all along the road. The acute fatigue that blanketed Stuart's men made them vulner-able as their senses were less able to detect and then to respond to any Federal incursion despite their expectation of enemy contact.

The steady movement of the horse jostled John Cooke awake. He realized that he "fell asleep every few minutes" during this part of the ride. Cooke admitted that Stuart had earlier extended him an invitation to ride ahead to Richmond, but Cooke had declined because his horse was "worn out."[15]

Despite his responsibility for leading the van, Lieutenant Robins fought to stay alert too. "I was constantly falling asleep, and awaking with a start when almost off my horse." John Mosby rode with Robins and expressed amazement over their uncontested passage toward Richmond. With the gunboats in the river to the left and Joseph Hooker's infantry somewhere to the right, he admitted, "[n]othing would have been easier than for him [McClellan] to have thrown a division of infantry as well as cavalry across our path." With these basic moves, Mosby believed that only a miracle of biblical proportions could have saved Stuart's raiders.[16]

Robins led the command past the steep southern face of Malvern Hill, which was only two weeks away from becoming a household name and being added to the war's list of bloody hallowed ground. The road continued several miles south of the quagmire called White Oak Swamp. As the sky began to lighten near dawn, Robins looked to the left across the fields of Strawberry Plains on Curl's Neck. Naked masts from enemy warships poked up above the high bank. He waited for the blasts from naval guns that signaled their sighting. However, the only noise was the steady creak of leather and clop of hooves. Never warned to be on the watch for Confederate cavalry, the U. S. Navy had either not posted lookouts high in the ships' rigging, the observers were asleep or else they had failed to notice the nearby passage of more than 1,300 riders, horses and mules. Years later, John Mosby still marveled that the "gap of several miles between his [Union] left and the James" allowed Stuart's men to slip through on the James River Road.[17]

Luck still rode with Jeb Stuart's cavalrymen.

CHAPTER 23

Safe Again

SUNDAY, JUNE 15, 1862

MORNING

A SHORT TIME AFTER passing the danger from the Federal gunboats on the James River, Lieutenant William Robins heard a voice hiss, "'Who goes there?'" Robins jerked himself alert and looked into the shadows next to the road. The challenge came from a 10th Virginia Cavalry picket. Relief coursed through Robins. Jeb Stuart's horsemen had reached Confederate lines again after beginning the ride some seventy-eight hours before with most of the time spent behind enemy lines. Robins soon shook hands with an impressed Colonel James Lucius Davis, who commanded the regiment.[1]

Robins then led the relieved parade of cavalrymen past the pottery factory at Bailey's Run and on through New Market. A mile later the vanguard received word to halt. The tired men dismounted and brushed dust off their sleeves as they pulled food, much of it purloined Federal edibles, out of their haversacks. Bleary-eyed and dirty, both horse and men provided quite a sight for the citizens. Perhaps the most amazing aspect about the expedition was the low casualty count. "We lost one man killed," noted Robins, "and a few wounded, and no prisoners." John Mosby clarified the numbers when he admitted that one drunken German, oversupplied with

Federal beverages, had been left by the road and captured near the Forge Bridge crossing.[2]

The Confederate cavalry soon continued on. The peals of Sunday church bells reached their ears; then, the spires of Richmond poked into view. John Mosby recognized a familiar figure coming their way. It was Jeb Stuart riding back to meet his men. Mosby expressed surprise because Stuart was "gay as a lark and showed no signs of weariness" despite two days and nights attached to a saddle with little sleep. Stuart seemed quite happy to see that his troopers were safe.[3]

The general had just come from the Dabbs house, where he had briefed General Lee moments after sunup. The ecstatic Lee issued hearty congratulations and then listened in rapt interest as Stuart highlighted the raid. Stuart described how the unanchored enemy right flank, manned by Fitz John Porter's 5th Corps, could be turned by a concentrated attack. Once Porter's men had been driven out of their Mechanicsville lines, the narrow, muddy Hanover County roads ensured they would have difficulty maneuvering. Stuart admitted that he had seen no evidence that McClellan planned to shift his supply base away from White House Landing, yet three days later, McClellan would order the transfer of some supplies over to the James River.[4]

No doubt, Stuart must have apologized to Lee for possibly exceeding the commanding general's intent. Stuart noted in his June 17 after-action report: "Although the expedition was prosecuted farther than was contemplated in your instructions I feel assured that the considerations which actuated me will convince you that I did not depart from their spirit, and that the boldness developed in the subsequent direction of the march was the quintessence of prudence."[5]

When Stuart and his two-man escort had reached Richmond earlier that morning, he had sent Richard Frayser to inform Mrs. Stuart of their safe return and then to the governor's mansion to brief Governor John Letcher of the mission's success. Upon arrival at the mansion, a servant brushed off Frayser's request for a visit and insisted that the governor was still in bed due to the early hour.

However, the persistent young trooper finally sat down with the Virginia leader, who listened as the corporal related the excitement and success of the raid. Frayser's perseverance paid off as the now enthusiastic Letcher noticed that the trooper had a broken saber. Letcher authorized Frayser to choose a replacement saber out of the nearby state arsenal.[6]

By the time the weary main column neared the boundary of Richmond, the morning sun which had been up for several hours had heated up the day. A Federal cavalryman manning the lines nearby recalled, "I feel like taking off my flesh and sitting in my bones in the shade to keep cool. I don't see how the soldiers manage to work on the fortifications this day for it is just about boiling hot." A newspaper correspondent who noted the lethargy of Union soldiers recorded that they "are weary of the dog-days heat of the last few days."[7]

A Jeff Davis Legion trooper observed that the long ride had also sapped the energy from the prisoners and the horses, but he added, "[i]t was a trip that I would not have missed for anything." A Richmond newspaperman saw a disheveled trooper watering "his jaded and faithful animal by a roadside spring." He queried the man about the expedition, and the soldier admitted that the experience had been difficult, but "I wouldn't have missed the trip for $1000 — history cannot show such another exploit as this of Stuart's." The 9th Virginia's corporal William Campbell noted forty-nine years after the war ended that the one incident that always comes to mind: "I recall none more splendidly conceived, more daringly executed, and showing more favorable results than Stuart's raid around McClellan at Richmond."[8]

However, not all the Southern cavalrymen seemed satisfied. One Georgia officer grumbled over the Jeff Davis Legion's continual placement in the rear of the column. He believed that Jeb Stuart gave preferential positioning to Virginia cavalry units to the detriment of troopers from other states.[9]

Lieutenant Colonel Martin's rear guards escorted the prisoners toward Shockoe Bottom, the valley between Church Hill and Capitol Square. The column neared the James River and approached the port at Rocketts Landing, where they stopped for rest and food. Several hours later amidst gathering clouds, they skirted the base of Chimborazo Hill, home to the large Confederate hospital, and rode between the brick warehouses of the commercial district. The heat and humidity gave birth to a drenching downpour, which cleansed some of the dust and sweat off the men and animals. Around 4 PM, the soaked riders drew rein in front of a three-story brick building at the corner of 20th and Cary streets. The 165 Union prisoners soon filed toward the entrance of the building. Overhead hung a sign that read "L. Libby & Son, Ship Chandler." The place had been built in 1845 to store import and export goods for ships docked on the nearby canal. Confederate authorities had seized the building to house the growing number of captured Yankees.[10]

After the prisoners entered the warehouse, the large thick doors of Libby Prison banged closed behind them. The Richmond *Dispatch* boasted the next day that the "abolition prisoners included eight Yankee sutlers" plus "11 negroes, 8 of whom were slaves." That evening, Braxton Garlick, owner of property around Garlick's Landing, arrived at the prison to identify several of his slaves who had earlier run away with the Union troops. Handlers next turned over the 260 captured horses and mules to quartermaster officials, who later distributed the animals to various regiments.[11]

As the large number of horsemen rode into the city, word quickly spread of their accomplishment — a raid that looped for about 110 miles all the way around the Federal army! People came out of their houses, and cheering throngs soon lined the streets. Women waved handkerchiefs and flags as their heroes passed.

The 9th Virginia Cavalry's Charles Chewning expressed his joy at surviving his first real test as a soldier and as a young man. "We are finally back very tired sore and hungry." He no doubt looked forward to relaxing in camp as they "came back with full bags of good eats and a lot of badly needed equipment." Two days later, after the "booty" was sorted, Chewning strutted around in a new pair of oversized "high boots" to replace his old shoes, which sported too many holes. The young trooper also expressed concern and prayers for his childhood friend, Private Lewis Alexander Ashton, who "hurt his back real bad when he fell off his horse at Old Church."[12]

In a letter written to his mother on June 18, Lieutenant Chis Dabney admitted, "I tell you I was about as tired as you ever find any individual." He exhibited the confidence gleaned from the previous days' work when he wrote, "we are going to whip the Yankees like the mischief in a few days." This youngest Stuart staff officer had left the University of Virginia and joined the army against the wishes of his parents in 1861. Stuart had even noted some reservations about the young man, yet his service as an aide-de-camp in 1862 confirmed his value to the general.[13]

The various regiments began to move in separate directions toward their old camps where the men longed for a peaceful sleep, unencumbered by the lurch of a horse or the fear of enemy attack. Rooney Lee's 9th Virginia had the farthest distance to ride to Mordecai farm, which was north of town on Brook Road. Soon a reporter from the Richmond *Dispatch* rode up to interview several troopers while the column moved through the city streets. The following morning the paper carried several articles that detailed the audacity of the ride and brought forth the names of Latane, von Borcke, Mosby, Farley, Frayser, and Robins into the public psyche for the first time. The name of Jeb Stuart had previously been in the papers, but now he became known as the leader of the great Chickahominy Raid. The mission's success brought a cavalier pride combined with a sense of accomplishment, not only to Stuart's men, but to the Confederacy and its people, who in this spring of 1862, craved any piece of positive news. Jeb Stuart and his troopers had given them something to celebrate.[14]

Eustace Moncure's squadron had swapped ends and now approached the city as the rearguard. Fearful that many of the grubby troopers might get separated from the command while traveling the alluring streets of Richmond, Moncure and his squadron mates patrolled back and forth to maintain order.[15]

Part of the 9th Virginia had continued on toward Brook Road while Moncure's squadron, weary and sweat-drenched from their provost marshal work, stopped several blocks from the capital building to rest. Moncure noted the time as about 12:30 PM, and the location on Marshall Street near 7th or 8th Street. He hailed a passing acquaintance who had just departed from a nearby church service. The gentleman, James T. Butler, lived nearby, and when he heard about the raid, he sent a servant to travel the nearby street ringing a dinner bell to summon others to come. The festive occasion quickly grew as throngs of people arrived on Marshal Street "to hear the news of the raid, and the bread and ham and Sunday dinners of those good church-going people, interspersed with a good deal of nice wine, was soon handed around to and devoured by a set of dirty, tired, sleepy cavalrymen." Moncure would later become a post-war judge in Virginia, and when asked about his favorite war remembrance, he quickly recalled the celebration and revelry of that hot Sunday afternoon of June 15.[16]

Heros von Borcke reached the staff bivouac site, and he quickly tended to his horse "who had carried me nobly through the severe fatigue." The fact that von Borcke's mount hauled the 250-pound German with his weighty weapons and accouterments back to Richmond without being wounded, killed or broken represented an unheralded addendum to the ride. Fatigue finally knocked over von Borcke as he revealed, "I fell fast asleep, and so continued during the whole day and night."[17]

Private Robert S. Young, a Mississippian in the Jeff Davis Legion, dismounted at camp and wished for the myriad enemy supplies they had either bypassed or burned. However, he knew that trying to gather everything would have taken too much time. "It would have been a loss of everything if we had of attempted to bring off wagons it was all that we could do to get through with the prisoners, horses & mules." Then, three days later, Young found himself broken down and unable to serve on picket duty. He leaned against a tree and used his canteen as a writing desk to let his brother know about "pains in my bones, head ache etc., ... severe fatigue and exposure." He then admitted, "I have a perfect dread of hospitals."[18]

Newspapermen, from both North and South, began to hear of the raid, and they prepared their stories that hailed the prowess of

Jeb Stuart. The headlines of the coming week ensured that Stuart's name would always be synonymous with chivalry and bravery. The Richmond *Examiner* on June 17 called the ride "one of the most brilliant affairs of the war, bold in its inception, and most brilliant in its execution." The Charleston *Mercury* stated several days later: "It is a question of whether the annals of warfare furnish so daring a deed."[19]

A June 17 article in the *New York Times* attracted the reader's eyes with bold headlines describing Stuart's expedition as "A Bold and Partially Successful Movement." A subsequent subtitle stated "Narrow Escape of A Railroad Train. A Panic at White House." Another correspondent for the *New York Times* agreed that Stuart's "affair excites as much admiration in the Union army as it does in Richmond. He then wrote, "we regard it as a feather of the very tallest sort in the rebel cap." Then a week later the same newspaper repeated the common question still in the minds of many Union men: "How they have come from the right, passed through the heart of our lines, and escaped by our left, is something no one seems able to comprehend."[20]

The 9th Virginia's corporal Robert Baylor heard that "in all about a million & a half dollars worth property" was destroyed on the raid. He acknowledged that "[i]t is considered one of the *most brilliant* affairs of the war." Yet, despite the successes, "the death of our Capt [Latane] throws a damper over the whole affair." He sadly admitted, "I feel as if I have lost a brother, almost a sister." Fellow 9th Virginian private Richard J. Norris believed the destruction amounted to "two million U.S. dollars worth of property." Three days later, Norris admitted to having "very sore [muscles] on account of our long & dangerous scout."[21]

A 4th Virginia trooper, twenty-five-year-old John Henry Timberlake, seemed happy to be back in camp. He wrote on June 16, "It is thought by Genl. Stuart that we damaged the Yankees to the amount of two millions of dollars. I am dressed in a full Yankee uniform. I have just been shaved & had my hair cut close to my head & had a good wash and feel much better than I have for several days." A few days later, a Richmond newspaper highlighted

the Hanover and New Kent scout work performed by lieutenants
Jones Christian and David Timberlake along with John Timberlake
and Richard Frayser. This guidance was of course the main reason
that Jeb Stuart decided to include local companies from the 3rd
and 4th Virginia Cavalry regiments.[22]

The 1st Virginia Cavalry's private William Z. Mead wrote his
mother six days later and admitted that he had participated in the
expedition and was safe "after hair breadth 'scapes and dangers
of flood and flu." He noted that "[w]e are comfortable, contented
and in fine health although the boys, as well as the horses, are
somewhat reduced by hard riding and slim rations." This well-read
trooper saluted his skinny mount "Rebel" and compared him to
Don Quixote's "Rocinante" as he noted the animal's faithful obedi-
ence: "All he asks for his services is as much as he can eat, for his
appetite is immeasurable and he is only allowed half rations like
his master." Mead denounced the "inaccurate accounts of the raid
in the papers" which included undue accolades that Mead believed
the editors gave to a rival regiment. "Undue prominence is given
to the 9th [Virginia Cavalry]," cited Mead, "and a few officers who
made much display after the privates had routed the foe." After he
caught up on some sleep he equated the expedition as "a dream —
the baseless fabric of a vision." Mead realized that he had been part
of something special because he indicated that he hoped to write a
magazine article about the expedition "as I think this exploit will
become one of the most exciting chapters of the war."[23]

The ride also elevated the status of John Mosby, who performed
much of the scouting work that brought success to the mission. Mosby
wrote his wife, Pauline, on June 16 to let her know that General
Stuart had promised him a commission. He claimed credit for the
idea of the ride when he wrote, "I returned yesterday with Genl
Stuart from the grandest scout of the War — I not only helped to
execute but was the first one who conceived & demonstrated that
it was practicable." He also notified her that he had sent her a spoil
of war, a small rug from a Yankee officer's tent, probably pillaged
at Old Church. He let her know that he hoped to see her soon:
"a good many ludicrous scenes I will narrate when I get home."[24]

Jeb Stuart visited Governor Letcher on June 16 at the executive mansion. A crowd soon formed and demanded to hear from their new hero. A *New York Times* article noted the visit and even referred to Stuart as "the bold dragoon" while citing some of his remarks. The cavalryman's sense of humor showed when he stated that "he had been to the Chickahominy to visit some of his old friends of the U. S. Army, but they very uncivilly turned their backs upon him."[25]

After the raid, the average Confederate horsemen carried a swagger in both appearance and attitude. The confidence boost helped to reinforce their superiority, if only in their own minds, as noted by early Stuart biographer John Thomason. "Its moral value was enormous: the Southern trooper was confirmed in his opinion that he could outride, outfight and outdare anything the Yankee nation might put on four legs, and for a full year the Confederate cavalry superiority was hardly disputed." The event also raised Jeb Stuart onto a pedestal, exalted by many Southern civilians and soldiers and many of their counterparts in the North. The Union cavalry would need another year of fighting experience mixed with a command restructure to be on par with the gray-clad horsemen.[26]

A stark contrast existed between the two opposing cavalry camps. Brigadier General Philip St. George Cooke rode into his headquarters' camp near Gaines' Mill at about 8 AM, on Sunday morning, June 15. He reportedly had been awake for about 36 straight hours. The beleaguered cavalry commander remained on his mount for a spell as he was "sitting sidewise on his horse, and looking fatigued and perfectly miserable." Colonel Rush later came down the same road. He stopped at a Dr. Tyler's, probably Dr. Wat Tyler's place some 10 miles from Tunstall's, "looking as cross as a savage." When asked whether he had seen the Rebels, Rush snapped that "'Yes, he saw his rear guard just as it passed the Swamp. He (Stuart) had gone in at the back door.'"[27]

The raid's penetration deep behind the Federal lines also left many blue-clad soldiers on edge. Brigadier General George W.

Morell's division stood near Gaines' Mill and he was "on thorns" over the raid. He would "not let a band play for fear of revealing his position to the rebel guerillas."[28]

Late in the afternoon of June 15, near Garlick's Landing, a patrol from the 8th Illinois Cavalry charged toward an 11th Pennsylvania Cavalry patrol. Fortunately, both units recognized the error and reined to a halt in time. Other Pennsylvanians admitted, "[f]rom the day after Stuart's raid until the 28th [June] there was ceaseless vigilance" behind Union lines. Days later, Philip St. George Cooke would receive orders from 5th Corps to be vigilant for another raid. Jeb Stuart's successful mission had molded the mind of the average Union soldier to see a gray-uniformed bogeyman behind every tree, especially well behind the Federal lines.[29]

Official Federal officer reports and newspaper accounts also cited the problems wrought by the myriad of loyal Southern civilians who lived behind the Union lines and offered aid and information to Confederate soldiers. In the wake of the ride, numerous citizens in Hanover and New Kent counties would be arrested for their loyal sympathies. They included J. A. Lipscomb who owned the Old Church Hotel, and his neighbor who owned Rockett's Hotel. Private Sidney M. Davis, 6th U. S. Cavalry, surveyed Captain Royall's burned Old Church camp and the "freshly made graves" of several 5th Regular troopers. He gained some satisfaction when they led Lipscomb away for "insulting language used toward our troops" and "for displaying the confederate flag."[30]

George McClellan and his staff did their best to downplay the raid, yet it became impossible to hide what historian Jeffry Wert called "a humiliating embarrassment." The parceling out of Union cavalry units ensured an inadequate pursuit. Stuart biographer Emory Thomas noted that the raid "fed McClellan's fears that he, not Lee, was in grave danger."[31]

Dr. Charles Tripler, McClellan's chief surgeon, wrote in early-1863: "On the 13th the enemy made a raid to our rear, doing but little harm. Our railway communications were not interrupted." Yet, this assessment does not consider the additional troops later pulled off the frontline to guard interior roads and escort wagon trains. Nor does Tripler give merit to the psychological effect that Stuart's riders had on the average Union soldier pulling picket, vidette or guard duty deep behind the lines during the remainder of the Peninsula Campaign.[32]

Union colonel William W. Averell later recognized the uniqueness of Stuart's leadership during the raid. He wrote, "This expedition was appointed with excellent judgment, and was conducted with superb address." Averell also recognized how Stuart had changed cavalry tactics: "This raid of Stuart's added a new feature to cavalry history."[33]

The information that Stuart gleaned from the expedition reinforced the idea for Robert E. Lee that the Union right flank was vulnerable, and this knowledge enabled Lee to make the confident decision to move Stonewall Jackson from the Shenandoah Valley to Richmond. The raid also highlighted the ineptitude and lack of communication that existed between the various Federal cavalry commands and McClellan's headquarters. The decentralized blue cavalry command structure could not respond to an emergency.

One trooper in the 2nd U. S Cavalry expressed surprise that various New York papers highlighted the enemy raid. The soldier wrote a friend: "I am truly surprised that the operations of Stewart with his scouting party should have created such apprehension in New York [as] it was regarded here only as being a bold dash by a brave and daring officer." This soldier, who was a McClellan supporter, chastised his friend for not seeing "the qualities of a great leader" in his commander.[34]

A correspondent for a New York newspaper believed the small numbers of Union cavalry near the Hanover Court House area emboldened the enemy to make the raid. He admitted that the enemy mission "was not wholly unsuccessful."[35]

The raid also represented the height of Philip St. George Cooke's storied military career. Whether beset by health problems related to heat, fatigue and stress, Cooke seemed incapable of a quick response to the enemy intrusion. He would again incur the wrath of Fitz John Porter for ordering a controversial cavalry charge during the Battle of Gaines' Mill on June 27.

It was likely early July when Cooke wrote an angry undated letter to his wife. Amidst an avalanche of ill will from fellow officers and McClellan's staff, Cooke revealed, "I am disgusted with this army, in everyway, there are many cowards in it, — you may defer fools too, — in high places — in fact I think it will never come to much, — or our cause either if there be not more military skill, and unity, — between Govt or people, & generals."[36]

On July 5, abandoned by McClellan's loyal cadre of officers and sensing his impending demise, Cooke resigned his command in frustration. He admitted that the Confederates had the best generals "who inspire confidence" in their men, yet he could not understand that "[t]his army still cheers McClellan, but they cheer every thing, — all the time; — after being well beaten." He indicated that he had lost confidence in his mounted arm when he wrote, "I don't believe in our cavalry; — the regular a skeleton, & and has lost its officers — no one understands it."[37]

Cooke would spend the next year on court-martial duty, and then he commanded the Baton Rouge District in the Union's Department of the Gulf from October 1863 to May 1864. He would close out the war in charge of recruiting and then spend the next twenty years trying to clear his tarnished name over his performance during the Peninsula Campaign. After the war, he moved his family to Michigan, where he retired from the U. S. Army in 1873.

Thirty years after the war ended, Wesley Merritt, a former Cooke aide and cavalry division commander, still seethed over McClellan's misuse of cavalry during the Peninsula Campaign. In an article designed to eulogize Cooke shortly after his 1895 death, Merritt complained of the "emasculated ranks of the thin right wing of what was left of Cooke's cavalry." He considered Stuart's raid inconsequential and especially lamented that the blame "was unworthily thrown on the cavalry and on General Cooke by the uninformed, owing to untruthful statements of those who know better, but were willing to accept a scapegoat." Merritt recalled that he watched as Cooke became more frustrated after the Battle of Gaines' Mill over the continued separation of cavalry units to division and brigade level.[38]

Stuart's deep raid also caused McClellan to admit the vulnerability of the White House Landing supply depot. On June 18, McClellan made plans to transfer some supplies via boat from White House to the James River. This prescient move to establish a secondary depot on the James would later prove valuable. However, over the next ten days, McClellan did little to strengthen Fitz John Porter's 5th Corps despite the accurate perception amongst some Northerners that the Confederate cavalry mission represented more than just a mere raid. A correspondent for the *New York Times* surmised on June 20, that Stuart's raid revealed "the disposition of our troops, and of the extent to which our rear is unprotected." He predicted that the next Rebel attack would be against the "weaker" right flank "to cut off our communications with York River, and seize the large quantity of supplies collected at the White House, on the Pamunkey." His forecast would prove quite accurate.[39]

George McClellan might not have thought about the possibility of changing his supply base without the raid. If anything, Stuart's expedition pushed the Federal commander to hedge his supply situation by bringing ships up both rivers. Thus, some Confederate officers believed that Stuart's raid should have only been a reconnaissance with a handful of men, not 1,200 cavalrymen thundering around in the enemy's rear highlighting the deficiencies of the White House Landing supply line. Hindsight enabled Stuart's detractors to know that the stalemate at the Battle of Mechanicsville on June 26 and the Confederate success at the Battle of Gaines' Mill the following day led to the capture of White House, but by then much of the supplies for the Army of the Potomac had already been removed by ship to the James River.

This fortuitous movement of supplies enabled Lieutenant Colonel Rufus Ingalls on June 28 to follow a contingency plan to abandon "the White House depot, leaving no public property behind of any value or use." With heavily laden Federal boats already at anchor on the James River east of City Point, the Army of the Potomac never faced the loss of its vital supply system. Without this preemptive move, the consequences to McClellan's army might have proved disastrous. Ingalls still noted: "It seems almost a miracle, our successful escape from the White House."[40]

Ingalls arrived at Haxall's Landing on the James near darkness on June 30. He met with McClellan on the eve of the Battle of Malvern Hill, and they selected Harrison's Landing as the new supply depot.[41]

However, not all the Federal material escaped from the Pamunkey River. Jeb Stuart arrived with his horsemen at White House on June 28 and found, "[n]ine large barges loaded with stores were on fire as we approached; immense numbers of tents, wagons, cars in long trains loaded and five locomotives, a number of forges, quantities of every species of quartermaster's stores and property, making a total of many millions of dollars — all more or less destroyed." Nearby, the bloated carcasses of hundreds of cavalry horses littered the estate of Mount Prospect. Retreating Union soldiers had destroyed the animals rather than risk them being saddled by approaching Confederate troopers.[42]

Harrison's Landing seemed a stronger position than White House Landing as it enabled the long-range guns from navy gunboats to protect both of McClellan's flanks. On July 6, in a dispatch to Jefferson Davis, Robert E. Lee recognized the risk of an attack against the new Federal position. Faced with the horrendous Confederate casualties at Malvern Hill on July 1, Lee feared the huge enemy naval shells "would prevent us from reaping any of the fruits of victory & expose our men to great destruction." However, George McClellan had seen and suffered enough damage from the guns of Lee's men. Over the next several weeks, Union soldiers would board transport boats and float down the James River — away from Richmond.[43]

With the benefit of seven months' hindsight, Brigadier General John G. Barnard, McClellan's chief engineer, noted on January 26, 1863, that "on leaving Williamsburg we should have crossed the Chickahominy and connected with the Navy in the James. We should have had a united army and the co-operation of the Navy, and probably would have been in Richmond in two weeks." Barnard realized that the need to link with McDowell and the use of the York/Pamunkey River supply route split McClellan's forces. He believed that the two above factors meant that "we lost essentially all that was worth going so far to gain, viz, the James River approach and the co-operation of the Navy."[44]

Jeb Stuart's accomplishment in mid-June 1862, allowed the soldiers and the civilians of the fledgling Confederacy to cheer about a positive event. Southern hopes lifted on the mission's success in the face of other 1862 Southern disasters: the fall of New Orleans and loss of the lower Mississippi River; the loss at the Battle of Shiloh; and the continued Union naval blockade from the Gulf to Virginia. Eighty years later, a similar daring mission led by Brigadier General Jimmie Doolittle's raiders, who piloted bombers off aircraft carriers [a first] and bombed a seemingly invincible Tokyo, would help swell America's pride amidst numerous setbacks in the Pacific at the beginning of World War II.

The audacity of Stuart's lightning mission also led to an evolution of Union and Confederate cavalry tactics. This deep raid's success ensured that other cavalry leaders would try to replicate the mission throughout the remainder of the war, albeit with mixed results. The addition of horse artillery that introduced fast, heavy firepower miles behind enemy lines represented a novel concept that would also be used in future conflicts. One lesson that Stuart seemed to have learned was the difficulties wrought by leaving the artillery at the column's rear on a raid. On future expeditions, the guns would ride near the front, which enabled them to be deployed easier. Also, the roads would be less churned near the front, which presented less stress as the horse teams pulled the gun carriages along.[45]

An elated Confederate war clerk, John Jones, noted the profound psychological difference amongst Richmonders in a diary entry he made on June 15. "What a change! No one now dreams of the loss of the capital." Jones failed to mention the reason for the optimism, but he could not have missed the festival atmosphere heralded by Jeb Stuart's triumphant return. John Mosby observed, "Richmond in fine spirits, — everybody says it is the greatest feat of the war. I never enjoyed myself so much in my life."[46]

Stuart's briefing to Robert E. Lee near sunrise on Sunday, June 15, signaled a green light for the Confederate army commander to continue plans for his offensive that would become known as The Seven Days' Battles. The next morning Lee sent a message directed to the Shenandoah Valley for Stonewall Jackson: "The present, therefore, seems to be favorable for a junction of your army and this."[47]

Jackson's nearly 18,000 troops began their move toward Richmond on June 17. The senior Confederate leadership wondered whether Jackson's men would be able to reach Richmond and reinforce Lee before McClellan could attack or would McClellan wait for more of his own reinforcements? The answer came via a letter written by the 4th U. S. Cavalry's private Charles Edward Bates while he served as a headquarters guard for McClellan's staff. Irritated with McClellan's excuses, Bates wrote his parents on June 19, "it is time something was being done besides throwing up dirt." Four days later, on June 23, Robert E. Lee would meet with all of his commanders at the Dabbs House to finalize the attack against the vulnerable Union right flank.[48]

Over seven days at the end of June, Lee's Army of Northern Virginia would push George McClellan's army away from Richmond toward Harrison's Landing on the James River. The war would continue for nearly three additional years and cost thousands of more lives before the Federal army under a different commander would have a similar opportunity to seize Richmond.

However, perhaps what is lost due to the overshadowing success of Robert E. Lee's offensive during those seven fateful days was the potential disaster faced by Jeb Stuart and his 1,200 cavalrymen two weeks earlier. A more aggressive Union pursuit mixed with less Confederate luck might have garnered a different outcome, and Stuart's fame might not ever have been launched. Several days after the expedition returned to Richmond, Lieutenant John Cooke asked General Stuart whether he had contemplated surrender if an overwhelming enemy force had appeared to trap the Confederates against the Chickahominy River. Stuart answered, "'No. One other course was left.'" When Cooke asked, "'What was that?'" Stuart replied, "'To *die game.*'" Perhaps this represented hyperbole, but in an era where honor amongst men stood for much, Jeb Stuart would not have enjoyed being taken prisoner, especially by his father-in-law.[49]

John Mosby certainly recognized the special nature of this "*reconnaissance* in force." "This raid is unique, and distinguished from all the others on either side during the war, on account of the narrow limits in which the cavalry was compelled to operate. From the time when he broke through McClellan's line on his right until he had passed around him on his left Stuart was enclosed by three unfordable rivers, over one of which he had to build a bridge to cross. During the whole operation the cavalry never drew a sabre except at the first picket post they encountered."[50]

Before he made his last cavalry ride in May 1864, Stuart told John Cooke that the 1862 Chickahominy Raid "'was the most dangerous of all my expeditions, if I had not succeeded in crossing the Chickahominy, I would have been ruined, as there was no way of getting out.'" Jeb Stuart, ever the realist, knew how desperate things might have been, not only for his men, but for his reputation during those three hot days in mid-June of 1862.[51]

Order of Battle

STUART'S RAID AROUND MCCLELLAN
ON JUNE 12–15, 1862

CONFEDERATE

Army of Northern Virginia, Cavalry Brigade

Brigadier General James Ewell Brown Stuart

- 1st Virginia Cavalry Regiment – Colonel Fitzhugh Lee

    4th Virginia Cavalry [4 companies] – Captain Robert E. Utterback

- 9th Virginia Cavalry Regiment [7 companies] – Colonel William Henry Fitzhugh "Rooney" Lee [note: minus companies A, H, & I on detached service]

    4th Virginia Cavalry [2 companies] – Captain William Beverly Wooldridge

- Jefferson Davis Legion [3 companies] – Lieutenant Colonel William Thompson Martin
  Company C – Southern Guards [Mississippi]
  Company E – Canebrake Legion [Alabama]
  Company F – Georgia Hussars [Georgia]

    Boykin Rangers [South Carolina] – Lieutenant John Chesnut

- Stuart Horse Artillery [1 section] – Lieutenant James Breathed
  1 twelve-pound howitzer & 1 rifled gun

UNION

Army of the Potomac, Cavalry Reserve

Brigadier General Philip St. George Cooke

1st Brigade – Brigadier General William H. Emory

- 5th U. S. Cavalry Regiment – Captain Charles J. Whiting

    Detached to Old Church on May 31:

    2nd Squadron – Co. A & C – Captain William B. Royall

    4th Squadron – Co. F & H – Captain James E. Harrison

- 6th U. S. Cavalry Regiment – Major Lawrence Williams

- 6th Pennsylvania Cavalry Regiment [Lancers] – Colonel
  Richard H. Rush

2nd Brigade – Colonel George A. H. Blake

- 1st U. S. Cavalry Regiment

- 8th Pennsylvania Cavalry Regiment

White House Landing Supply Depot – Lieutenant Colonel Rufus
Ingalls

- 11th Pennsylvania Cavalry Regiment – Colonel Josiah Harlan

- 93rd New York Infantry Regiment

- 3rd U. S. Infantry Regiment [2 companies]

- 1st New York Artillery [1 section] – 2 rifled guns

The Burial of Captain William Latane, 9th Virginia Cavalry

THE DUST HAD FINALLY SETTLED after the cavalry fight near Linney's Corner. Sergeant John Latane sat on the ground as he cradled his dead older brother's head in his lap. The twenty-four-year-old tried to control his emotions as he looked down into his brother's pale lifeless face. He flicked his hands at the vulture-like flies that seemed attracted to the uneven circles of blood that stained William Latane's coat. Colonel Rooney Lee and many others had already dismounted, removed their hats and expressed sorrow. Most of them had ridden on, drawn toward the enemy troopers somewhere to the east. Colonel Rooney Lee was gone too, but he had given John permission to stay behind to bury the body.

Perhaps John Latane entertained thoughts of getting his brother back to Essex County but doing so would require crossing the Pamunkey River and then meandering through King William County before crossing the Mattaponi River. High water and dangerous travel through enemy-held territory would have jeopardized this idea.

Corporal Stephen W. Mitchell, "being the stoutest man present," was selected to bear the body from the field." The twenty-eight-year-old Mitchell mounted his horse and then several men gently lifted Captain Latane's body and placed it in front of Mitchell's saddle. John Latane hopped on his horse, and the pair continued downhill toward the Totopotomoy Creek bottom.

A short time later an ox-cart caught up with the small funeral party. Several 9th Virginia troopers hailed the black boy driving the cart. Bags of corn destined for a nearby grist mill still filled the cart bed as the driver had been unable to sneak past Union patrols to deliver the grain. The cart and driver had come from Westwood, the farm of Dr. William S. P. Brockenbrough, a Confederate surgeon. The driver was the slave son of the Brockenbrough's cook.[1]

John Latane's friends shoved the corn to the side and lifted William's body onto the bed for the journey to Westwood. John gave his horse to one of the troopers and he then climbed aboard the cart. The cart continued northwest on the same road earlier traveled by the Confederate column. The driver and John both scanned the road ahead for Union troops. Three miles later they came to Haw's Shop, scene of the earlier skirmish with the 5th U. S. Cavalry pickets. The driver swung the reins to the right, and the cart made a hard east turn toward the Pamunkey River. Westwood stood some two miles down this road.

The cart driver had certainly warned John Latane that Union cavalry had been on picket around Westwood, but as they arrived the place seemed clear. However, with a Union outpost nearby, John Latane would need to exercise caution. The driver steered the cart into the back yard as John Latane sat concealed in the bed "riding with his brother's head in his lap."[2]

Catherine Brockenbrough looked out a window of Westwood and saw the cart approach. She suspected nothing was amiss until one of her servants ran in and said that there was a dead soldier aboard. She came outside and met the cart, where she gasped at the unexpected cargo. A quick glance around still showed no Union horsemen, so she had the servants carry the body inside the house. She must have harbored the fear that one of the servants might reveal to returning Federal troops the presence of the dead officer.

Mrs. Brockenbough urged John Latane to leave before Union troops returned. She convinced the distraught young man that she would ensure that his brother received a proper Christian burial.

During John Latane's brief time at Westwood, a "heavily armed" blue-clad cavalryman appeared along the road, but he did not stop.[3]

John Latane needed another horse to escape so the Westwood matron called a servant to lead him a short distance through the woods to nearby Summer Hill plantation which was run by her niece, Mrs. William B. Newton. She knew that the soldier might find another mount there.[4]

As the pair approached the majestic Summer Hill, they watched and listened for any sounds of Yankee cavalry. Their arrival startled one of the Newton women, as she sat on the porch reading a book. She thought they were Yankees. Mrs. Willoughby Newton, sister-in-law of Mrs. Brockenbrough, agreed to give the young sergeant their only horse, which was mostly blind. Latane went down to the barn and saddled the disabled horse and soon departed to find his colleagues.[5]

The ladies of Summer Hill then hustled over to Westwood to "assist in preparing the body for the burial." When they arrived,

Summer Hill today. Author photo.

they found that some of the servants had already cleaned the dust and caked blood off his uniform and face. He had been shot four times and "one ball had entered the region of his heart and passed out at the back." One of the ladies clipped a lock of Captain Latane's hair for his family. A Westwood servant named Aaron rode to find Reverend George Carraway to see if he could perform the burial. Carraway spent much time on the local roads as he pastored both Hanover Court House's St. Paul's Episcopal Church and Old Church's Immanuel Episcopal Church. A carpenter, probably a Westwood slave, sawed and hammered some nearby boards for a coffin.[6]

Aaron soon returned from his unsuccessful search for Reverend Carraway. He had been unable to get past Union cavalry pickets who actively patrolled most Hanover roads in search of Jeb Stuart's men. Due to the heat and the deteriorating body condition, Catherine Brockenbrough knew that she and her Summer Hill relatives would have to bury Captain Latane soon.

On Saturday, June 14, the women seemed blessed because Union soldiers had moved miles away from Westwood and Summer Hill toward Tunstall's Station on the now cold trail of Stuart's raiders. As evening approached, the wagon cart that carried Captain William Latane's casket proceeded to Summer Hill. The procession then continued to the small Summer Hill family graveyard located about a half-mile east of the plantation house.

Several servants had dug the grave alongside Lieutenant William B. Phelps' burial spot. Phelps was a family member from the 1st Virginia Infantry, who had been mortally wounded at the Battle of Dranesville [Virginia] in December 1861. Mrs. Willoughby Newton performed the service while several young girls dropped flowers on the grave.[7]

Mrs. Willoughby Newton noted in her June 14 diary that Captain Latane "and our precious W. [Willie Phelps] lie side by side, martyrs to a holy cause." She and her relatives expressed some anxiety about the fate of Jeb Stuart and his men as she wrote, "I know that Gen. S. is thought to be reckless and I can't help feeling very anxious."[8]

Brockenbrough Family graveyard near Summer Hill. Author Photo.

Headstone for Captain William Latane. Headstone on right is for Lieutenant William Phelps, a Brockenbrough relative, who had succumbed to battle wounds in January 1862. Author Photo.

Aaron had indicated that Yankee soldiers vowed vengeance for the raid and that "they will shoot black and white." On June 16, Union cavalry intercepted a servant carrying letters from the women to soldier relatives. Several of these letters would soon appear in New York newspapers.[9]

Yankee cavalry pickets returned to Westwood and Summer Hill on June 17 and an angry Mrs. Willoughby Newton wrote, "We doubtless have the will to do them harm enough, but, surrounded and watched as we are, the power is wanting." The new guard was composed of regular cavalry whom she found "much more decent than the volunteers." She wondered whether the vitriolic anti-Union tone found in the confiscated letters resulted in the large number of guards at the two homesteads as: "It is so absurd to see the great fellows on their horses, armed from head to foot, with their faces turned toward us, standing at our yard-gate, guarding women and children, occasionally riding about on the gravel-walks, plucking roses, with which they decorate their horses' heads."[10]

Only days after the last spade of dirt was dropped on the fresh grave at Summer Hill, the life of Captain William Latane took on mythological significance in the South. The bravado of the young fallen cavalry officer leading his men in a thunderous collision of horses and men against the enemy begged for remembrance, but a subsequent poem and painting added a romantic flourish to the event.

Southerners seemed enthralled with John R. Thompson's 1862 poem titled "The Burial of Latane" amidst its wide critical acclaim. Thompson had previously served as the editor at the *Southern Literary Messenger*. His poem eulogized Latane, but it also drew attention to the huge wartime sacrifices rendered by Southern women highlighted by their selflessness as they wept over the grave of a warrior who was but a stranger to them.

Newspaper stories about the burial and Thompson's poem no doubt inspired an artist named William D. Washington. The twenty-eight-year-old Clarke County, Virginia native hired several

Richmond women and young girls to serve as models for his rendition of the graveyard scene. He finished the work in late 1864, and it drew further attention to the sacrifices of both soldier and citizen by ensuring that by war's end, the name of Captain William Latane would be known throughout the South.[11]

APPENDIX C

The Old Church Decision

S HORTLY AFTER Stuart's Chickahominy Raid ended, some Confederate officers expressed criticism over his decision to continue toward Tunstall's Station instead of returning to Richmond via Hanover Court House. Some historians have questioned the wisdom of the move too, as they believed that the extension of the raid southeast of Old Church alerted George McClellan to the vulnerability of his White House Landing supply line. Others criticized Stuart for taking so many men on the ride instead of sending a handful of scouts to gather the same information.

Historian Jennings Cropper Wise noted that "while it [raid] was a brilliant feat, its results were adverse to Lee and far-reaching." Wise believed that the raid alerted McClellan to his vulnerable right flank, yet McClellan had expressed concerns about protecting his Pamunkey River line well before Stuart ever launched his expedition. McClellan had complained about the need to extend his right flank to the Pamunkey River and he seemed to prefer a battlefront that stretched only between the Chickahominy and James rivers.[1]

A shortened front would have allowed McClellan to consolidate his lines and enabled the Federal navy to sweep this area with their guns. Therefore, McClellan probably decided to hedge his supply situation by ordering boats to move supplies from White House Landing to the James River, three days after Stuart's mission ended.

Little Mac did not reveal what inspired this move which has allowed critics to focus on the raid as the cause.

Could Stuart have turned back toward Hanover Court House from Old Church and safely brought General Lee the valuable information about the terrain and the Union troop positions on the right flank? John Thomason asserted in his 1930 biography titled *Jeb Stuart:* "Stuart could, as the events turned out, have retreated up the Pamunkey, a little north of the road by which he came." Yet, General Stuart had no access to this hindsight as he sought to make numerous rapid decisions while riding through the Hanover County countryside. Thomason stated, "Being a trained officer, he assumed — as he had been taught to assume — that the enemy would use good judgment, and block this line of retreat at once. But Cooke proved incapable, and Stuart could have gotten out." Stuart no doubt was surprised over his father-in-law's slow reaction to the raid, but again the Rebel cavalry leader could not have foreseen the situation. Plus, a move to pass north of Hanover Court House would have left Stuart's men little room to maneuver with the column's right shoulder against the river.

Thomason does assert that "Stuart's ride applied a very powerful stimulus to his [McClellan's] careful brain," forcing the Union commander to craft plans to transfer his supply base to the James River. Thomason also provides more conjecture when he states that had Stuart turned back after Old Church then McClellan might not "have been ready for that change of base which saved his army from complete disaster." This again is pure speculation.[2]

Burke Davis in his biography, *Jeb Stuart: The Last Cavalier,* noted that the raid had barely ended before critics questioned what Stuart had actually accomplished, save giving McClellan an unsubtle warning about his vulnerable right flank. Yet amazingly, the commander for the Army of the Potomac did nothing to strengthen this right flank. Daily forays by small Confederate cavalry scouts proved this as Stonewall Jackson's men made their trek from the Shenandoah Valley destined to soon change the strategic situation near Richmond.[3]

Jubal Early noted that while Stuart's raid gained valuable information for Lee, "it also served to convince McClellan of the necessity of a change of his base to James river, which for us was the most dangerous position for him to occupy." E. Porter Alexander later considered the "forced reconnaissance of the enemy's rear" with 1,200 cavalrymen a "grave error" for it made McClellan well aware of his supply line vulnerability on the right flank. Alexander believed that the same information that Lee needed could have been gathered by a handful of scouts, similar to the mission performed by John Mosby on June 9–10. However, Alexander's analysis has the benefit of hindsight — abilities that Generals Lee and Stuart did not have on those fateful days of June 1862.[4]

Even Confederate soldiers at the company level wondered about the ramifications of the raid. An astute infantry lieutenant, Virgil A. S. Parks, from the 17th Georgia feared that "General Stuart's unrivaled feat" awakened McClellan to his vulnerable supply and communications line from the White House to the Chickahominy River. Parks wrote on June 21, "The whole thing seems fabulous; but the reality of Gen. Stuart's having been among their wagon trains, commissary and quartermaster's stores, and sutler's shops, is too plainly felt by the enemy to ignore."[5]

However, some of this criticism is debunked by a careful reading of Lee's June 11 order to Stuart. Lee wanted Stuart "to make a secret movement to the rear of the enemy." Certainly the enemy's rear could be interpreted as the York River Railroad. The order also urged Stuart to capture grain and cattle and "destroy his wagon trains" on the roads from Piping Tree Ferry which is east of Old Church. Lee also urged Stuart to "take every means in your power to save and cherish those you do take." The next paragraph of the order indicated that "[a] large body of infantry, as well as cavalry, was reported near the Central Railroad." If Stuart had contemplated launching his expedition with fewer men, this warning about possible large enemy numbers would have probably changed his mind.[6]

On this expedition, General Stuart had to make numerous decisions in short order, while under some duress. Unlike his critics, he did not have the benefit of hindsight. He also read General Lee's orders and he took prudent precautions to make sure that he had enough men, with enough firepower, to fight their way through any enemy obstacles. If he had sent only a handful of men on the reconnaissance or he had turned back at Old Church, the poignant words of John Thomason come to mind: "Still military history would be poorer by a fine and daring thing."[7]

Route of the Ride – Day One Question, June 12, 1862

T HROUGH THE YEARS, there has been some disagreement about the route that Jeb Stuart's troopers took on that first day of June 12, 1862 after they departed the Mordecai Farm area on Brook Road [Turnpike]. The accepted or "traditional" route for many years has been noted in many secondary sources and even followed by numerous historians who have led bus tours. This route seems to have been plotted out by members of the Richmond Civil War Round Table in 1956. The segment was then used by the 1961 Richmond Civil War Centennial Committee and the Virginia Civil War Commission.

This "traditional" route begins at the intersection of Azalea and Brook roads, yet I consider the formal departure point for the expedition was Mrs. Mordecai's farm [camp of the 9th Virginia Cavalry] located 1¼ miles to the southwest in the middle of present day Bryan Park. The "traditional" route moves from Azalea Road north on Brook Road about 2.9 miles to a left turn onto Mountain Road and then along Greenwood Road [Rt. 625] to a right turn on Old Washington Highway [Rt. 626]. The route then crosses a narrow portion of the Chickahominy River to a left turn onto Cedar Lane [Rt. 623]. After a short distance turn right onto Elmont Road [Rt. 626 again] which crosses the R. F. & P. Railroad at the spot formerly known as Kilby's Station. The route then continues north to a left turn onto Route 54 skirting the west edge of Ashland before turning right onto Independence Road [Rt. 669] and then makes several turns before arriving at the evening bivouac spot on Winston Farm.

Yet, my research and study has failed to reveal any primary source — either a map, a report or a letter — that supports this "traditional" route on day one of June 12, 1862. Nor could I find any evidence to explain why the "traditional route" for day one became the standard. One possible reason might be that the famed Richmond historian Douglas Southall Freeman looked over the official sketch map that accompanied Stuart's official report of the expedition and deemed it "untrustworthy" as seen in Freeman's *Lee's Lieutenants* on page 287. However, Freeman does not explain why or what part of this official expedition map he believes is inaccurate.

This official sketch map is displayed in color in *The Official Military Atlas of the Civil War* on page XXI, map 9 and it was drawn by one of the staff topographic engineers. The map would have certainly been approved by General Stuart prior to being submitted with his report. Therefore, lacking any evidence to the contrary, I believe the map has to be accepted as valid.

After spending hours looking at numerous period and current maps, I believe the route portrayed on this "Pamunkey Expedition" map reveals that the Confederate cavalrymen crossed the railroad south of the Chickahominy River and looped well west of Ashland on day one.

Specifically, I believe that Stuart's men turned left off the Brook Road [Turnpike] just south of Yellow Tavern and moved northwest on Hungary Road to Hungary Spring Station where they crossed the R. F. & P. Railroad. They then turned right onto a series of farm roads that intersected with Mountain Road west of the railroad tracks. They probably turned right onto Mountain Road and then made an immediate left and moved north on a small road that went by Dr. John M. Sheppard's place which is present day Sheppard Crump Memorial Park and the Meadow Farm Museum. They then probably continued north on a farm lane/road to intersect with what period maps refer as the Plank Road which is present day Greenwood Road [Rt. 625]. They then made a left turn onto Greenwood Road [Rt. 625] and crossed the Chickahominy River and then made a right turn to go north toward Kilby's Station. The column then made a left turn onto what is today named Cedar Lane [Rt. 623]. Scouts would have ridden to Kilby's Station to gather waiting cavalrymen and then rejoined the column now headed northwest to support Stuart's ruse that the troopers were headed toward Louisa County and the Shenandoah Valley.

They continued to an intersection with Courthouse Road [also known as Ashland Road Rt. 666], and turned right. After a short distance they stayed left onto Hughes Road which is now called Blanton Road [Rt. 666]. They continued on this road to an intersection with a road from Ashland, today called Independence Road [Rt. 669]. This intersection is just south of Independence Church which is where this routing rejoins with the "traditional" 1956 route. The column then zigged and zagged several times until crossing the railroad again and halting to bivouac in the rolling fields of the Winston farm near sundown on June 12.

The big difference is that *The Official Military Atlas* map shows the column crossing the railroad and turning north to parallel the railroad west of the tracks. The "traditional" route has the column paralleling the tracks east of the railroad until crossing at Kilby's Station.

My main reason for supporting this newer day one route is that it closely matches the sketch map that accompanied Stuart's report. This newer route also gets Stuart's long column off of Brooke Road [Turnpike] sooner to avoid bumping into a Union patrol or being spotted by Union spies. The move toward Hungary Station also gets them headed northwest quicker toward Louisa County. The newer route also keeps the column nearly two miles west of Ashland which would have helped prevent detection by both Union cavalry and spies whereas the "traditional " route had the column skirt the western boundary of Ashland.

Directions for Tracing
Stuart's Route Today

FOR CURRENT DOWNLOADABLE Driving Tour Directions

Go to www.AngleValleyPress.com

Or www.JohnFoxBooks.com

Destruction of White House. On June 28, 1862, Union troops abandoned the supply depot here and burned what supplies could not be shipped away. The White House went up in flames and all that remained were the chimneys. MOLLUS, USAHEC.

Remains of White House circa 1954. Charles R. Knight Collection.

Notes

Abbreviations

MOLLUS — Military Order of the Loyal Legion of the U. S.

NARA — National Archives and Records Administration, Washington, D.C.

NPS — National Park Service

OR — War of the Rebellion: A Compilation of the Official Records of the Union and Confederate Armies. 130 volumes

SHSP — Southern Historical Society Papers

USAHEC — U. S. Army History and Education Center, Carlisle, Pennsylvania

VHS — Virginia Historical Society, Richmond, Va.

Notes

Preface

1   *OR,* vol. 5, 777.

2   Averell, "With the Cavalry on the Peninsula," Edited by Robert U. Johnson and Clarence C. Buel, *Battles and Leaders of the Civil War,* vol. 2, New York: The Century Co., 1956, 430.

3   Mosby, *The Memoirs of Colonel John S. Mosby.* Edited by Charles Wells Russell. Boston, MA: Little, Brown, and Company, 1917, 119.

4   Cooke, *Wearing of the Gray,* 190.

Chapter 1: On to Richmond

1   Carter, "The Sixth Regiment of Cavalry," *The Maine Bugle,* October 1896, 295–296.

2   Jones, *A Rebel War Clerk's Diary*, 75.

3   Ibid. 76–77; "The War News," Richmond *Dispatch*, May 15, 1862.

4   Telegram from George McClellan to wife, May 15, 1862. Copy in Bound Volume #170, research library, Richmond National Battlefield Park.

5   "The War News," Richmond *Dispatch*, May 15, 1862; "Notice," Richmond *Dispatch*, May 15, 1862; "Save Richmond", *Richmond Dispatch*, May 15, 1862.

6   Untitled Article, *Richmond Examiner*, May 14, 1862 (as reprinted in *Charleston Mercury*, May 16, 1862).

7   Thomas, *Robert E. Lee*, 223; Robert E. L. Krick, "Letters Cast New Light on the Burial of Latane," *Hanover County Historical Society Bulletin.* vol. 64, Summer 2001, 5; Hewett, Trudeau, and Suderow, eds. *Supplement to the Official Records of the Union and Confederate Armies*, vol. 56, 835.

8   McGuire, *Diary of a Southern Refugee During the War*, i.

9   Ibid., 117.

10   Jones, *A Rebel War Clerk's Diary*, 77–78.

11   Ibid., 79.

12   Sears, ed., *The Civil War Papers of George B. McClellan*, 264.

13   Wolseley, *The American Civil War*, p. 136.

Chapter 2: White House Landing on the Pamunkey River

1   *OR*, vol. 11, pt. 1, 164–165.

2   Ibid., 205.

3   Mewborn, "A Wonderful Exploit: Jeb Stuart's Ride Around the Army of the Potomac," *Blue & Gray Magazine*, August 1998, 7; "From Our Army Correspondents," *New York Times,* June 20, 1862.

4   Moore Jr., *Moore's Complete Civil War Guide to Richmond*, 175; Coulling, *The Lee Girls*, 101–102; Sears, *To the Gates of Richmond*, 104.

5   Thomas, *Robert E. Lee*, 223; Robert E. L. Krick, "Letters Cast New Light on the Burial of Latane. *Hanover County Historical Society Bulletin.* Vol. 64, Summer 2001, p. 5; Hewett, Trudeau, Suderow, eds. *Supplement to the Official Records of the Union and Confederate Armies.* vol. 56, 835; Smith, "We Have It Damn Hard Here, 33; Mason, "Anecdotes of the Peninsular Campaign: part IV, Origin of the Lee Tomatoes," Edited by Robert U. Johnson and Clarence C. Buel, *Battles and Leaders of the Civil War*, vol. II, 277; Coulling, *The Lee Girls*, 103. The three Lee ladies returned to Confederate lines under a flag of truce on June 10.

6   *OR*, vol. 11, pt. 1, 159.

7   Grant, *Personal Memoirs of U. S. Grant*, vol. 2, 104. Ingalls has a spot in the U. S. Army Quartermaster Hall of Fame located at Ft. Lee, Virginia near Petersburg, Va.

8   Carter, *From Yorktown to Santiago*, 33; Davis, *Common Soldier, Uncommon War*, 136; Pennsylvania, Eleventh Cavalry Regiment, *History of the Eleventh Pennsylvania Volunteer Cavalry*, 39.

9   Kautz Biography, August V. Kautz Papers, 35, USAHEC.

10   Andrew Wallace, "General August V. Kautz and the Southwestern Frontier," Doctoral dissertation, 1967, privately published. Copy in August V. Kautz Papers, Kautz Collection, USAHEC.

11   Kautz, "Reminiscences of the Civil War," USAHEC, 9. Williams' father was an engineer captain who had been killed at Monterey during the Mexican War.

12   Pennsylvania, Eleventh Cavalry Regiment, *History of the Eleventh Pennsylvania Volunteer Cavalry*, 38–39.

13   Davis, *Common Soldier, Uncommon War*, 139.

14   Ibid., 135.

15   Ibid., 133, 135.

16   *OR*, vol. 11, pt. 1, 205, 186.

17   Ibid., 186, 200.

18   Townsend, *Rustics in Rebellion*, 121.

19   Ibid., 125–126. Townsend did not reveal the names of these officers but he did cite that a particular colonel lived a lavish life "that rivaled anything in Broadway" and even compared him to "Napoleon III." Townsend's reference here might have been aimed at Lieutenant Colonel Rufus Ingalls. Townsend indicated that the evacuation and subsequent fire that destroyed millions of dollars of supplies at the landing might have been started to cover up this misuse of government equipment.

20   *OR*, vol. 11, pt. 1, 159, 169.

21   Ibid., 159; *OR*, vol. 11, pt. 3, p. 178.

22   Pennsylvania, Eleventh Cavalry Regiment. *History of the Eleventh Pennsylvania*, 39.

23   *OR*, vol. 11, pt 1, 162–163.

24   Ibid., 158–159.

25   Wert, *The Sword of Lincoln*, 82.

Chapter 3: Jeb Stuart and Philip St. George Cooke: The In-Law Problem

1   Brennan, *"To Die Game": Gen. J. E. B. Stuart, CSA*, 6, 16.

2   *Official Register of the Officers and Cadets of the United States Military Academy*, West Point, N.Y.; Brennan, *"To Die Game"*, 8.

3   Wert, *A Glorious Army*, 16.

4   Davis, *JEB Stuart*, 34.

5   Thomas, *The Bold Dragoon*, 41. Stuart married Flora on November 14, 1855.

6   Ibid., 37, 39, 46–50.

7   Ibid., 52–53.

8   Ibid., 54–58; Davis, *JEB Stuart*, 8, 10–11.

9   Jeb Stuart letter from Ft. Wise, Kansas dated March 4, 1861, William Alexander Stuart Papers, 1861–1889, VHS.

10 Duncan, editor. *Letters of J. E. B. Stuart to His Wife — 1861*. 19; Mitchell, editor. *The Letters of Major General James E. B. Stuart*, 250.

11 Duncan, editor. *Letters of J. E. B. Stuart to His Wife — 1861*, 19.

12 von Borcke, *Memoirs of the Confederate War for Independence*, vol. 1, 48; Mitchell, editor. *The Letters of Major General James E. B. Stuart*, 254. Stuart must have been quite familiar with Lawrence Williams because he referred to him by only first and last name, no rank or unit, in the letter. The familiarity probably dated to West Point since Williams graduated in 1852, two years ahead of Stuart.

13 Brennan, *"To Die Game"*, 6, 16; Duncan, editor. *Letters of J. E. B. Stuart to His Wife — 1861*, 29.

Chapter 4: More Indecision Near Richmond

1   "Rush's Lancers in Virginia," Philadelphia *Inquirer,* June 17, 1862.

2   *OR*, vol. 11, pt. 3, 191; Smith, *"We Have It Damn Hard Here"*, 26; Gracey, *Annals of the Sixth Pennsylvania Cavalry*, v; Taylor, *Philadelphia in the Civil War 1861–1865*, 162.

3   Smith, *"We Have It Damn Hard Here,"* 25, 27.

4   *OR*, vol. 11, pt. 3, 189, 193.

5   Jones, *A Rebel War Clerk's Diary*, 78.

6   *OR*, vol. 11, pt. 3, 192.

7   Letter to "Dear Parents," written about May 29, 1862, Charles Edward Bates Papers, VHS.

8   "The Union Cavalry," *Journal of the United States Cavalry Association*, 11; *OR*, vol. 11, pt. 3, 36.

9   Wert, *The Sword of Lincoln*, 41.

10 *OR*, vol. 5, 777.

11 Miller, editor. *The Peninsula Campaign of 1862: Yorktown to the Seven Days*, vol. 3, 83, 87–90.

12 Wert, *The Sword of Lincoln*, 41.

13 "The Union Cavalry," *Journal of the United States Cavalry Association*, 87.

14 *Official Register of the Officers and Cadets of the United States Military Academy, West Point, N.Y.*

15 "The Union Cavalry," *Journal of the United States Cavalry Association*, 79.

16 Ibid., 84.

17 Smith, *"We Have It Damn Hard Here,"* 3–4; White, John C. "A Review of the Services of the Regular Army During the Civil War." Serialized article from an unknown periodical believed to be dated 1909 — located at USAHEC under 6th U. S. Cavalry.

18 Jones, *A Rebel War Clerk's Diary*, 79.

Chapter 5: Big Decisions for General Lee

1   Davis, *Common Soldier, Uncommon War*, 152; Kautz, "Reminiscences of the Civil War," Kautz Papers, 13, USAHEC.

2   Sears, editor, *The Civil War Papers of George B. McClellan*, 277–278, 281, 287.

3   Davis, *Common Soldier, Uncommon War*, 152.

4   Alexander, *Fighting for the Confederacy*, 91; Alexander, *Military Memoirs of a Confederate*, 110–111.

5   Letter of Jeb Stuart to "My Dear Brother, Camp Qui Vive Jan 6th 1862," William Alexander Stuart Papers, 1861–1889, VHS; Duncan, editor. *Letters of J. E. B. Stuart to His Wife — 1861*, 27.

6   Jones, *A Rebel War Clerk's Diary*, 82.

7   Sears, editor, *The Civil War Papers of George B. McClellan*, 244–245.

8   Lee, *Lee's Dispatches*, 8.

9   Letter to "Dear Parents", Camp Lincoln Va June 19th 1862", Charles Edward Bates Papers, 1858–1865, VHS.

10 Daniel, Richmond *Examiner*, June 10, 1862.

11 Lee, *Lee's Dispatches*, 5–7.

12 *OR*, vol. 11, pt. 2, p. 490.

13 Murray, *My Mother Used To Say: A Natchez Belle of the Sixties*, 130.

14 Ibid.

15 Gordon Family Papers, Georgia Historical Society Library. These chiggers, the size of a pinhead, succeeded in burrowing under the skin and creating an itchy red bump. The unfortunate officer and many of his fellow soldiers found themselves covered with these ugly welts which took weeks to heal.

16 *OR*, vol. 11, pt. 1, 1020; *OR*, vol. 11, pt. 3, p. 203.

17 *OR*, vol. 11, pt. 1, p. 1020; Arlington National Cemetery website burial record of Brigadier General William Bedford Royall. Royall received several brevet promotions for gallant and meritorious service and he retired in 1887 as a brigadier general. He is buried in Arlington Cemetery's section 1.

18 Kautz, "Reminiscences of the Civil War," Kautz Papers, 13, USAHEC.

19 Ibid., 13–14.

20 Carter, *From Yorktown to Santiago*, 44; Kautz, "Reminiscences of the Civil War," Kautz Papers, 14, USAHEC.

21 Davis, *Common Soldier, Uncommon War*, 154.

22 Kautz, "Reminiscences of the Civil War," Kautz Papers, 10, USAHEC. Kautz wrote that be believed that Williams did have contact with Confederate soldiers and friends during his absences. He doubted that Williams gave the enemy any valuable information but instead wanted to make friends in the event that the South was successful; Davis, *Common Soldier, Uncommon War*, 139; Carter, *From Yorktown to Santiago*, 35–36. Lawrence Williams' brother, William, was promoted to a Confederate colonel but due to strange circumstance he and his adjutant were arrested by Union authorities in Franklin, Tennessee while dressed in Union uniforms in June 1863. They both were hung the next day as spies.

23 Kautz, "Reminiscences of the Civil War," Kautz Papers, 8, USAHEC.

24 Carter, *From Yorktown to Santiago*, 35–36.

25 *OR*, vol. 11, pt.1, 45; *OR*, vol. 11, pt 1, 46.

26 Styple, editor, *Writing and Fighting the Civil War*, 105.

27 *OR*, vol. 11, pt 1, p.46.

Chapter 6: What Is On the Union Right Flank?

1 Mitchell, editor. *The Letters of Major General James E. B. Stuart*, 254–256 ; Cooke, *Wearing of the Gray*, 175; Freeman, *Lee's Lieutenants*, 277; Thomas, Bold Dragoon, 109.

2 *OR*, vol. 11, pt. 2, 490.

3 von Borcke, *Memoirs of the Confederate War for Independence*, vol. 1, 34–37.

4   Trout, *They Followed the Plume*, 274.

5   von Borcke, *Memoirs of the Confederate War for Independence*, vol. 1, 21–22.

6   Blackford, *War Years with Jeb Stuart*, 69; Sorrel, *Recollections of a Confederate Staff Officer*, 66.

7   Blackford, *War Years with Jeb Stuart*, 69; Wert, *Cavalryman of the Lost Cause*, 103.

8   Sorrel, *Recollections of a Confederate Staff Officer*, 66.

9   Mosby, "The Ride Around General McClellan," *SHSP* (1898) vol. 26, 247.

10   Mosby, *The Memoirs of Colonel John S. Mosby*, 6–9.

11   Wert, *Cavalryman of the Lost Cause*, 93.

12   Mosby "The Ride Around General McClellan," *SHSP* (1898) vol. 26, 246–247.

13   Wert, *Cavalryman of the Lost Cause*, 71; Mosby, *Mosby's War Reminiscences*, 218.

14   Mosby, "The Ride Around General McClellan," *SHSP* (1898) vol. 26, 247; Driver, *1st Virginia Cavalry*, 165, 215, 240.

15   Mosby, *Mosby's War Reminiscences*, 220.

16   Ibid.

17   Mosby, "The Ride Around General McClellan," *SHSP* (1898) vol. 26, 248; Wert, *Cavalryman of the Lost Cause*, 93.

18   Mosby, "The Ride Around General McClellan," *SHSP* (1898) vol. 26, 248.

19   Ibid.

20   Sorrel, *Recollections of a Confederate Staff Officer*, 67.

Chapter 7: The Battles of George McClellan

1   *OR*, vol. 11, pt. 3, p. 210.

2   *OR*, vol. 11, pt.1, p. 46; *OR*, vol. 11, pt. 3, p. 216.

3   Miller, editor. *The Peninsula Campaign of 1862: Yorktown to the Seven Days*, vol. 1, 19.

4   Sears, *To the Gates of Richmond*, p. 163.

5   "Kearney vs. McClellan," *Indianapolis Daily Journal*, October 12, 1864.

6   "Hooker on McClellan," *National Tribune*, November 14, 1907.

7   *OR*, vol. 11, pt. 1, 27.

8   *OR*, vol. 11, pt. 1, 28.

9   Ibid.

10   Wolseley, *The American Civil War*, 136.

11   Lincoln, *The Collected Works of Abraham Lincoln*, vol. 2, 216.

12   *OR,* vol. 11, pt. 3, 210.

13   Sears, editor, *The Civil War Papers of George B. McClellan,* 278.

14   Ibid., 293

15   *OR,* vol. 11, pt. 3, 225. McCall arrived at White House on June 10 with about 10,000 men and this left McDowell with another 30,000 troops.

16   Sears, editor, *The Civil War Papers of George B. McClellan,* 289, 296.

17   Townsend, *Rustics in Rebellion,* 126.

Chapter 8: Planning for the Great Chickahominy Raid

1   *OR,* vol. 11, pt. 3, p. 590.

2   Ibid.

3   Ibid.

4   Ibid.

5   Ibid., 589.

6   Sears, editor, *The Civil War Papers of George B. McClellan,* 297.

7   *OR,* vol. 11, pt. 3, 216, 224–225; Sears, *The Civil War Papers of George B. McClellan,* 297.

8   Order from R.B. Marcy to General, June 7, 1862. "Letters, Telegrams, Reports, and Lists Received by the Cavalry Corps, 1861–1865," NARA.

9   Smith, *"We Have It Damn Hard Here,* 40–41; Wittenberg, *Rush's Lancers,* 14; Gracey, *Annals of the Sixth Pennsylvania Cavalry,* vii.

10   Blackford, *War Years with Jeb Stuart,* 72.

11   Smith, *"We Have It Damn Hard Here",* 42.

12   McGuire, *Diary of a Southern Refugee During the War,* 141.

13   Letter to "Dear Parents," May 24, 1862. Theodore Sage letters, Harrisburg CWRT Collection, USAHEC

14   McGuire, *Diary of a Southern Refugee During the War,* 141–142; "Editorial Correspondence of the New York Times," *New York Times,* June 20, 1862.

15   Smith, *"We Have It Damn Hard Here",* 42.

Chapter 9: The Raid Begins

1   *OR,* vol. 11, pt. 3, p. 590.

2   von Borcke, *Memoirs of the Confederate War for Independence,* vol. 1, 37; Cooke, *Wearing of the Gray,* 175–176.

3   Duncan, editor. *Letters of J. E. B. Stuart to His Wife — 1861,* 25–26.

4   Ibid., p. 23.

5   Mosby, *The Memoirs of Colonel John S. Mosby*, 112.

6   Bond, Frank A. "Fitz Lee in Army of Northern Virginia," *Confederate Veteran*, vol. 6, 420.

7   *Report of the Secretary of War*, U.S. War Department, 1853. See H.W. Readnour dissertation.

8   Mewborn, "A Wonderful Exploit: Jeb Stuart's Ride Around the Army of the Potomac," *Blue & Gray Magazine*, August 1998, 10.

9   Beale, R. L. T. *History of the Ninth Virginia Cavalry*, 16–17; Stiles, *4th Virginia Cavalry*, 12.

10 Thomas, *Robert E. Lee*, 171, 178;

11 Stiles, *4th Virginia Cavalry*, 12.

12 Jesse Roderick Sparkman Civil War Diary, Mississippi State University Libraries; Hopkins, *The Little Jeff*, 60. Martin would be promoted to brigadier general at the end of the year and later command a division in the western theater.

13 *OR*, vol. 11, pt. 1, 1044–1045; "Late From the South," Philadelphia *Inquirer*, June 20, 1862. The second cannon has variously been described as a three-inch ordnance rifle, a six-pound English rifle, and Ed Bearss claims a "rifled 12-pounder Blakely" in his article in Miller, William J., editor. *The Peninsula Campaign of 1862: Yorktown to the Seven Days*, vol. 1, 45. The question seems to be which type of *rifled* cannon accompanied the column? Jeb Stuart in a January 18, 1862 letter noted that the Stuart Horse Artillery had "four (twelve pound) Howitzers, one Blakely (twelve pound) Rifle, one (six pound) and two Mountain Howitzers." This letter might give credence to the Bearss' claim that the rifled piece was a Blakely. For this letter see Adele Mitchell, *The Letters of Major General James E. B. Stuart*, 250; Mewborn, "A Wonderful Exploit: Jeb Stuart's Ride Around the Army of the Potomac," *Blue & Gray Magazine*, August 1998, 10; Moore, Robert H. II, *The 1st and 2nd Stuart Horse Artillery*, 15, 174.

14 Murray, *My Mother Used To Say*, 130.

15 Robins, W. T. "Stuart's Ride Around McClellan," Edited by Robert U. Johnson and Clarence C. Buel, *Battles and Leaders of the Civil War*, vol. 2, 271; Beale, G. W., *A Lieutenant of Cavalry in Lee's Army*, 24.

16 Robins, W. T. "Stuart's Ride Around McClellan," Edited by Robert U. Johnson and Clarence C. Buel, *Battles and Leaders of the Civil War*, vol. 2, 271. Several historians like Ed Bearrs and Emory Thomas have indicated that by about June 10 that Stuart's cavalry headquarters had shifted from the Charles City Road east of Richmond to the area around Mrs. Mordecai's farm north of Richmond. I believe that Stuart still had his headquarters east of Richmond, probably along the Charles City Road at the Waddell house. Just east of the Charles City Road area was where the bulk of McClellan's troops gathered

plus Dabbs House, Lee's headquarters, was near the Charles City Road cavalry headquarters of Stuart; von Borcke, *Memoirs of the Confederate War for Independence,* vol. 1, 37.

17   Mosby, "The Ride Around McClellan," *SHSP* (1898) vol. 26, 248; von Borcke, *Memoirs of the Confederate War for Independence,* vol. 1, 37.

18   The Journal of Charles R. Chewning, 3, Handley Library Archives — Stewart Bell Jr. Archives Room.

19   Brown, *Stringfellow of the Fourth,* 121.

20   *OR,* vol. 11, pt. 1, p. 1036.

21   Robins, "Stuart's Ride Around McClellan," Edited by Robert U. Johnson and Clarence C. Buel, *Battles and Leaders of the Civil War,* vol. II, 271.

22   Brown, *Stringfellow of the Fourth,* 121.

23   Duncan, editor. *Letters of J. E. B. Stuart to His Wife — 1861,* 22–23; Mewborn, "A Wonderful Exploit: Jeb Stuart's Ride Around the Army of the Potomac," *Blue & Gray Magazine,* August 1998, 46; Krick, Robert E. L., *Staff Officers in Gray,* 87. Burke would be wounded twice in August 1862 and then killed in November in an ambush at Shepherdstown. He was buried in that town's Elmwood Cemetery.

24   Captain William D. Farley, Compiled Service Records of Confederate General and Staff Officers, and Non-Regimental Enlisted Men, NARA; Krick, Robert E. L., *Staff Officers in Gray,* 125; Trout, *They Followed the Plume,* 106–108; *OR,* vol. 11, pt. 1, 445.

25   Trout, *They Followed the Plume,* 111; Wert, *Cavalryman of the Lost Cause,* 87; Freeman, *Lee's Lieutenants,* vol. 1, 280; Cooke, *Wearing of the Gray,* 142.

26   Stiles, *4th Virginia Cavalry,* 139; Jesse Roderick Sparkman Civil War Diary, Mississippi State University Libraries.

27   Letter from W. H. F. Lee to wife, 25 June 1862, Lee Family Papers, 1824–1918,VHS; Cooke, *Wearing of the Gray,* 176.

28   Brown, *Stringfellow of the Fourth,* 121.

29   Beale, G. W., *A Lieutenant of Cavalry in Lee's Army,* 24–25; Richmond *Dispatch,* June 16, 1862; Mewborn, "A Wonderful Exploit: Jeb Stuart's Ride Around the Army of the Potomac." *Blue & Gray Magazine,* August 1998, 12; Letter of William Z. Mead to "My Dearest Mother, Cavalry Camp 1 Cavalry, June 21, 1862," typescript and copy of original sent to author from descendant J.B. Mead. Mead's account of the signal rockets came in a letter he wrote six days after the ride ended so the events would have been fresh in his mind, although the time of midnight might be inaccurate.

30   Brown, *Stringfellow of the Fourth,* 122; Krick, Robert K. *9th Virginia Cavalry,* 95.

31   Beale, *A Lieutenant of Cavalry in Lee's Army*, 25; Krick, Robert K. *9th Virginia Cavalry*, 85.

Chapter 10: First Contact at Hanover Court House

1   Davis, *Common Soldier, Uncommon War*, 153–154.

2   Ibid., 154–155.

3   *OR*, vol. 11, pt. 1, p. 1036.

4   Mosby, "The Ride Around General McClellan," *SHSP* (1898) vol. 26, 249; Brown, *Stringfellow of the Fourth*, 122.

5   Mewborn, "A Wonderful Exploit: Jeb Stuart's Ride Around the Army of the Potomac." *Blue & Gray Magazine*, August 1998, 12; *OR*, vol. 11, pt. 1, 1036.

6   Cooke, *Wearing of the Gray*, 176–177.

7   Davis, *Common Soldier, Uncommon War*, 155; Mewborn, "A Wonderful Exploit: Jeb Stuart's Ride Around the Army of the Potomac." *Blue & Gray Magazine*, August 1998, 12. Mewborn referred to the prisoner as a Corporal Sweeney.

8   Property Claim by Family of Clevars S. Chisholm, Southern Claims Commission, Hanover County VA., NARA.

9   *OR*, vol. 11, pt. 1, 1036.

Chapter 11: Haw's Shop to Totopotomoy Creek: A Running Fight

1   *OR*, vol. 11, pt.1, 1021.

2   Pennsylvania, Eleventh Cavalry Regiment, *History of the Eleventh Pennsylvania Volunteer Cavalry*, 40.

3   *OR*, vol. 11, pt. 1, 1021–1022.

4   McCormick, "Fighting Them Over" *National Tribune*, February 21, 1901.

5   Ibid. McCormick does not seem to look favorably on Lt. Leib thus some of this article, written well after the war, might be embellished.

6   *OR*, vol. 11, pt. 1, p. 1022.

7   Krick, Robert K., *9th Virginia Cavalry*, 100; Beale, G. W. *A Lieutenant of Cavalry in Lee's Army*, 25; *OR*, vol. 11, pt. 1, 1037.

8   *OR*, vol. 11, pt. 1, 1022.

9   Frassanito, *Grant and Lee*, 162.

10   "From Our Army Correspondents," *New York Times*, June 21, 1862; *Immanuel Episcopal Church: A Timeline*, Immanuel Episcopal Church. When 1865 came, Carraway hung his head as he walked the grounds and surveyed the damaged interior of the parish building at Immanuel Episcopal Church.

Union troops had spent much time in the area during the 1864 Overland Campaign and he accorded them the blame for what he saw. He recorded, "God's house has been robbed and shamefully desecrated."

11   *OR*, vol. 11, pt. 1, 1020, 1022.

12   Ibid.

13   Ibid., 1022.

14   Ibid.

15   Ibid., 1020, 1024.

16   Ibid., 1022.

17   Krick, Robert K., *9th Virginia Cavalry*, 65; Franklin and Pruett, editors. *Civil War Letters of Dandridge William and Naomi Bush Cockrell, 1862–1863*, 5–6.

18   Brown, *Stringfellow of the Fourth*, 123.

19   Ibid; Krick, Robert K., *9th Virginia Cavalry*, 6.

20   "The Scout," Richmond *Daily Dispatch*, June 17, 1862.

21   Robins, "Stuart's Ride Around McClellan," Edited by Robert U. Johnson and Clarence C. Buel, *Battles and Leaders of the Civil War*, vol. II, 271.

22   *OR*, vol. 11, pt. 1, 1037; "The Scout," Richmond *Daily Dispatch*, June 17, 1862; Frayser, "Riding Around McClellan's Army with Jeb Stuart," Philadelphia *Weekly Times*, vol. 7, no. 24, August 4, 1883; von Borcke, *Memoirs of the Confederate War for Independence*, vol. 1, 38.

23   Letter of Robert S. Young, Lewis Leigh Collection, USAHEC.

24   *OR*, vol. 11, pt. 1, 1022.

25   Robins, "Stuart's Ride Around McClellan," Edited by Robert U. Johnson and Clarence C. Buel, *Battles and Leaders of the Civil War*, vol. II, 271.

26   Ibid; von Borcke, *Memoirs of the Confederate War for Independence*, vol. 1. 39.

27   Beale, G. W., *A Lieutenant of Cavalry in Lee's Army*, 25–26; Beale, R. L. T., *History of the Ninth Virginia Cavalry*, 17.

28   Beale, G. W., *A Lieutenant of Cavalry in Lee's Army*, 26; Beale, R. L. T., *History of the Ninth Virginia Cavalry*,17,

29   *OR*, vol. 11, pt. 1, 1022.

30   Robins, "Stuart's Ride Around McClellan," Edited by Robert U. Johnson and Clarence C. Buel, *Battles and Leaders of the Civil War*, vol. II, 271; von Borcke, *Memoirs of the Confederate War for Independence*, vol. 1, 39.

31   *OR*, vol. 11, pt. 1, 1022; von Borcke, *Memoirs of the Confederate War for Independence*, vol. 1, 38.

32   Cooke, *Wearing of the Gray*, 177; Beale, G.W., *A Lieutenant of Cavalry in Lee's Army*, 26.

33 Beale, G. W., *A Lieutenant of Cavalry in Lee's Army*, 24, 26.

34 *OR*, vol. 11, pt. 1, 1022.

35 Robins, "Stuart's Ride Around McClellan," Edited by Robert U. Johnson and Clarence C. Buel, *Battles and Leaders of the Civil War*, vol. II, 1956, 271.

36 von Borcke, *Memoirs of the Confederate War for Independence*, vol. 1, 39; Robins, "Stuart's Ride Around McClellan," Edited by Robert U. Johnson and Clarence C. Buel, *Battles and Leaders of the Civil War*, vol. II, 1956, p. 271.

37 Cooke, *Wearing of the Gray*, 177; Beale, G. W., *A Lieutenant of Cavalry in Lee's Army*, 27.

38 *OR*, vol. 11, pt. 1, 1022–1023. Leib stated that his men retreated about two miles, yet the distance from Totopotomoy Creek Bridge to Linney's Corner is slightly less than one mile.

39 *OR*, vol. 11, pt. 1, 1020; Mosby, *The Memoirs of Colonel John S. Mosby*, 112; *OR*, vol. 11, pt. 1, p. 1020.

Chapter 12: Collision Near Linney's Corner

1 Beale, R. L. T., *History of the Ninth Virginia Cavalry*, 17–18; Moncure, "Brief Memoranda of some of the Engagements" *Bulletin of the Virginia State Library*, vol. XVI, July 1927, 68.

2 Cooke, *Wearing of the Gray*, 177; *OR*, vol. 11, pt. 1, 1037.

3 Beale, G. W., *A Lieutenant of Cavalry in Lee's Army*, 26.

4 Beale, R. L. T., *History of the Ninth Virginia Cavalry*, 17–18; Campbell, "Stuart's Ride and Death of Latane," *SHSP* (1914), vol. 39, 88–89; Krick, Robert K. *9th Virginia Cavalry*, 62, 89; "Sketch of William Campbell's Life," typescript copy in Bound Volume #31, research library, Richmond National Battlefield Park.

5 Robins, "Stuart's Ride Around McClellan," Edited by Robert U. Johnson and Clarence C. Buel, *Battles and Leaders of the Civil War*, vol. II, 272.

6 Ibid.; *OR*, vol. 11, pt. 1, p. 1037.

7 Beale, R. L. T., *History of the Ninth Virginia Cavalry*, 17–18; McClellan, H.B., *The Life and Campaigns of Major-General J. E. B. Stuart*, 56.

8 *OR*, vol. 11, pt. 1, 1020, 1023–1024.

9 Ibid., 1020.

10 Freeman, *Lee's Lieutenants*, vol. 1, 285. Freeman estimated the time as 3 p.m.; Campbell, "Stuart's Ride and Death of Latane," *SHSP* (1914), vol. 39, 89; Robins, "Stuart's Ride Around McClellan," Edited by Robert U. Johnson and Clarence C. Buel, *Battles and Leaders of the Civil War*, vol. II, 1956, 272.

11 *OR*, vol. 11, pt. 1, 1020.

12   Robins, "Stuart's Ride Around McClellan," Edited by Robert U. Johnson
     and Clarence C. Buel, *Battles and Leaders of the Civil War*, vol. II, 1956, 272.

13   Salmon, "The Burial of Latane." *Virginia Cavalcade*, vol. 28, no. 3, winter
     1979, 118–129; Richmond *Dispatch*, June 16, 1862.

14   "The Scout," Richmond *Dispatch*, June 17, 1862; Compiled Service Records
     of Confederate Soldiers Who Served in Organizations from the State of
     Virginia, NARA; Krick, Robert K. *9th Virginia Cavalry*, 56.

15   Robins, "Stuart's Ride Around McClellan," Edited by Robert U. Johnson
     and Clarence C. Buel, *Battles and Leaders of the Civil War*, vol. II, 272; Beale,
     R. L. T., *History of the Ninth Virginia Cavalry*, 18; H.B. McClellan, *The Life and
     Campaigns of Major-General J. E. B. Stuart*, relates the legend yet McClellan
     initially served in the 3rd Va. Cavalry and did not join Stuart's staff until
     1863. There is no evidence to show that H.B. McClellan was on the raid.

16   *OR*, vol. 11, pt. 1, 1024.

17   Ibid.; Probably Benjamin Evans who NPS website lists as sergeant from
     Co. C, 5th US Cav., see http://www.nps.gov/civilwar/soldiers-and-sailors-
     database.htm

18   Campbell, "Stuart's Ride and Death of Latane," *SHSP* (1914), vol. 39, 89;
     "Sketch of William Campbell's Life," typescript copy in Bound Volume #31,
     research library, Richmond National Battlefield Park.

19   Campbell, "Stuart's Ride and Death of Latane," *SHSP* (1914), vol. 39, 89;
     Krick, Robert K. *9th Virginia Cavalry*, 91; "Sketch of William Campbell's
     Life," typescript copy in Bound Volume #31, research library, Richmond
     National Battlefield Park.

20   *OR*, vol. 11, pt. 1, p. 1023.

21   J.A.H. "Rebel Dash on Pamunkey River — Capt. W.B. Royall," probably
     Philadelphia area newspaper from late June 1862 located on www.fold3.
     com; *OR*, vol. 11, pt. 1, 1023; Mewborn, "A Wonderful Exploit: Jeb Stuart's
     Ride Around the Army of the Potomac," *Blue & Gray Magazine*, August
     1998, 14. McLean would be incarcerated at Richmond's Libby Prison until
     he was exchanged. Apparently his wounds never fully healed as he died ten
     months later from inflammation of the brain.

22   "The Scout," Richmond *Dispatch*, June 17, 1862; Robins, "Stuart's Ride
     Around McClellan," Edited by Robert U. Johnson and Clarence C. Buel,
     Battles and Leaders of the Civil War, vol. II, 1956, 272.

23   *OR*, vol. 11, pt. 1, 1024.

24   J.A.H. "Rebel Dash on Pamunkey River — Capt. W.B. Royall" probably
     Philadelphia area newspaper from late June 1862 located on www.fold3.com

25   *OR*, vol. 11, pt. 1, p. 1021.

26 "Sketch of William Campbell's Life," typescript copy in Bound Volume #31, research library, Richmond National Battlefield Park; Campbell, "Stuart's Ride and Death of Latane." *SHSP* (1914), vol. 39, 89.

27 Krick, Robert K. *9th Virginia Cavalry*, 80, 105; "Sketch of William Campbell's Life," typescript copy in Bound Volume #31, research library, Richmond National Battlefield Park; Krick, Robert K. *9th Virginia Cavalry*, 85.

28 Letter of Chiswell Dabney, "Dear Mother, Hd Qrs Caval' Brigade June 18th 1862," Saunders Family Papers, 1798–1903, VHS.

29 Cooke, *Wearing of the Gray*, 178; Mosby, *The Memoirs of Colonel John S. Mosby*, 112.

30 Beale, G. W., *A Lieutenant of Cavalry in Lee's Army*, 26.

31 Letter of R.J. Norris, "Camp Young, June 18th '62," offered for sale by Museum Quality Americana at www.mqamericana.com in March 2013.

32 *OR*, vol. 11, pt. 1, 1037.

Chapter 13: A Momentous Decision at Old Church

1 *OR*, vol. 11, pt. 1, p. 1024. There was no infantry assigned to Stuart's reconnaissance nor any other separate Confederate infantry in the area; Miller, editor. *The Peninsula Campaign of 1862: Yorktown to the Seven Days*, vol. 1, 94. Ed Bearrs refers to the Hanovertown Ferry Road as Bosher's Ferry Road.

2 Miller, editor. *The Peninsula Campaign of 1862: Yorktown to the Seven Days*, vol. 1, 91.

3 *OR*, vol. 11, pt. 1, 1037.

4 The Journal of Charles R. Chewning, Company E, 9th Virginia Cavalry, CSA. 4, Handley Library Archives — Stewart Bell Jr. Archives Room.

5 Cooke, *Wearing of the Gray*, 178.

6 *OR*, vol. 11, pt. 1, 1021, 1023. At the field hospital, orderlies disrobed the brave officer and discovered at least four saber slashes; Smith, *"We Have It Damn Hard Here,"* 45. Smith reported that Royall also had two bullet wounds yet Royall's official report and the account by J.A.H. only makes reference to blade cuts, not bullet wounds; J.A.H., "Rebel Dash on Pamunkey River — Capt. W.B. Royall" probably Philadelphia area newspaper from late June 1862 located on www.fold3.com. J.A.H.'s account based on an interview at Royall's Philadelphia hospital bedside on June 26, 1862 makes no mention of any bullet wounds.

7 Mewborn, "A Wonderful Exploit: Jeb Stuart's Ride Around the Army of the Potomac," *Blue & Gray Magazine*, August 1998, 16.

8 *OR*, vol. 11, pt. 1, 1023.

9 Ibid., 1023–1024.

10   Letter of R.J. Norris, "Camp Young, June 18th '62," offered for sale by Museum Quality Americana at www.mqamericana.com in March 2013.

11   Frayser, "Riding Around McClellan's Army with Jeb Stuart," Philadelphia *Weekly Times*, August 4, 1883; von Borcke, *Memoirs of the Confederate War for Independence*, vol. 1, 40.

12   Driver, *1st Virginia Cavalry*, 37; Driver, *First and Second Maryland Cavalry, C.S.A.*, 240.

13   Driver, *1st Virginia Cavalry*, 37–38; *OR*, vol. 11, pt.1, 1043; Mewborn, "A Wonderful Exploit: Jeb Stuart's Ride Around the Army of the Potomac," *Blue & Gray Magazine*, August 1998, 16.

14   *OR*, vol. 11, pt. 1, 1037; Mosby, *The Memoirs of Colonel John S. Mosby*. 112.

15   Cooke, *Wearing of the Gray*, 178, 181.

16   Letter of Chiswell Dabney, "Dear Mother, Hd Qrs Caval' Brigade June 18th 1862," Saunders Family Papers, 1798–1903, VHS.

17   Beale, R. L. T., *History of the Ninth Virginia Cavalry*, 18; *OR*, vol. 11, pt. 1, p. 1037; von Borcke, *Memoirs of the Confederate War for Independence*, vol. 1, 40.

18   Compiled Service Records of Confederate Soldiers Who Served in Organizations from the State of Virginia, NARA; Mewborn, "A Wonderful Exploit: Jeb Stuart's Ride Around the Army of the Potomac," *Blue & Gray Magazine*, August 1998, 16; *OR*, vol. 11, pt.1, 1043–1044.

19   Mewborn, "A Wonderful Exploit: Jeb Stuart's Ride Around the Army of the Potomac," *Blue & Gray Magazine*, August 1998, 16; Price, *Across the Continent With the Fifth Cavalry*, 107; *OR*, vol. 11, pt. 1, 1020–1021.

20   Mosby, *Mosby's War Reminiscences: Stuart's Cavalry Campaigns*, 223–224.

21   *OR*, vol. 11, pt. 1, 1037.

22   Thomas, *Bold Dragoon*, 118; *OR*, vol. 11, pt. 1, p. 1038.

23   Beale, R. L. T., *History of the Ninth Virginia Cavalry*, 18; Robins, "Stuart's Ride Around McClellan," Edited by Robert U. Johnson and Clarence C. Buel, *Battles and Leaders of the Civil War*, vol. II, 1956, 272; Letter of William Z. Mead to "My Dearest Mother, Cavalry Camp 1 Cavalry, June 21, 1862," typescript copy from J.B. Mead.

24   Mosby, *The Memoirs of Colonel John S. Mosby*, 112.

25   Mosby, "The Ride Around General McClellan," *SHSP* (1898) vol. 26, 250; Mosby, *Mosby's War Reminiscences*, 224; *OR*, vol. 11, pt. 1, p. 1038.

26   *OR*, vol. 11, pt. 1, p. 1038.

Chapter 14: Deeper Behind Federal Lines

1   McClellan, H.B., *The Life and Campaigns of Major-General J. E. B. Stuart,* 62; Frayser, "Riding Around McClellan's Army with Jeb Stuart." Philadelphia *Weekly Times,* vol. 7, no. 24, August 4, 1883; Nanzig, *3rd Virginia Cavalry,* 108; Mosby, *The Memoirs of Colonel John S. Mosby,* 112.

2   Robins, "Stuart's Ride Around McClellan," Edited by Robert U. Johnson and Clarence C. Buel, *Battles and Leaders of the Civil War,* vol. II, 272; Mewborn, "A Wonderful Exploit: Jeb Stuart's Ride Around the Army of the Potomac," *Blue & Gray Magazine,* August 1998, 16; "False Reports of a Battle Corrected," *New York Times,* June 22, 1862.

3   Cooke, *Wearing of the Gray,* 179.

4   Ibid., 179–180. Beale, R. L. T., *History of the Ninth Virginia Cavalry,* 18.

5   *OR,* vol. 11, pt. 1, p. 1038.

6   Beale, G. W. *A Lieutenant of Cavalry in Lee's Army,* 27.

7   *OR,* vol. 11, pt. 1, 1008.

8   Ibid., 1007, 1009.

9   Ibid., 1008, 1010.

10 Ibid., 1015–1016.

11 Ibid., 1010, 1015; Carter, *From Yorktown to Santiago,* 47; *OR,* vol. 11, pt. 1, 1025.

12 *OR,* vol. 11, pt. 1, 1008, 1029–1030.

13 "Reminiscences of the Civil War," August V. Kautz Papers, 14, USAHEC.

14 *OR,* vol. 11, pt. 1, p. 1007, 1025.

15 "Reminiscences of the Civil War," August V. Kautz Papers, 14, USAHEC.

16 *OR,* vol. 11, pt. 1, p. 1025.

17 Ibid.

18 Ibid., 1010.

19 Ibid.

20 Ibid.

21 Ibid., 1006, 1010.

22 Letter of Lt. Emlen Newbold Carpenter to "E.N. Carpenter, June 20, 1862, Camp before Richmond, June 20 1862," Alexander R. Chamberlin Papers Collection — Officer's letters Jun 6, 1861 — Nov. 16, 1864, USAHEC.

23 "Former Germantown Academy Students in the Civil War," Germantown Academy Papers, Parry Family Collection (officer's bio sketches 1861–1865), USAHEC. This info comes from "To Preserve the Union G.A. Alumni in

the Civil War" by Edward O. Parry '39 an article in unknown magazine but probably Germantown Academy alumni magazine.

24 Smith, *"We Have It Damn Hard Here,"* 44.

25 *OR*, vol. 11, pt. 1, 1010; Smith, *"We Have It Damn Hard Here,"* 44. Smith indicated that Warren's infantry arrived about 6 p.m. and replaced cavalry on line so they could return to camp for provisions.

26 *OR*, vol. 11, pt. 1, 1006.

27 Ibid., 1010.

28 "Reminiscences of the Civil War," August V. Kautz Papers, 14, USAHEC.

Chapter 15: Panic on the Pamunkey River

1 Mosby, "The Ride Around General McClellan," *SHSP* (1898) vol. 26, 250.

2 Mosby, *The Memoirs of Colonel John S. Mosby*, 113–114; *OR*, vol. 11, pt. 1, 164.

3 "False Reports of a Battle Corrected," *New York Times*, June 22, 1862.

4 Mosby, *The Memoirs of Colonel John S. Mosby*, 113–114.

5 *OR*, vol. 11, pt. 1, 207.

6 Beale, G. W., *A Lieutenant of Cavalry in Lee's Army*, 28.

7 Cooke, *Wearing of the Gray*, 180.

8 Ibid., 180–181.

9 Krick, Robert K. *9th Virginia Cavalry*, 6, 84, 91; McMurry, *Virginia Military Institute Alumni in the Civil War*, 157; Frayser, "Riding Around McClellan's Army with Jeb Stuart." Philadelphia *Weekly Times*, vol. 7, no. 24, August 4, 1883; *OR*, vol. 11, pt. 1, 1038, 1044; McClellan, H.B., *The Life and Campaigns of Major-General J. E. B. Stuart*, 60.

10 "Our Peninsula Letter," Philadelphia *Inquirer*, June 17, 1862.

11 *OR*, vol. 11, pt.1, 1028.

12 "From Gen. McClellan's Army," *New York Times*, June 21, 1862; Mewborn, "A Wonderful Exploit: Jeb Stuart's Ride Around the Army of the Potomac," *Blue & Gray Magazine*, August 1998, 19.

13 R.J. Norris letter, "Camp Young, June 18th '62," offered for sale by Museum Quality Americana at www.mqamericana.com in March 2013.

14 *OR*, vol. 11, pt.1, 1028.

15 Ibid., 1032–1033, 1038; "Our Peninsula Letter," Philadelphia *Inquirer*, June 17, 1862; Mewborn, "A Wonderful Exploit: Jeb Stuart's Ride Around the Army of the Potomac," *Blue & Gray Magazine*, August 1998, 17.

16 Mewborn, "A Wonderful Exploit: Jeb Stuart's Ride Around the Army of the Potomac," *Blue & Gray Magazine*, August 1998, 17; *OR*, vol. 11, pt. 1,

1033–1034; "False Reports of a Battle Corrected," *New York Times,* June 22, 1862.

17 "Our Army Correspondence," Philadelphia *Inquirer,* June 20, 1862.

18 Townsend, *Rustics in Rebellion,* 118–119.

19 Ibid., 119–120.

20 *OR,* vol. 11, pt. 1, 1031. Hanover and Hanovertown Ferry are the same river crossing spot.

21 "From the Army Before Richmond," Philadelphia *Inquirer,* June 24, 1862; *OR,* vol. 11, pt. 1 1031.

22 "From the Army Before Richmond," Philadelphia *Inquirer,* June 24, 1862.

23 Pennsylvania, Eleventh Cavalry Regiment, *History of the Eleventh Pennsylvania,* 40; Henry Lyle Letters, Harrisburg CWRT Collection, Daniels Collection, June 16, 1862, USAHEC.

24 *OR,* vol. 11, pt. 1, 1031–1032.

25 Ibid., 1032, 1038; Pennsylvania, Eleventh Cavalry Regiment, *History of the Eleventh Pennsylvania,* 40.

Chapter 16: Cutting the Union Supply Line at Tunstall's Station

1 Mosby, *The Memoirs of Colonel John S. Mosby,* 114–115; "The Scout," Richmond *Dispatch,* June 17, 1862.

2 Mosby, John S. "The Ride Around General McClellan," *SHSP* (1898) vol. 26, 251; "The Scout," Richmond *Dispatch,* June 17, 1862.

3 Mosby, *The Memoirs of Colonel John S. Mosby,* 114–115; Mosby, John S., *Mosby's War Reminiscences,* 229; Richmond *Daily Examiner,* June 17, 1862.

4 Letter of Christian Geisel to sister dated June 19th 1862, Christian Geisel Collection, 1862–1868, Pennsylvania State Archives.

5 Smith, *"We Have It Damn Hard Here,"* 45; Wittenberg, *Rush's Lancers,* 46.

6 "From the Army Before Richmond," Philadelphia *Inquirer,* June 24, 1862; Frayser, "Riding Around McClellan's Army with Jeb Stuart." Philadelphia *Weekly Times,* vol. 7, no. 24, August 4, 1883; Cooke, *Wearing of the Gray,* 182; "From the Army Before Richmond" Philadelphia *Inquirer,* June 24, 1862]

7 Robins, "Stuart's Ride Around McClellan," Edited by Robert U. Johnson and Clarence C. Buel, *Battles and Leaders of the Civil War,* vol. II, 272; *OR,* vol. 11, pt.1, 1038.

8 Robins, "Stuart's Ride Around McClellan," Edited by Robert U. Johnson and Clarence C. Buel, *Battles and Leaders of the Civil War,* vol. II, 273.

9 Cooke, *Wearing of the Gray,* 181.

10 *OR,* vol. 11, pt. 1, 1045.

11 Cooke, *Wearing of the Gray,* 181–182.

12 Jeb Stuart letter to "My Dear Brother from Fort Wise K.T., January 18th 1861," William Alexander Stuart Papers, 1861–1889, VHS; Jeb Stuart letter to "My Dear Brother, Camp Beverly Oct 4th 1861," William Alexander Stuart Papers, 1861–1889, VHS.

13 *OR,* vol. 11, pt. 1, 1045.

14 Ibid.; Mosby, *The Memoirs of Colonel John S. Mosby,* 116; "The Scout," Richmond *Daily Dispatch,* June 17, 1862,

15 Beale, R. L. T., *History of the Ninth Virginia Cavalry,* 19.

16 von Borcke, *Memoirs of the Confederate War for Independence,* vol. 1, 41.

17 Cooke, *Wearing of the Gray,* 181.

18 Robins, "Stuart's Ride Around McClellan," Edited by Robert U. Johnson and Clarence C. Buel, *Battles and Leaders of the Civil War,* vol. II, 273.

19 Ibid.; "Arrival of Prisoners," Richmond *Dispatch,* June 16, 1862; "From Gen. McClellan's Army," *New York Times,* June 21, 1862; Mewborn, "A Wonderful Exploit: Jeb Stuart's Ride Around the Army of the Potomac." *Blue & Gray Magazine,* August 1998, 20.

20 Cooke, *Wearing of the Gray,* 182.

21 "Sketch of William Campbell's Life," typescript copy in Bound Volume #31, research library, Richmond National Battlefield Park.

22 Cooke, *Wearing of the Gray,* 183; Robins, "Stuart's Ride Around McClellan," Edited by Robert U. Johnson and Clarence C. Buel, *Battles and Leaders of the Civil War,* vol. II, 273.

23 Cooke, *Wearing of the Gray,* 182–183; Brown, *Stringfellow of the Fourth,* 129.

24 *OR,* vol. 11, pt. 1, 1044; Robins, "Stuart's Ride Around McClellan," Edited by Robert U. Johnson and Clarence C. Buel, *Battles and Leaders of the Civil War,* vol. II, 27; *OR,* vol. 11, pt. 1, 1038–1039.

25 "From Gen. McClellan's Army," *New York Times,* June 21, 1862; "Our Peninsula Letter," Philadelphia *Inquirer,* June 17, 1862; "False Reports of a Battle Corrected," *New York Times,* June 22, 1862; Mewborn, "A Wonderful Exploit: Jeb Stuart's Ride Around the Army of the Potomac," *Blue & Gray Magazine,* August 1998, 20; Beale, G. W., *A Lieutenant of Cavalry in Lee's Army,* 28.

26 Beale, R. L. T., *History of the Ninth Virginia Cavalry,* 19; "Our Peninsula Letter," Philadelphia *Inquirer,* June 17, 1862; Cooke, *Wearing of the Gray,* 18; von Borcke, *Memoirs of the Confederate War for Independence,* vol. 1, 42; "From Our Army Correspondents, *New York Times,* June 20, 1862.

27 Robins, W. T. "Stuart's Ride Around McClellan," Edited by Robert U. Johnson and Clarence C. Buel, *Battles and Leaders of the Civil War,* 273; "From Our

Army Correspondents," *New York Times,* June 20, 1862; "Our Peninsula Letter," Philadelphia *Inquirer,* June 17, 1862.

28 "The Scout," Richmond *Daily Dispatch,* June 17, 1862; Moncure, "Brief Memoranda," *Bulletin of the Virginia State Library,* Vol. XVI, July 1927, 68; von Borcke, *Memoirs of the Confederate War for Independence,* vol. 1, 42. The blunderbuss was a shortened musket with a flared muzzle that could fire a single bullet or multiple projectiles. It was an early form of a shotgun.

29 Cooke, *Wearing of the Gray,* 183; *OR,* vol. 11, pt. 1, p. 1039, 1032.

30 Beale, R. L. T., *History of the Ninth Virginia Cavalry,* 20; Mewborn, "A Wonderful Exploit: Jeb Stuart's Ride Around the Army of the Potomac," *Blue & Gray Magazine,* August 1998, 21; "From Gen. McClellan's Army," *New York Times,* June 17, 1862; "From Our Army Correspondents," *New York Times,* June 21, 1862.

31 Mosby, *The Memoirs of Colonel John S. Mosby,* 116.

32 *OR,* vol. 11, pt.1, p. 1038, 1014.

33 Ibid., 1038; Beale, R. L. T., *History of the Ninth Virginia Cavalry,* 20.

34 Mewborn, "A Wonderful Exploit: Jeb Stuart's Ride Around the Army of the Potomac." *Blue & Gray Magazine,* August 1998, 46.

35 Cooke, *Wearing of the Gray,* 183.

36 Letter from W. H. F. Lee to wife, 25 June 1862, Lee Family Papers, 1824–1918, VHS.

37 Frayser, "Riding Around McClellan's Army with Jeb Stuart," Philadelphia *Weekly Times,* vol. 7, no. 24, August 4, 1883.

38 Townsend, *Rustics in Rebellion,* 120; Gracey, *Annals of the Sixth Pennsylvania Cavalry,* 50; "From Gen. McClellan's Army," *New York Times,* June 21, 1862. This article about Tunstall's Station burning was reprinted by NYT from *Richmond Examiner,* June 16.

39 *OR,* vol. 11, pt. 1, p. 1039.

40 Moncure, "Brief Memoranda," *Bulletin of the Virginia State Library,* Vol. XVI, July 1927, 68.

41 Cooke, *Wearing of the Gray,* 183.

42 Letter of Chiswell Dabney, "Dear Mother, Hd Qrs Caval' Brigade June 18th 1862," Saunders Family Papers, 1798–1903, VHS.

43 von Borcke, *Memoirs of the Confederate War for Independence,* vol. 1. 43.

44 Cooke, *Wearing of the Gray,* 183. This must have been a different bridge from Black Creek Bridge as maps show they had to cross two creeks within one-quarter mile of leaving Tunstalls.

45 Robins, "Stuart's Ride Around McClellan," Edited by Robert U. Johnson and Clarence C. Buel, *Battles and Leaders of the Civil War*, vol. II, 272; *OR,* vol. 11, pt. 1, p. 1038.

Chapter 17: Chaos at White House Landing

1   *OR,* vol. 11, pt. 1, p. 1032.

2   Pennsylvania, Eleventh Cavalry Regiment, *History of the Eleventh Pennsylvania,* 39; *OR,* vol. 11, pt. 1, p. 1032.

3   *OR,* vol. 11, pt. 1, 1032; Miller, editor. *The Peninsula Campaign of 1862: Yorktown to the Seven Days,* vol. 1, 127; Mewborn, "A Wonderful Exploit: Jeb Stuart's Ride Around the Army of the Potomac," *Blue & Gray Magazine,* August 1998, 21.

4   *OR,* vol. 11, pt. 1, 1032, 246.

5   Krick, Robert K., *Civil War Weather in Virginia,* 62.

6   Townsend, *Rustics in Rebellion,* 120.

7   *OR,* vol. 11, pt. 1, 1032–1033.

8   Ibid., 269–270.

9   "From Gen. McClellan's Army," *New York Times,* June 17, 1862; "From Our Army of Correspondents," *New York Times,* June 20, 1862.

Chapter 18: The Fog of War

1   *OR,* vol. 11, pt. 1, 1005–1006.

2   Ibid., 1006–1007.

3   Ibid., 1025.

4   Ibid., 1025–1026.

5   Ibid., 1010.

6   Ibid., 1030, 1007.

7   Ibid., 273, 1007.

8   Ibid., 1010–1011, 1030.

9   Ibid., 1012.

10 Ibid., 1006.

11 Ibid., 1006, 1016.

Chapter 19: A Brief Respite at Talleysville

1   Thomason, *JEB Stuart,* 149.

2   *OR*, vol. 11, pt. 1, 1039; Cooke, *Wearing of the Gray*, 184; Unknown newspaper article, James Ewell Brown Stuart Papers, VHS; "False Reports of a Battle Corrected," *New York Times*, June 22, 1862; Richmond *Dispatch*, June 16, 1862.

3   *OR*, vol 11, pt. 1, 1039; Robins, "Stuart's Ride Around McClellan," Edited by Robert U. Johnson and Clarence C. Buel, *Battles and Leaders of the Civil War*, vol. II, 273.

4   Beale, G. W., *A Lieutenant of Cavalry in Lee's Army*, 29; Robins, "Stuart's Ride Around McClellan," Edited by Robert U. Johnson and Clarence C. Buel, *Battles and Leaders of the Civil War*, vol. II, 273.

5   Moncure, "Brief Memoranda," *Bulletin of the Virginia State Library*, Vol. XVI, July 1927, 68; von Borcke, *Memoirs of the Confederate War for Independence*, vol. 1, 43.

6   Beale, G. W., *A Lieutenant of Cavalry in Lee's Army*, 29.

7   Cooke, *Wearing of the Gray*, 185.

8   Ibid.

9   Frayser, "Riding Around McClellan's Army with Jeb Stuart." Philadelphia *Weekly Times*, vol. 7, no. 24, August 4, 1883.

10   Letter of John Reynolds to "My Dear Ellie, June 10, 1862," Reynolds Family Papers, Franklin and Marshall College.

11   "Letters, Telegrams, Reports, and Lists Received by the Cavalry Corps, 1861–1865," NARA.

12   Ibid.

13   *OR*, vol. 11, pt. 1, p. 1028.

14   Ibid., 1044, 1028; Brown, *Stringfellow of the Fourth*, 131. Brown indicated that the body might be one of the soldiers who had stepped off train and then fell under the wheels as he tried to climb back onboard.

15   *OR*, vol. 11, pt. 1, p. 1028.

16   "Letters, Telegrams, Reports, and Lists Received by the Cavalry Corps, 1861–1865," NARA.

17   Ibid.

18   *OR*, vol. 11, pt. 1, 1014; Letter of Lt. Emlen Newbold Carpenter to "E.N. Carpenter, June 20, 1862, Camp before Richmond, June 20 1862."Alexander R. Chamberlin Papers Collection — Officer's letters Jun 6, 1861 — Nov. 16, 1864, USAHEC.

Chapter 20: Trapped?

1   Cooke, *Wearing of the Gray*, 184; Freeman, *Lee's Lieutenants*, 295; Mewborn, "A Wonderful Exploit: Jeb Stuart's Ride Around the Army of the Potomac,"

Blue & Gray Magazine, August 1998, 47. While John Cooke indicated that the Rooney Lee incident happened shortly after leaving Tunstall's, I agree with several historians who believe that the incident happened between Talleysville and the Chickahominy River.

2   Letter of Robert S. Young, Lewis Leigh Collection, USAHEC.

3   Robins, "Stuart's Ride Around McClellan," Edited by Robert U. Johnson and Clarence C. Buel, *Battles and Leaders of the Civil War*, vol. II, 1956, 273; Cooke, *Wearing of the Gray*, 186.

4   Cooke, *Wearing of the Gray*, 186.

5   von Borcke, *Memoirs of the Confederate War for Independence*, vol. 1, 63.

6   Elting and McAfee, editors. *Military Uniforms in America*. vol. 3, 78.

7   *OR*, vol. 11, pt. 1, p. 1017.

8   Ibid., 1011.

9   Ibid., 1018; Gracey, *Annals of the Sixth Pennsylvania Cavalry*, iv, 51.

10 Elting and McAfee, editors. *Military Uniforms in America*, vol. 3, 78.

11 *OR*, vol. 11, pt. 1, 1018.

12 Ibid.

13 Letter of Lt. Emlen Newbold Carpenter to "E.N. Carpenter, June 20, 1862, Camp before Richmond, June 20 1862."Alexander R. Chamberlin Papers Collection — Officer's letters Jun 6, 1861 — Nov. 16, 1864, USAHEC.

14 *OR*, vol. 11, pt. 1, 1018–1019.

15 Ibid., 1019. Morris indicated that after passing St. Peter's Church his men stopped at Mrs. Christian's house and Mr. Apperson's house. Two dwellings owned by persons named Apperson, located southeast of St. Peter's Church, appear on the *Atlas to Accompany the Official Records of the Union and Confederate Armies*, map #XIX. Morris' men probably then rode west toward Talleysville on the road that connected New Kent and Talleysville.

16 *OR*, vol. 11, pt. 1, 1018–1019.

17 Nanzig, *3rd Virginia Cavalry*, 101.

18 "City Point," *Harper's Weekly*, June 21, 1862, 395; "Freak of the Fresh," Richmond *Dispatch*, June 13, 1862; "Across the Chickahominy," *Harper's Weekly*, June 21, 1862, 396.

19 Cooke, *Wearing of the Gray*, 186; Frayser, "Riding Around McClellan's Army with Jeb Stuart," Philadelphia *Weekly Times*, vol. 7, no. 24, August 4, 1883; Beale, G. W., *A Lieutenant of Cavalry in Lee's Army*, 29. Cooke's account, written in 1867, noted that Rooney Lee attempted to swim with his horse. Frayser also supports this version when he said in his article that Rooney Lee and others "plunged into the flood with the heads of their horses turned upstream." George Beale claimed that Rooney Lee disrobed and

then swam himself across. However, George Beale's account was written well after the war, which is why I believe that Cooke's and Frayser's fresh account is probably most accurate.

20 Letter of William Z. Mead to "My Dearest Mother, Cavalry Camp 1 Cavalry, June 21, 1862," typescript copy from J.B Mead in Personal Collections.

21 Beale, G. W., *A Lieutenant of Cavalry in Lee's Army*, 30.

22 McClellan, *The Life and Campaigns of Major-General J. E. B. Stuart*, 63–64; Moncure, "Brief Memoranda," *Bulletin of the Virginia State Library*, vol. XVI, July 1927, 68.

23 Beale, G. W., *A Lieutenant of Cavalry in Lee's Army*, 30; McClellan, H.B., *The Life and Campaigns of Major-General J. E. B. Stuart*, 63–64.

24 Richmond *Dispatch*, June 16, 1862.

25 Beale, R. L. T., *History of the Ninth Virginia Cavalry*, 20; Beale, G. W., *A Lieutenant of Cavalry in Lee's Army*, 30.

26 Beale, R. L. T., *History of the Ninth Virginia Cavalry*, 20; Krick, Robert K., *9th Virginia Cavalry*, 57.

27 Cooke, *Wearing of the Gray*, 187; Frayser, "Riding Around McClellan's Army with Jeb Stuart," Philadelphia *Weekly Times*, vol. 7, no. 24, August 4, 1883.

28 Robins, "Stuart's Ride Around McClellan," Edited by Robert U. Johnson and Clarence C. Buel, *Battles and Leaders of the Civil War*, vol. II, 274; Beale, R. L. T., *History of the Ninth Virginia Cavalry*, 20. Rooney Lee shouted across the river for those men who had already crossed to remain there; McClellan, H.B., *The Life and Campaigns of Major-General J. E. B. Stuart*, 63–64.

29 Cooke, *Wearing of the Gray*, 187.

30 von Borcke, *Memoirs of the Confederate War for Independence*, vol. 1, 44; McClellan, H.B., *The Life and Campaigns of Major-General J. E. B. Stuart*, 64; *OR*, vol. 11, pt. 1, 1039; Frayser, "Riding Around McClellan's Army with Jeb Stuart." Philadelphia *Weekly Times*, vol. 7, no. 24, August 4, 1883.

31 McClellan, H.B., *The Life and Campaigns of Major-General J. E. B. Stuart*, 64; Freeman, *R. E. Lee*, vol. 2, 99.

32 von Borcke, *Memoirs of the Confederate War for Independence*, vol. 1, 44; *OR*, vol. 11, pt. 1, 1039.

33 Cooke, *Wearing of the Gray*, 187; von Borcke, *Memoirs of the Confederate War for Independence*, vol. 1, 44.

34 *OR*, vol. 11, pt. 1, 1039; Cooke, *Wearing of the Gray*, 187–188; Beale, G. W., *A Lieutenant of Cavalry in Lee's Army*, 30.

35 *OR*, vol. 11, pt. 1, 1039; Mosby, "The Ride Around General McClellan," *SHSP* (1898) vol. 26, 253; "The Scout," Richmond *Daily Dispatch*, June 17, 1862; Thomason, *JEB Stuart*, 6.

36　*OR*, vol. 11, pt. 1, 1040.

37　Frayser, "Riding Around McClellan's Army with Jeb Stuart." Philadelphia *Weekly Times*, vol. 7, no. 24, August 4, 1883.

38　Cooke, *Wearing of the Gray*, 188.

39　Ibid., 187–188; von Borcke, *Memoirs of the Confederate War for Independence*, vol. 1, 44; McClellan, H.B., *The Life and Campaigns of Major-General J. E. B. Stuart*, 65.

40　Beale, G. W., *A Lieutenant of Cavalry in Lee's Army*, 30.

41　Robins, "Stuart's Ride Around McClellan," Edited by Robert U. Johnson and Clarence C. Buel, *Battles and Leaders of the Civil War*, vol. II, 274; von Borcke, *Memoirs of the Confederate War for Independence*, vol. 1, 44.

42　Beale, R. L. T., *History of the Ninth Virginia Cavalry*, 21.

43　Cooke, *Wearing of the Gray*, 188; Mosby, *Mosby's War Reminiscences*, 233; Mosby, *The Memoirs of Colonel John S. Mosby*, 118.

44　Mosby, *Mosby's War Reminiscences*, 233; Mosby, "The Ride Around General McClellan," *SHSP* (1898) vol. 26, 254.

Chapter 21: "Hope To Punish Them"

1　*OR*, vol. 11, pt. 1, p. 1014, 1017; Miller, editor. *The Peninsula Campaign of 1862: Yorktown to the Seven Days*, vol. 1, 132.

2　*OR*, vol. 11, pt. 1, p. 1017.

3　Ibid., 1019.

4　Ibid., 1005.

5　Ibid., 1017, 1019.

6　Moncure, "Brief Memoranda," *Bulletin of the Virginia State Library*, vol. XVI, July 1927, 68; von Borcke, *Memoirs of the Confederate War for Independence*, vol. 1, 44–45.

7　Cooke, *Wearing of the Gray*, 189; *OR*, vol. 11, pt. 1, 1039.

8　Beale, G. W., *A Lieutenant of Cavalry in Lee's Army*, 31.

9　von Borcke, *Memoirs of the Confederate War for Independence*, vol. 1, 45.

10　Cooke, *Wearing of the Gray*, 188; Robins, "Stuart's Ride Around McClellan," Edited by Robert U. Johnson and Clarence C. Buel, *Battles and Leaders of the Civil War*, vol. II, 274.

11　Beale, R. L. T., *History of the Ninth Virginia Cavalry*, 21.

12　Letter of Lt. Emlen Newbold Carpenter to "E.N. Carpenter, June 20, 1862, Camp before Richmond, June 20 1862." Alexander R. Chamberlin Papers Collection — Officer's letters Jun 6, 1861 — Nov. 16, 1864, USAHEC.

13 *OR*, vol. 11, pt. 1, 1017.

14 Robins, "Stuart's Ride Around McClellan," Edited by Robert U. Johnson and
    Clarence C. Buel, *Battles and Leaders of the Civil War*, vol. II, 1956, 274–275.

15 Letter of Lt. Emlen Newbold Carpenter to "E.N. Carpenter, June 20, 1862,
    Camp before Richmond, June 20 1862." Alexander R. Chamberlin Papers
    Collection — Officer's letters Jun 6, 1861 — Nov. 16, 1864, USAHEC; Miller,
    editor. *The Peninsula Campaign of 1862: Yorktown to the Seven Days*, vol. 1, 134.
    The bridge was in full flames as Morris' men approached and they watched
    parts of it drop into the water.

16 Letter of Lt. Emlen Newbold Carpenter to "E.N. Carpenter, June 20, 1862,
    Camp before Richmond, June 20 1862." Alexander R. Chamberlin Papers
    Collection — Officer's letters Jun 6, 1861 — Nov. 16, 1864, USAHEC; *OR*,
    vol. 11, pt. 1, 1017.

17 Robins, "Stuart's Ride Around McClellan," Edited by Robert U. Johnson
    and Clarence C. Buel, *Battles and Leaders of the Civil War*, vol. II, 274–275.

18 Letter of Lt. Emlen Newbold Carpenter to "E.N. Carpenter, June 20, 1862,
    Camp before Richmond, June 20 1862."Alexander R. Chamberlin Papers
    Collection — Officer's letters Jun 6, 1861 — Nov. 16, 1864, USAHEC; *OR*,
    vol. 11, pt. 1, p.1017.

19 Mosby, *Mosby's War Reminiscences,*234; Mewborn, "A Wonderful Exploit: Jeb
    Stuart's Ride Around the Army of the Potomac," *Blue & Gray Magazine*,
    August 1998, 49; Compiled Service Records of Confederate Soldiers Who
    Served in Organizations from the State of Virginia, Record of John Jacob
    Schwartz, NARA; Driver, *1st Virginia Cavalry*, 224.

20 *OR*, vol. 11, pt. 1, 1017.

21 Ibid.

22 Ibid; Miller, editor. *The Peninsula Campaign of 1862: Yorktown to the Seven
    Days*, vol. 1, 130.

23 *OR*, vol. 11, pt. 1, 1008, 1014; Miller, editor. *The Peninsula Campaign of 1862:
    Yorktown to the Seven Days*, vol. 1, 135. The artillery section came from Stephen
    Weed's Co. I, 5th U. S. Light Artillery.

24 *OR*, vol. 11, pt. 1, p. 1012.

25 Ibid., 1012, 1009.

26 Ibid., 1008.

27 Letter of Lt. Emlen Newbold Carpenter to "E.N. Carpenter, June 20, 1862,
    Camp before Richmond, June 20 1862." Alexander R. Chamberlin Papers
    Collection — Officer's letters Jun 6, 1861 — Nov. 16, 1864, USAHEC.
    Brigadier General Turner Ashby was Stonewall Jackson's fiery cavalry com-
    mander in the Shenandoah Valley. Carpenter probably was not aware that
    Ashby had been killed in action earlier in the month on June 6.

28   *OR*, vol. 11, pt. 1, 1030–1031; G.K. Warren letter to Brother, June 16, 1862, Gouverneur K. Warren Papers, New York State Library.

29   *OR*, vol. 11, pt. 1, p.1008.

30   Ibid., 1045.

Chapter 22: Headed for Richmond

1   Beale, G. W., *A Lieutenant of Cavalry in Lee's Army*, 31; Robins, "Stuart's Ride Around McClellan," Edited by Robert U. Johnson and Clarence C. Buel, *Battles and Leaders of the Civil War*, vol. II, 274.

2   Cooke, *Wearing of the Gray*, 189.

3   Frayser, "Riding Around McClellan's Army with Jeb Stuart." Philadelphia *Weekly Times*, vol. 7, no. 24, August 4, 1883; Mewborn, "A Wonderful Exploit: Jeb Stuart's Ride Around the Army of the Potomac," *Blue & Gray Magazine*, August 1998, 49; Davis, *JEB Stuart*, 127. There seems to be some discrepancy about where Stuart's staff stopped to rest in the late afternoon of June 14. John E. Cooke and H.B. McClellan believed it was the home of Thomas Christian while Richard Frayser, a native of the area, wrote that it was the home of Judge Isaac Christian. Maybe the staff or parts of the staff stopped at both places or there was confusion over the same last names. I tend to believe the Frayser account since he was a local, and Judge Christian's place was more distant from the Chickahominy River crossing, which would lessen the chance of the staff being surprised by Union cavalry.

4   Mosby, *Mosby's War Reminiscences*, 234.

5   Frayser, "Riding Around McClellan's Army with Jeb Stuart." Philadelphia *Weekly Times*, vol. 7, no. 24, August 4, 1883; Nomination Form for Woodburn in Charles City County, Va., National Register of Historic Places, National Park Service, U. S. Department of the Interior — see website listing in bibliography; McClellan, H.B., *The Life and Campaigns of Major-General J. E. B. Stuart*, 66; Cooke, *Wearing of the Gray*, 189.

6   McClellan, H.B., *The Life and Campaigns of Major-General J. E. B. Stuart*, 66; Robins, "Stuart's Ride Around McClellan," Edited by Robert U. Johnson and Clarence C. Buel, *Battles and Leaders of the Civil War*, vol. II, 275.

7   Cooke, *Wearing of the Gray*, 190.

8   McClellan, H.B., *The Life and Campaigns of Major-General J. E. B. Stuart*, 66; *OR*, vol. 11, pt. 1, p. 1040.

9   *OR*, vol. 11, pt. 3, 229, 235.

10   Frayser, "Riding Around McClellan's Army with Jeb Stuart." Philadelphia *Weekly Times*, vol. 7, no. 24, August 4, 1883.

11   Robins, "Stuart's Ride Around McClellan," Edited by Robert U. Johnson and Clarence C. Buel, *Battles and Leaders of the Civil War*, vol. II, 275.

12   Ibid.

13   Beale, G. W., *A Lieutenant of Cavalry in Lee's Army*, 31.

14   Moncure, "Brief Memoranda," *Bulletin of the Virginia State Library*, vol. XVI, July 1927, 69.

15   Cooke, *Wearing of the Gray*, 190.

16   Mosby, *Mosby's War Reminiscences*, 235.

17   Robins, "Stuart's Ride Around McClellan," Edited by Robert U. Johnson and Clarence C. Buel, *Battles and Leaders of the Civil War*, vol. II, 275; Mosby, *The Memoirs of Colonel John S. Mosby*, 110.

Chapter 23: Safe Again

1   Robins, "Stuart's Ride Around McClellan," Edited by Robert U. Johnson and Clarence C. Buel, *Battles and Leaders of the Civil War*, vol. II, 275.

2   Ibid; Mosby, *Mosby's War Reminiscences*, 234.

3   Mosby, *Mosby's War Reminiscences*, 235; Mosby, *The Memoirs of Colonel John S. Mosby*, 119; Eggleston, *A Rebel's Recollections*, 115.

4   Miller, William J., editor. *The Peninsula Campaign of 1862: Yorktown to the Seven Days*, vol. 1, 139–140.

5   *OR*, vol. 11, pt. 1, p. 1036.

6   Frayser, "Riding Around McClellan's Army with Jeb Stuart." Philadelphia *Weekly Times*, vol. 7, no. 24, August 4, 1883.

7   Letter to "Dear Parents, Camp near Richmond June 15th 1862," Charles Edward Bates Papers, 1858–1865, VHS; "From Our Army Correspondents," *New York Times*, June 21, 1862.

8   Hopkins, *The Little Jeff*, 63–64; Richmond *Dispatch*, June 16, 1862; Campbell, "Stuart's Ride and Death of Latane," *SHSP* (1914), vol. 39, 90.

9   Hopkins, *The Little Jeff*, 64

10   Moore, *Moore's Complete Civil War Guide to Richmond*, 77.

11   "Arrival of Prisoners," Richmond *Dispatch*, June 16, 1862; *OR*, vol. 11, pt. 1, 1039; "Arrival of Prisoners," Richmond *Whig*, June 16, 1862; "A Brilliant Reconnaissance By Stuart's Cavalry," Richmond *Daily Examiner*, June 17, 1862; *OR*, vol. 11, pt. 1, 1039.

12   Journal of Charles R. Chewning, Handley Library Archives, typescript; Krick, Robert K., *9th Virginia Cavalry*, 56. Ashton would be discharged in April 1863 at age 29 due to a spine injury sustained in that fall.

13   Letter of Chiswell Dabney "Dear Mother, Hd Qrs Caval' Brigade June 18th 1862," Saunders Family Papers, 1798–1903, VHS; Duncan, editor. *Letters of J. E. B. Stuart to His Wife — 1861*, 25.

14 Beale, G. W., *A Lieutenant of Cavalry in Lee's Army*, 31–32.

15 Moncure, "Brief Memoranda," *Bulletin of the Virginia State Library*, vol. XVI, July 1927, 69.

16 Ibid.

17 von Borcke, *Memoirs of the Confederate War for Independence*, vol. 1, 45.

18 Letter of Robert S. Young, Lewis Leigh Collection, USAHEC.

19 "A Brilliant Reconnaissance By Stuart's Cavalry," Richmond *Examiner*, June 17, 1862; *Charleston Mercury*, June 20, 1862.

20 "From Gen. McClellan's Army," *New York Times*, June 17, 1862; "From Gen. McClellan's Army," *New York Times*, June 21, 1862; "False Reports of a Battle Corrected," *New York Times*, June 22, 1862.

21 Robert P. Baylor letter, "Richmond June 15th 1862," VHS; R.J. Norris letter, "Camp Young, June 18th '62," offered for sale by Museum Quality Americana at www.mqamericana.com in March 2013. Norris would be wounded at Brandy Station just under a year later on June 9, 1863 and succumb to his wounds at Richmond's Hospital #21 in July.

22 J.H. Timberlake Letter "Dear Gertie Richmond Va., June 16th 1862," copy in Bound Volume #20, research library, Richmond National Battlefield Park; "Valuable Guides," Richmond *Dispatch*, June 20, 1862; Stiles, *4th Virginia Cavalry*, 139.

23 Letter of William Z. Mead to "My Dearest Mother, Cavalry Camp 1 Cavalry, June 21, 1862," typescript copy given to author from J.B Mead.

24 Letter of John Mosby to "My dearest Pauline, Richmond, Monday June 16th 1862," John Singleton Mosby Papers, 1855–1922, VHS.

25 "Gen. Stuart; Scarcity of Food," *New York Times*, June 24, 1862; Brown, *Stringfellow of the Fourth*, 136.

26 Thomason, *JEB Stuart*, 154–155.

27 Thomas, *Bold Dragoon*, 124. Thomas stated 36 hours awake for Cooke.; Hubbell, editor. "Notes and Documents," *The Journal of Southern History*, volume VII, 531; Gracey, *Annals of the Sixth Pennsylvania Cavalry*, 52.

28 Hubbell, editor. "Notes and Documents," *The Journal of Southern History*, volume VII, 531.

29 Pennsylvania, Eleventh Cavalry Regiment, *History of the Eleventh Pennsylvania*," 41–42; *OR*, vol. 11, pt. 3, 242–243.

30 "From Our Army Correspondents," *New York Times*, June 21, 1862; Davis, *Common Soldier, Uncommon War*, 157.

31 Wert, *The Sword of Lincoln*, 95; Thomas, *Bold Dragoon*, 123.

32 *OR*, vol. 11, pt.1, 189.

33   Averell, "With the Cavalry on the Peninsula," Edited by Robert U. Johnson and Clarence C. Buel, *Battles and Leaders of the Civil War*, vol. II, 430.

34   Letter of Thomas A. Carpenter, June 22, 1862, Bulkley Family Papers 1855–1865, Missouri Historical Society.

35   Whit, "From Before Richmond," *Herkimer* (N.Y.) *Tribune*, June 19, 1862.

36   Letter of Gen. Philip St. George Cooke [only one page of letter in file and date is unknown] to his wife Rachel W. (Herzog) Cooke, Cooke Family Papers, 1823–1953, VHS.

37   Ibid.

38   Merritt, "Life and Services of General Philip St. George Cooke, U. S. Army," *Journal of the United States Cavalry Association*, vol. viii, no. 29, June 1895, 88–89.

39   "Editorial Correspondence of the New York Times," *New York Times*, June 20, 1862.

40   *OR*, vol. 11, pt.1, p. 165.

41   Ibid.

42   *OR*, vol. 11, pt. 2, 517; Johnston, *Echoes of 1861–1961*, 67.

43   Dowdey and Manarin, editors. *The Wartime Papers of R. E. Lee*, 209.

44   *OR*, vol. 1, pt. 1, 130.

45   Wise, *The Long Arm of Lee*, vol. 1, 206; Bridges, *Fighting With Stuart*, 53.

46   Jones, *A Rebel War Clerk's Diary*, 82; Mosby, *The Memoirs of Colonel John S. Mosby*, 120;

47   *OR*, vol. 11, pt. 3, 602.

48   Letter of Charles E. Bates to "Dear Parents, Camp Lincoln Va June 19th 1862," Charles Edward Bates Papers, 1858–1865, VHS.

49   Cooke, *Wearing of the Gray*, 180.

50   Mosby, *Mosby's War Reminiscences*, 239.

51   Cooke, *Wearing of the Gray*, 190.

Appendix B: The Burial of Captain William Latane, 9th Virginia Cavalry

1   Campbell, "Stuart's Ride and Death of Latane." *SHSP* (1914), vol. 39, 89; R. C. S. "The Burial of Latane." *SHSP* (1896), vol. 24, 193.

2   "Letter from Your Wife to My Dearest Husband, Summer Hill, June 20, 1862," *New York Times*, June 15, 1862.

3   Ibid.

4   McGuire, *Diary of a Southern Refugee During the War*, 142–143.

5   Ibid.; Editorial Correspondence of the New York Times," *New York Times,* June 20, 1862.

6   McGuire, *Diary of a Southern Refugee During the War,* 143; Salmon, "The Burial of Latane," *Virginia Cavalcade,* vol. 28, no. 3, winter 1979, 122; "Editorial Correspondence of the New York Times," *New York Times,* June 20, 1862.

7   McGuire, *Diary of a Southern Refugee During the War,* 143.

8   "Letter from Your Wife to My Dearest Husband, Summer Hill, June 20, 1862," *New York Times,* June 15, 1862.

9   Ibid.; McGuire, *Diary of a Southern Refugee During the War,* 143–145.

10   McGuire, *Diary of a Southern Refugee During the War,* 144–145. The Brockenbrough and Newton women harbored intense dislike for the volunteer cavalry from the 6th Pennsylvania Cavalry or Rush's Lancers.

11   Salmon, "The Burial of Latane," *Virginia Cavalcade,* vol. 28, no. 3, winter 1979, 123–127.

Appendix C: The Old Church Decision

1   Wise, *The Long Arm of Lee,* vol. 1, 206.Wise was commandant of VMI when this book published in 1915.

2   Thomason, *JEB Stuart,* 154–155.

3   Davis, *JEB Stuart: The Last Cavalier,* 129–130.

4   Early, "Letter from Gen. J. A. Early." *SHSP* (1877), vol. 5, 57; Alexander, *Military Memoirs of a Confederate,* 113–114.

5   Parks, "Letter from V.A.S.P., Camp Near the Chickahominy, June 21, 1862." *Savannah Republican,* June 26, 1862.

6   *OR,* vol. 11, pt. 3, 590.

7   Thomason, *JEB Stuart,* 154–155.

Bibliography

ABBREVIATIONS

NARA — National Archives and Records Administration, Washington, D.C.

NPS — National Park Service

OR — U. S. War Department War of the Rebellion: A Compilation of the Official Records of the Union and Confederate Armies.

SHSP — Southern Historical Society Papers

USAHEC — U. S. Army History and Education Center, Carlisle, Pennsylvania

VHS — Virginia Historical Society, Richmond, Va.

MANUSCRIPTS & IMAGES

Franklin and Marshall College — Archives & Special Collections, Martin Library, Lancaster, Pennsylvania.
  Reynolds Family Papers, John Fulton Reynolds (1820–1863), Series X.

Georgia Historical Society Library, Savannah, Georgia
  Gordon Family Papers.

Handley Library Archives — Stewart Bell Jr. Archives Room, Winchester, Virginia
  The Journal of Charles R. Chewning, typescript.
  Images as noted.

Historical Society of Pennsylvania, Philadelphia, Pennsylvania
  Thomas W. Smith Letters, 1862–1864.

Immanuel Episcopal Church, Mechanicsville, Virginia
  Immanuel Episcopal Church: A Timeline.

Library of Congress, Wahington, D.C.
  Images as noted.

Mississippi State University Libraries, Mississippi State, Mississippi
  Jesse Roderick Sparkman Civil War Diary.

Missouri Historical Society, St. Louis, Missouri
Letter of Thomas A. Carpenter, June 22nd/62. Bulkley Family Papers 1855–1865.

Museum of the Confederacy, Richmond, Virginia
Image as noted.

National Archives [NARA], Washington, D. C.
Compiled Service Records of Confederate General and Staff Officers, and Non-Regimental Enlisted Men.
Compiled Service Records of Confederate Soldiers Who Served in Organizations from the State of Virginia.
Images as noted.
"Letters, Telegrams, Reports, and Lists Received by the Cavalry Corps, 1861–1865." RG 393, part 2, entry 1449.
Southern Claims Commission, Hanover County VA, claim no. 48636, Property Claim by Family of Clevars S. Chisholm, M1407.

National Park Service, Richmond National Battlefield Park, Richmond, Virginia
"Sketch of William Campbell's Life" typescript copy, 9th Va. Cav.
Jeremy Gilmer maps.
Telegram from George McClellan to wife, May 15, 1862. Copy in USA Generals and Staff red book, vol. 170.
J.H. Timberlake Letters [4th Va Cav] June–Oct 1862 "Vol. 1.
Gouvernour K. Warren maps.

New York State Library, Albany, New York
Gouverneur Kemble Warren Papers, 1848–1882.

Pennsylvania State Archives, Harrisburg, Pennsylvania
Christian Geisel Collection, 1862–1868,

Private Collections
Letter of William Z. Mead to "My Dearest Mother, Cavalry Camp 1 Cavalry, June 21, 1862," typescript and copy of original sent to author from descendant J.B. Mead.
Charles R. Knight collection of images sent to author.

Richmond Civil War Round Table, Richmond, Virginia
"Stuart's Ride Around McClellan, 1862: Official Log of the Trip" assembled by committee members around 1956.

St. Peter's Episcopal Church, New Kent, Virginia
"The First Church of the First Lady" church history assembled by History and Archives Committee, 2000.

U. S. Army History and Education Center [USAHEC], Carlisle, Pennsylvania
Emlen Newbold Carpenter, Alexander R .Chamberlin Papers Collection — Officer's letters Jun 6, 1861–Nov. 16, 1864.
Images from various CWP collections.

Germantown Academy Papers, Parry Family Collection, Officers
    Biographical Sketches 1861–1865.
August V. Kautz Papers, "Reminiscences of the Civil War" and Biography.
Henry Lyle Letters, Daniels Collection, Harrisburg CWRT Collection.
MOLLUS images as noted.
Theodore Sage letters, Harrisburg CWRT Collection.
Andrew Wallace, "General August V. Kautz and the Southwestern
    Frontier," dissertation privately printed in Tucson, AZ., 1967.
Robert S. Young letter, Lewis Leigh Collection.

Virginia Historical Society [VHS], Richmond, Virginia
    Charles Edward Bates, Papers, 1858–1865.
    Robert P. Baylor letter, "Richmond June 15th 1862".
    Cooke Family Papers, 1823–1953.
    Lee Family Papers, 1810–1914.
    Lee Family Papers, 1824–1918.
    John Singleton Mosby Papers, 1855–1922.
    Saunders Family Papers, 1798–1903.
    James Ewell Brown Stuart Papers.
    William Alexander Stuart Papers, 1861–1889.
    Wickham Family Papers, 1754–1977.

PUBLISHED PRIMARY SOURCES

Alexander, E. Porter. *Military Memoirs of a Confederate: A Critical Narrative.*
    New York, NY: Charles Scribner's Sons, 1907.

——. *Fighting for the Confederacy: The Personal Recollections of General Edward
    Porter Alexander,* edited by Gary W. Gallagher, Chapel Hill, N.C.: The
    University of North Carolina Press, 1989.

Beale, G. W. *A Lieutenant of Cavalry in Lee's Army.* Boston, MA.: The Gorham
    Press, 1918.

Beale, R. L. T. *History of the Ninth Virginia Cavalry, in the War Between the States.*
    Richmond, VA: B. F. Johnson Publishing Company, 1899.

Blackford, W. W. *War Years with Jeb Stuart.* New York, NY: Charles Scribner's
    Sons, 1945.

Cooke, John Esten. *Wearing of the Gray: Being Personal Portraits, Scenes and
    Adventures of the War.* New York, NY: E. B. Treat & Co., 1867.

——. *Hammer and Rapier.* New York, NY: Carleton, 1870.

Cooke, Philip St. George. *The 1862 U.S. Cavalry Tactics.* Washington, D.C.:
    Government Printing Office, 1862.

Davis, George B, Leslie J. Perry, Joseph W. Kirkley, *Atlas to Accompany the
    Official Records of the Union and Confederate Armies.* Washington, D.C.:
    Government Printing Office, 1891–1895.

Davis, Sidney Morris. *Common Soldier, Uncommon War*. Bethesda, MD.: John H. Davis, 1994.

Dowdey, Clifford and Louis Manarin, eds. *The Wartime Papers of R. E. Lee*. New York, NY: Bramhall House, 1961.

Duncan, Bingham, ed. *Letters of J. E. B. Stuart to His Wife — 1861*. Atlanta, GA.: The Library, Emory University, 1943.

Eggleston, George Cary. *A Rebel's Recollections*. Bloomington, IN.: Indiana University Press, 1959.

Franklin, Pauline and Mary V. Pruett, eds. *Civil War Letters of Dandridge William and Naomi Bush Cockrell, 1862–1863*. Lively, VA.: Brandylane Publishers, 1991.

Gracey, S. L. *Annals of the Sixth Pennsylvania Cavalry*. E. H. Butler & Co., 1868.

Grant, Ulysses S. *Personal Memoirs of U. S. Grant*, New York, NY: The Century Co., 1895.

Hewett, Janet B., Noah A. Trudeau, Bryce A. Suderow, eds. *Supplement to the Official Records of the Union and Confederate Armies*. Vol. 56, Wilmington, NC: Broadfoot Publishing Co., 1997.

Johnston, Robert U. and Clarence C. Buel. *Battles and Leaders of the Civil War*, 4 vols. New York: The Century Co., 1956.

Jones, John B. *A Rebel War Clerk's Diary*. Edited by Earl S. Miers. New York, N.Y.: Sagamore Press, Inc., 1958.

Lee, Robert E. *Lee's Dispatches: Unpublished Letters of General Robert E. Lee*. Edited by Douglas Southall Freeman, New York, NY: G.P. Putnam's Sons, 1957.

Lincoln, Abraham. *The Collected Works of Abraham Lincoln*. vol. 2. Edited by Roy P. Basler, New Brunswick, N.J.: Rutgers University Press, 1953.

McClellan, George B. *The Civil War Papers of George B. McClellan: Selected Correspondence, 1860–1865*. Edited by Stephen W. Sears. New York, NY: Ticknor & Fields, 1989.

McClellan, H. B. *The Life and Campaigns of Major-General J. E. B. Stuart: Commander of the Cavalry of The Army of Northern Virginia*. Secaucus, NJ.: The Blue & Grey Press, 1993.

McGuire, Judith B. *Diary of a Southern Refugee During the War*. Harrisonburg, VA.: Sprinkle Publications, 1996.

Mitchell, Adele H., ed. *The Letters of Major General James E. B. Stuart*. Stuart-Mosby Historical Society, 1990.

Mosby, John S. *Mosby's War Reminiscences: Stuart's Cavalry Campaigns*. New York: Dodd, Mead and Company, 1898.

——. *The Memoirs of Colonel John S. Mosby*. Edited by Charles Wells Russell. Boston, MA: Little, Brown, and Company, 1917.

Price, George F. *Across the Continent With the Fifth Cavalry*. New York, NY: D. Van Nostrand, 1883.

Richardson, James D. *A Compilation of the Messages and Papers of the Confederacy Including the Diplomatic Correspondence 1861–1865*. vols. 1–2, Nashville, TN: United States Publishing Company, 1906.

Russell, Charles Wells, ed. *The Memoirs of Colonel John S. Mosby*. Boston, MA: Little, Brown, & Co., 1917.

Smith, Thomas W. *"We Have It Damn Hard Here": The Civil War Letters of Sergeant Thomas W. Smith, 6th Pennsylvania Cavalry*. Edited by Eric J. Wittenberg. Kent, OH.: The Kent State University Press, 1999.

Sneden, Robert Knox. *Images of the Storm*. Edited by Charles F. Bryan, James C. Kelly, and Nelson D. Lankford. New York, NY: The Free Press, 2001.

Sorrel, G. Moxley. *Recollections of a Confederate Staff Officer*. Edited by Bell Irvin Wiley. Jackson, TN.: McCowat-Mercer Press, Inc., 1958.

Styple, William B. ed., *Writing & Fighting from the Army of Northern Virginia: A Collection of Confederate Soldier Correspondence*. Kearny, NJ: Belle Grove Publishing Co., 2003.

——. *Writing and Fighting the Civil War: Soldier Correspondence to the New York Mercury*. Kearny, N.J.: Belle Grove Publishing Company, 2004.

Townsend, George Alfred. *Rustics in Rebellion: A Yankee Reporter on the Road to Richmond, 1861–65*. Chapel Hill, NC: The University of North Carolina Press, 1950.

U. S. War Department. *Report of the Secretary of War*, 1853.

U. S. War Department. *War of the Rebellion: A Compilation of the Official Records of the Union and Confederate Armies*. 130 vols. Washington, D. C.: U. S. Government Printing Office, 1880–1901.

von Borcke, Heros. *Zwei Jahre Im Sattel Und Am Feinde*. Berlin: Ernst Siegfried Mittler und Sohn, 1886.

——. *Memoirs of the Confederate War for Independence*, vol. 1. New York: Peter Smith, 1938.

Wolseley, Field Marshal Viscount [Garnet Joseph Wolesey]. *The American Civil War: An English View*. Edited by James A. Rawley. Charlottesville, VA.: The University of Virginia Press, 1964.

Young, Bennett H. *Confederate Wizards of the Saddle: Being Reminiscences and Observations of One Who Rode with Morgan*. Boston, MA.: Chapple Publishing Co., 1914.

PUBLISHED SECONDARY SOURCES

Bates, Samuel P. *History of the Pennsylvania Volunteers, 1861–1865*, 4 vols., Harrisburg, PA.: B. Singerly, 1869.

Brennan, Patrick. *"To Die Game": Gen. J. E. B. Stuart, CSA*. Gettysburg, PA.: Farnsworth House Military Impressions, 1998.

Bridges, David P. *Fighting With Stuart: Major James Breathed and the Confederate Horse Artillery*. Arlington, VA.: Breathed Bridges Best, Inc., 2006.

Brown, R. Shepard. *Stringfellow of the Fourth*. New York: Crown Publishers, Inc., 1960.

Burton, Brian K. *Extraordinary Circumstances: The Seven Days Battles*. Bloomington, IN.: Indiana University Press, 2001.

Carter, W. H. *From Yorktown to Santiago: With the Sixth U. S. Cavalry*. Austin, TX.: State House Press, 1989.

Coulling, Mary P. *The Lee Girls*. Winston-Salem, NC: John F. Blair, 1987.

Cozzens, Peter and Robert I. Girardi. *The New Annals of the Civil War*. Mechanicsburg, PA: Stackpole Books, 2004.

Crute, Joseph H. Jr. *Confederate Staff Officers, 1861–1865*. Powhatan, VA.: Derwent Books, 1982.

Davis, Burke. *JEB Stuart: The Last Cavalier*, New York, NY: Rinehart & Company, Inc., 1957.

Driver, Robert J., Jr. *1st Virginia Cavalry*. Lynchburg, VA.: H. E. Howard, Inc., 1991.

——. *First and Second Maryland Cavalry, C.S.A.* Charlottesville, VA.: Howell Press., 1999.

Elting, John R., and Michael J. McAfee, eds. *Military Uniforms in America*: *Long Endure: The Civil War Period, 1852–1867*. vol. 3.Novato, CA.: Presidio Press, 1982.

Fishel, Edwin C. *The Secret War for the Union: The Untold Story of Military Intelligence in the Civil War*. Boston, MA.: Houghton Mifflin Company, 1996.

Frassanito, William A. *Grant and Lee: The Virginia Campaigns 1864–1865*. New York, NY: Charles Scribner's Sons, 1983.

Freeman, Douglass Southall. *R. E. Lee: A Biography*. vol. 2. New York: Charles Scribner's Sons, 1934.

——. *Lee's Lieutenants: A Study in Command*. vol. 1. New York: Charles Scribner's Sons, 1945.

Glatthaar, Joseph T. *General Lee's Army: From Victory to Collapse*. New York, NY.: Free Press, 2008.

Hageman, E. R., ed. *Fighting Rebels and Redskins: Experiences in the Army Life of Colonel George B. Sanford*. Norman, OK.: University of Oklahoma Press, 1969.

Holzer, Harold and Craig L. Symonds, eds. *The New York Times Complete Civil War, 1861–1865*. New York: Black Dog & Leventhal Publishers, Inc., 2010.

Hopkins, Donald A. *The Little Jeff: The Jefferson Davis Legion, Cavalry, Army of Northern Virginia.* Shippensburg, PA: White Mane Books, 1999.

Johnston, J. Ambler. *Echoes of 1861–1961.* Richmond, VA.: Richmond Civil War Roundtable.

Krick, Robert E. L. *Staff Officers in Gray: A Biographical Register of the Staff Officers in the Army of Northern Virginia.* Chapel Hill, NC: The University of North Carolina Press, 2003.

Krick, Robert K. *9th Virginia Cavalry.* Lynchburg, VA.: H. E. Howard, Inc., 1982.

——. *Civil War Weather in Virginia.* Tuscaloosa, AL.: The University of Alabama Press, 2007.

McMurry, Richard M. *Virginia Military Institute Alumni in the Civil War: In Bello Praesidium.* Lynchburg, VA.: H. E. Howard, Inc., 1999.

Miller, Francis T., ed. *The Photographic History of the Civil War in Ten Volumes.* vol. 4, New York, NY: The Review of Reviews Co., 1912.

Miller, William J., ed. *The Peninsula Campaign of 1862: Yorktown to the Seven Days.* vol. 1. Campbell, CA.: Savas Woodbury Publishers, 1993.

——. *The Peninsula Campaign of 1862: Yorktown to the Seven Days,* vol. 2. Da Capo Press, 1995.

——. *The Peninsula Campaign of 1862: Yorktown to the Seven Days,* vol. 3. Campbell, CA.: Savas Publishing Co., 1997.

Moore, Robert H. *The 1st and 2nd Stuart Horse Artillery.* Lynchburg, VA.: H. E. Howard, Inc., 1985.

Moore, Samuel J. T. Jr., *Moore's Complete Civil War Guide to Richmond.* 1978.

Murray, Elizabeth Dunbar. *My Mother Used To Say: A Natchez Belle of the Sixties.* Boston, MA: The Christopher Publishing House, 1959.

Nanzig, Thomas P. *3rd Virginia Cavalry.* Lynchburg, VA.: H. E. Howard, Inc., 1989.

Ness, George T., Jr. *The Regular Army on the Eve of the Civil War.* Baltimore, MD.: Toomey Press, 1990.

Official Register of the Officers and Cadets of the United States Military Academy, West Point, N.Y.

Pennsylvania, Eleventh Cavalry Regiment. *History of the Eleventh Pennsylvania Volunteer Cavalry Together with a Complete Roster of the Regiment and the Regimental Officers.* Philadelphia, PA.: Franklin Printing Company, 1903.

Pitts, Hugh Douglas. *High Meadow: Where Robert E. Lee Drew His Sword.* Richmond, VA: Henrico County Historical Society, 1999.

Reed, Rowena. *Combined Operations in the Civil War.* Annapolis, MD.: Naval Institute Press, 1978.

Sears, Stephen W., ed. *The Civil War Papers of George B. McClellan: Selected Correspondence 1860–1865,* New York, NY: Ticknor & Fields, 1989.

——. *To the Gates of Richmond: The Peninsula Campaign.* New York: Ticknor & Fields, 1992.

Smith, H. H. *J. E. B. Stuart : A Character Sketch.* Ashland, VA. [located USAHEC].

Starr, Stephen Z. *The Union Cavalry in the Civil War.* Baton Rouge, LA: Louisiana State University Press, 1979.

Stiles, Kenneth L. *4th Virginia Cavalry.* Lynchburg, VA.: H. E. Howard, Inc., 1985.

Swinton, William. *Campaigns of the Army of the Potomac.* Secaucus, N.J.: The Blue & Grey Press, 1988.

Taylor, Frank H. *Philadelphia in the Civil War 1861–1865.* Philadelphia, PA: 1913.

Thomas, Emory M. *Bold Dragoon: The Life of J. E. B. Stuart.* New York: Harper & Row, Publishers, 1986.

——. *Robert E. Lee: A Biography.* New York, NY: W. W. Norton & Company, 1995.

Thomason, John W. Jr. *JEB Stuart,* New York, NY: Charles Scribner's Sons, 1930.

Trout, Robert J. *They Followed the Plume: The Story of J.E.B. Stuart and His Staff.* Mechanicsburg, PA: Stackpole Books, 1993.

——. *Galloping Thunder: The Story of the Stuart Horse Artillery Battalion.* Mechanicsburg, PA.: Stackpole Books, 2002.

——. *"The Hoss": Officer Biographies and Rosters of the Stuart Horse Artillery Battalion.* Myerstown, PA.: JebFlo Press, 2003.

Union Army, The. vol. 1, Federal Publishing Company, 1908.

Union Army, The: A History of Military Affairs in the Loyal States. vol. viii, Wilmington, N.C.: Broadfoot Publishing Co., 1998.

Warner, Ezra J. *Generals in Blue: lives of the Union Commanders.* Baton Rouge, LA.: Louisiana State University Press, 1964.

Waugh, John C. *The Class of 1846, From West Point to Appomattox: Stonewall Jackson, George McClellan and their Brothers.* New York, NY: Ballantine Books, 1994.

Wert, Jeffry D. *The Sword of Lincoln: The Army of the Potomac.* New York, NY.: Simon & Schuster, 2005.

——. *Cavalryman of the Lost Cause: Biography of J. E. B. Stuart.* New York, NY.: Simon & Schuster, 2008.

——. *A Glorious Army: Robert E. Lee's Triumph, 1862–1863.* New York, NY: Simon & Schuster, 2011.

Wise, Jennings Cropper. *The Long Arm of Lee: Or the History of the Artillery of the Army of Northern Virginia*, vol. 1. Lynchburg, VA: J. P. Bell Co., 1915.

Wittenberg, Eric J. *Rush's Lancers: The Sixth Pennsylvania Cavalry in the Civil War*. Yardley, PA.: Westholme Publishing, LLC. 2007.

ARTICLES

Averell, William W. "With the Cavalry on the Peninsula." Edited by Robert U. Johnson and Clarence C. Buel, *Battles and Leaders of the Civil War*, vol. 2, New York: The Century Co., 1956, p. 429–433.

Bearrs, Edwin C. "...Into the Very Jaws of the Enemy... Jeb Stuart's Ride Around McClellan." *The Peninsula Campaign of 1862: Yorktown to the Seven Days*. vol. 1, edited by William J. Miller. Campbell, CA: Savas Woodbury Publishers, 1993, p. 71–143.

Bond, Frank A. "Fitz Lee in Army of Northern Virginia." *Confederate Veteran*, vol. 6, 1898, p. 420.

Breathed, Frank. "In Memorium — Major James Breathed." *Confederate Veteran*, vol. 15, 1908, p. 574–575.

Campbell, William. "Stuart's Ride and Death of Latane." *SHSP* (1914), vol. 39: 86–90.

Carter, William H. "The Sixth Regiment of Cavalry." *The Maine Bugle*, October 1896, p. 295–296.

Charleston Mercury. June 20, 1862.

Daniel, John M. Richmond *Examiner*, June 10, 1862.

Early, Jubal A. "Letter from Gen. J. A. Early." *SHSP* (1877), vol. 5, p. 50–60.

Frayser, Richard E. "Annals of the War, Chapters of Unwritten History, Three Days in the Saddle: A Narrative of Stuart's Raid in the Rear of the Army of the Potomac, Riding Around McClellan's Army with Jeb Stuart." Philadelphia *Weekly Times*, vol. 7, no. 24, August 4, 1883. [reprinted in Cozzens & Girardi, *The New Annals of the Civil War*,101–112.]

——. "A Narrative of Stuart's Raid in the Rear of the Army of the Potomac." *SHSP* (1883), vol. 11, p. 505–517. *[This is same article by Frayser that appeared in Philadelphia Weekly Times cited above.]*

——. "General Jeb Stuart." *SHSP* (1898), vol. 26, p. 87–93.

Harper's Weekly. "City Point." June 21, 1862, p. 395.

Harper's Weekly. "Across the Chickahominy." June 21, 1862, p. 396.

Hubbell, Jay B., ed. "Notes and Documents: The War Diary of John Esten Cooke." *The Journal of Southern History*, volume VII, number 4, November 1941.

Indianapolis Daily Journal, "Kearney vs. McClellan." October 12, 1864.

J.A.H. "Rebel Dash on Pamunkey River — Capt. W.B. Royall." Probably Philadelphia area newspaper from late June 1862 located on www.fold3 .com.

Journal of the United States Cavalry Association. "The Union Cavalry." vol. v, no. 16, March 1892, p. 9–15.

Krick, Robert E. L. "Letters Cast New Light on the Burial of Latane." *Hanover County Historical Society Bulletin,* vol. 64, Summer 2001.

Mason, W. Roy. "Anecdotes of the Peninsular Campaign: part IV, Origin of the Lee Tomatoes." Edited by Robert U. Johnson and Clarence C. Buel, *Battles and Leaders of the Civil War,* vol. 2, New York: The Century Co., 1956, p. 277.

Matthews, H. H. "A Maryland Confederate: Recollections of Major James Breathed." *SHSP,* vol. 30, 1902, p. 346–348.

McCormick, John. "Fighting Them Over." *National Tribune,* February 21, 1901.

Merritt, Wesley. "Life and Services of General Philip St. George Cooke, U. S. Army." *Journal of the United States Cavalry Association.* vol. viii, no. 29, June 1895, 79–92.

Mewborn, Horace. "A Wonderful Exploit: Jeb Stuart's Ride Around the Army of the Potomac." *Blue & Gray Magazine,* August 1998.

Military Collector & Historian: Journal of the Company of Military Collectors and Historians. vol. vi, no. 1, March 1954, p. 102.

Miller William J. " 'Scarcely any Parallel in History': Logistics, Friction and McClellan's Strategy for the Peninsula Campaign." *The Peninsula Campaign of 1862: Yorktown to the Seven Days,* vol. 2. Da Capo Press, 1995, p. 129–188.

Moncure, E. C. "Brief Memoranda of some of the Engagements of the Civil War in which Judge E. C. Moncure took part." *Bulletin of the Virginia State Library,* vol. XVI, July 1927, p. 66–70.

Mosby, John S. "The Ride Around General McClellan." *SHSP* (1898), vol. 26, 246–254.

Parks, Virgil A. S. "Letter from V.A.S.P., Camp Near the Chickahominy, June 21, 1862." *Savannah Republican,* June 26, 1862.

National Tribune, "Hooker on McClellan," November 14, 1907.

New York Times, "From Gen. McClellan's Army." June 17, 1862.

New York Times, "Letter from Your Wife to My Dearest Husband, Summer Hill," June 20, 1862 — also republished in Hanover County Historical Bulletin, vol. 64, Summer 2001.

New York Times, "Editorial Correspondence of the New York Times." June 20, 1862.

New York Times, "From Our Army Correspondents." June 20, 1862.

New York Times, "From Our Army Correspondents." June 21, 1862.

New York Times, "From Gen. McClellan's Army." June 21, 1862.

New York Times, "False Reports of a Battle Corrected." June 22, 1862.

New York Times, "Gen. Stuart; Scarcity of Food." June 24, 1862.

O'Neill, Robert. " 'What Men We Have Got are Good Soldiers & Brave Ones Too': Federal Cavalry Operations in the Peninsula Campaign." *The Peninsula Campaign of 1862: Yorktown to the Seven Days*, vol. 3, edited by William J. Miller. Campbell, CA.: Savas Publishing Co., 1997, p. 79–142.

Parks, Virgil A. S. "Camp Near the Chickahominy, June 21, 1862." *Savannah* [Ga.] *Republican,* June 26, 1862.

Philadelphia *Inquirer.* "Our Peninsula Letter." June 17, 1862.

Philadelphia *Inquirer.* "Rush's Lancers in Virginia." June 17, 1862.

Philadelphia *Inquirer.* "Late From the South." June 20, 1862

Philadelphia *Inquirer.* "Our Army Correspondence." June 20, 1862.

Philadelphia *Inquirer.* "From the Army Before Richmond." June 24, 1862.

R. C. S. "The Burial of Latane." *SHSP* (1896), vol. 24, p. 192–194.

Richmond *Daily Examiner.* June 17, 1862.

Richmond *Dispatch.* "The War News." May 15, 1862, p.3, c1;

Richmond *Dispatch.* "Notice." May 15, 1862.

Richmond *Dispatch.* "Save Richmond." May 15, 1862.

Richmond *Dispatch.* "Freak of the Fresh." June 13, 1862

Richmond *Dispatch.* "Arrival of Prisoners." June 16, 1862

Richmond *Dispatch.* June 16, 1862.

Richmond *Dispatch.* "Arrival of Prisoners." June 16, 1862.

Richmond *Dispatch.* "The Scout." June 17, 1862

Richmond *Dispatch.* "Valuable Guides." June 20, 1862.

Richmond *Examiner.* "A Brilliant Reconnaissance By Stuart's Cavalry." June 17, 1862.

Richmond *Whig.* "Arrival of Prisoners," June 16, 1862.

Robins, W. T. "Stuart's Ride Around McClellan," Edited by Robert U. Johnson and Clarence C. Buel, *Battles and Leaders of the Civil War*, vol. 2, New York: The Century Co., 1956, p. 271–275.

Salmon, Emily J. "The Burial of Latane." *Virginia Cavalcade*, winter 1979, vol. 28, no. 3, p. 118–129.

Scribner, Robert L. "Chickahominy Canter." *Virginia Cavalcade*, autumn 1954, vol. 4, no. 2, p. 26–28.

Whit. "From Before Richmond." *Herkimer* (N.Y.) *Tribune,* June 19, 1862.

White, John C. "A Review of the Services of the Regular Army During the Civil War." Serialized article from an unknown periodical believed to be dated 1909 — located at USAHEC under 6th U. S. Cavalry.

DISSERTATIONS

Readnour, Harry Warren [Wynnwood, OK]. "General Fitzhugh Lee, 1835–1905: A Biographical Study." Charlottesville, VA: University of Virginia, Corcoran Department of History, 1971. [found at W&L archives] http://leearchive.wlu.edu/reference/theses/readnour/index.html#intro

Wallace, Andrew. "General August V. Kautz and the Southwestern Frontier." Doctoral dissertation, 1967, privately published, copy at USAHEC.

WEBSITES

Arlington National Cemetery website burial record of Brigadier General William Bedford Royall, http://www.arlingtoncemetery.net/wbroyall.htm

Civil War Richmond, Inc. http://mdgorman.com/

Harper's Weekly from 1861–1865 on the internet. http://www.sonofthesouth.net/leefoundation/the-civil-war.htm

Southern Claims Commission, Hanover County VA, claim no. 48636 by family of Clevars S. Chisholm, NARA, M1407, this info also available on www.fold3.com

R.J. Norris letter, "Camp Young, June 18th '62," offered for sale by Museum Quality Americana on March 2013 at www.mqamericana.com

National Park Service Civil War Soldiers and Sailors database — http://www.nps.gov/civilwar/soldiers-and-sailors-database.htm

U. S. Department of the Interior, National Park Service — National Register of Historic Places — Nomination Form for Woodburn in Charles City County, Va. [Judge Issac Christian's house] http://www.dhr.virginia.gov/registers/Counties/CharlesCity/018-0052_Woodburn_1978_Final_Nomination.pdf

U. S. Military Historical Records — see http://www.fold3.com/

Index

About the Author

J OHN J. FOX III IS THE AUTHOR OR EDITOR of numerous books and articles about the Civil War. He graduated from Washington & Lee University and served in the U. S. Army as an armor officer and aviator. He lives with his family in Virginia's Shenandoah Valley.